WORLD WAR II
TOLD THROUGH
100 ARTIFACTS

DR. ALLAN R. MILLETT
SENIOR MILITARY ADVISOR FOR THE
NATIONAL WORLD WAR II MUSEUM
AND
MAJOR GENERAL
JULIAN THOMPSON

This edition published in 2019 by Cavendish Square Publishing, LLC
243 5th Avenue, Suite 136, New York, NY 10016

Website: cavendishsq.com

This publication represents the opinions and views of the author based on his or her personal
experience, knowledge, and research. The information in this book serves as a general guide
only. The author and publisher have used their best efforts in preparing this book and disclaim
liability rising directly or indirectly from the use and application of this book.

All websites were available and accurate when this book was sent to press.

Cataloging-in-Publication Data

Names: Millett, Allan R. | Thompson, Julian.
Title: World War II told through 100 artifacts / Dr. Allan R. Millett and Julian Thompson.
Description: New York : Cavendish Square, 2019. | Series: War told through artifacts | Includes bibliography and index.
Identifiers: ISBN 9781502644640 (pbk.) | ISBN 9781502644664 (library bound)
Subjects: LCSH: World War, 1939-1945–Juvenile literature. | World War, 1939-1945–Antiquities–Juvenile literature. | World War,
1939-1945–Equipment and supplies–Juvenile literature.
Classification: LCC D743.7 M55 2019 | DDC 940.53–dc2

Printed in the United States of America

CONTENTS

INTRODUCTION

The 100 objects in this book all have a vital connection with World War II. Some were conceived before that war, and others during it, but all formed an essential part of the "tapestry" of that conflict. The aim in this book is to produce pictures and text that resonate with readers, whether they are experts on World War II or approaching the subject for the first time. Only objects were chosen, not people. The choice ranges from the biggest object, the Atlantic Wall, to an ampoule of penicillin. The big objects include the Maginot Line, the two Mulberry Harbors, and the Bridge over the Kwai River—or, to give it its proper name at the time, the Mae Klong. The smaller objects include Churchill's cigar and insignias for the U.S. Airborne Division, the SS, and the Desert Rats, as well as Australian divisional patches.

It was important to include objects associated with the Germans, Japanese, and Italians, as well as British, American, Soviet, Australian, and other Allied nations who used some of the same equipment. Three of the most famous tanks of the war appear here: the Soviet T-34, the German Tiger, and American Sherman; this last used extensively by the British as well. The Italians were the first to use human torpedoes to attack ships; other nations quickly followed suit, and their torpedoes also appear in the book. Numerous vehicles became famous in World War II, none more so than the ubiquitous Jeep, though the amphibious DUKW (Duck) was probably a close second. Arguably the most deadly

antitank gun of World War II, the German 88-mm, appears in both its guises: antitank and antiaircraft.

Several documents appear in the book. Right at the beginning is the piece of paper that the British Prime Minister, Neville Chamberlain, waved for the crowd to see when he returned to London after meeting Adolf Hitler in Munich, telling them that this guaranteed "Peace in our time." Just 11 months later, Hitler issued his first war directive ordering the invasion of Poland and World War II had begun. Another document, created by President Roosevelt and Prime Minister Churchill on board HMS *Prince of Wales* at Placentia Bay Newfoundland in August 1941, became adapted as the Charter of the United Nations. The final document did not see the light of day until a month after it was written: a note penned by General Eisenhower to be used in the event of the failure of the Normandy landings of June 6, 1944.

As well as the Spitfire, the other aircraft depicted in the book include the famous "Flying Fortress" B-17 bomber, the Mustang, and the Bf 109 Messerschmitt, along with the "String bag" Swordfish and the Lancaster bomber. The carrier U.S.S. *Enterprise* (the celebrated "Big E") is here, along with the *Graf Spee*, and the "little ships" of Dunkirk.

It is hoped that readers will enjoy reading about the chosen items in *World War II Told through 100 Artifacts*, and find the book both informative and perhaps that it throws a light on some generally less well known facts.

ABOVE: One of the most iconic items of the Second World War, the British Mark III combat helmet.

◼ Peace in Our Time

On the afternoon of September 30, 1938, the Prime Minister of the United Kingdom, Neville Chamberlain, left Munich in a British Airways Super Lockheed Electra and landed at Heston airport, near today's Heathrow. A huge crowd greeted him. Facing a battery of microphones, he waved a piece of paper, saying, "This morning I had another talk with the German Chancellor, Herr Hitler, and here is a paper which bears his name as well as mine." The police cleared a route through the mob to enable him to drive to Buckingham Palace, where he appeared on the balcony with the King and Queen. That evening, he addressed a crowd from an upper window in Downing Street. "My good friends, this is the second time in our history that there has come back from Germany to Downing Street peace with honor. I believe it is peace in our time."

Chamberlain's visit to Munich was his third trip to see Hitler in 15 days as a result of a crisis concerning Czechoslovakia. In 1938 Czechoslovakia's total population of around 14 million included some three million German speakers, most of whom lived in an area known as Sudetenland. In early September, the Sudetenlanders, stoked by Hitler's inflammatory speeches and with strong Nazi support, rioted, demanding union with Germany. By September 15, the Czech authorities had restored order, but there was an atmosphere of mounting tension across Europe.

That day, Chamberlain flew to the Berghof, Berchtesgaden, to persuade Hitler not to invade Czechoslovakia. He proposed that where more than half of the population desired union with Germany they should be granted their wish, to which Hitler agreed. The French reluctantly joined the British in putting pressure on President Beneš of Czechoslovakia to agree. Chamberlain returned to London, but Hitler, in a classic blackmailer's ploy, said the concessions were insufficient.

On September 22, Chamberlain flew to meet Hitler at the Dreesen Hotel in Bad Godesberg, one of Hitler's favorite watering holes. Chamberlain was inclined to concede to Hitler's demands, but was opposed by his own Cabinet. On September 23, the Czechs mobilized and the British Royal Navy was deployed to war stations. Britain prepared for war. Chamberlain broadcast on September 27: "How horrible, fantastic, incredible it is that we should be digging trenches and trying on gas-masks here because of a quarrel in a faraway country between people of whom we know nothing."

An appeal to Benito Mussolini, First Marshal of the Empire of Italy, to mediate signaled to Hitler that the French and British would crumble. On September 29, Chamberlain flew to Munich along with Édouard Daladier, the French Prime Minister. They met Hitler and Mussolini at the Führerbau, the new neoclassical Nazi party headquarters. Here they accepted terms put forward by Mussolini but drafted by the German Foreign Office, conceding virtually all Hitler's demands. The next morning Chamberlain met Hitler in his private apartment, for what the former described as "a very friendly and pleasant talk," during which they signed the paper that Chamberlain showed at Heston.

German troops occupied Sudetenland immediately. They delayed occupying the rest of Czechoslovakia until May 1939, Hitler declaring, "I shall not occupy Prague for six months or so. I can't bring myself to do such a thing to the old fellow at the moment."

Strategic experts still disagree over whether the year's delay before the outbreak of World War II benefited Germany or the Allies. Perhaps Chamberlain's climbdown caused Hitler to underestimate the British, to his ultimate cost. In August 1939 he said to his generals, "Our enemies are small worms. I saw them at Munich."

We, the German Führer and Chancellor and the British Prime Minister, have had a further meeting today and are agreed in recognising that the question of Anglo-German relations is of the first importance for the two countries and for Europe.

We regard the agreement signed last night and the Anglo-German Naval Agreement as symbolic of the desire of our two peoples never to go to war with one another again.

We are resolved that the method of consultation shall be the method adopted to deal with any other questions that may concern our two countries, and we are determined to continue our efforts to remove possible sources of difference and thus to contribute to assure the peace of Europe.

Neville Chamberlain

September 30. 1938.

LEFT: Chamberlain at Heston airport on September 30, 1938, on his return from Munich.

ABOVE: The paper with Hitler's and Chamberlain's signature.

OVERLEAF: Chamberlain greeted by an SS guard of honor on his arrival at Munich. The German foreign minister von Ribbentrop is on Chamberlain's left.

8

■₂ Führer Directive Number 1

From the moment Adolf Hitler became Chancellor of Germany in January 1933, he had directed the country's armed forces with political aims, ordering a program of rearmament in direct violation of the terms of the Treaty of Versailles (1920) and readying the military for a series of aggressive actions aimed at constructing a Greater German Reich. His direction of (and interference in) military affairs was characterized by a series of directives to the army. More general and forward-looking than simple orders, these *Führerdirektivs* tended to be of a strategic nature, beginning in autumn 1933 with the "Directive for the Armed Forces in the Event of Sanctions" and continuing in March 1938 with a "Directive 1," which ordered the Anschluss that annexed Austria. To enable his will to be transmitted throughout the armed forces with a minimum of political interference or modification by the traditional military hierarchy, Hitler decided on February 4, 1938, to replace the old Defense Ministry with the OKW (*Oberkommando der Wehrmacht*, High Command of the Armed Forces) headed up by one of his own placemen, General Wilhelm Keitel (an officer so unpopular with operational officers for his slavish subservience to Hitler's will that he became known as *Lakeitel*, "lackey").

Plans for the projected assault on Poland (known as "Case White") were first circulated on April 3, 1939, but the assault was delayed until the fall to give time to isolate the country diplomatically and to broker the agreement with the Soviet Union on Poland's dismemberment, which bore fruit with the Nazi–Soviet Pact of August 24.

By the fourth week in August, all was ready; Hitler gambled that France and Britain would lack the political will to intervene on behalf of Poland, and this is reflected in the first of a new series of *Führerdirektivs*. Directive Number 1, dated August 31, 1939, self-servingly summarized the scenario in its opening words: "Since the situation on Germany's eastern frontier has become intolerable and all political possibilities of peaceful settlement have been exhausted, I have decided upon a solution by force." A brief invocation of Case White as the template for the coming operation against Poland is followed by a much longer section concerned with the West. Germany's armed forces are ordered at all costs to respect the neutrality of Holland, Belgium, Luxembourg, and Switzerland and warned that the blame for hostilities opening in western Europe must be laid firmly at the door of Britain and France. Whenever, however, either of those two countries might engage in aggressive moves against Germany, then the neutrality of the others could be violated with impunity in order to outflank the French defensive positions.

The declarations of war by Britain and France against Germany on September 3 provided Hitler with this pretext,

leading to the issue of *Führerdirectiv* 2 ("For the Conduct of the War") the same day. The series continued until Directive 51 (of November 3, 1943), which gave orders for the disposition of the army to fight against the Allied opening of a second front in the West. Long before this, the style of the directives had turned from strategic judgments to Hitler's more typical micromanaging of operational military matters, which undercut operational officers' authority and undermined any rational direction of the war effort. From November 1943, with the war turning defensive, Hitler abandoned the *Führerdirektiv* format in favor of a series of ad hoc *Führer* orders and orders of the day, a stream which only finally ceased on April 15, 1945, just a fortnight before his suicide, with a last, hopeless call for resistance against the "Bolshevik" onslaught.

ABOVE: The German invasion of Poland, September 1, 1939.

RIGHT: Hitler's Directive Number 1, issued on August 31, 1939, ordered the invasion of Poland.

Der Oberste Befehlshaber der Wehrmacht   Berlin, den 31.8.39.
OKW/WFA Nr. 170 /39 g.K.Chefs. L I

         8 Ausfertigungen
         2. Ausfertigung.

Weisung Nr. 1
für die Kriegführung.

1.) Nachdem alle politischen Möglichkeiten erschöpft sind, um auf friedlichem Wege eine für Deutschland unerträgliche Lage an seiner Ostgrenze zu beseitigen, habe ich mich zur gewaltsamen Lösung entschlossen.

2.) Der Angriff gegen Polen ist nach dem für Fall Weiss getroffenen Vorbereitungen zu führen mit den Abänderungen, die sich beim Heer durch den inzwischen fast vollendeten Aufmarsch ergeben.

     Aufgabenverteilung und Operationsziel bleiben unverändert.

     Angriffstag: ..1.9.39..

     Angriffszeit ....

     Diese Zeit gilt auch für die Unternehmungen Gdingen - Danziger Bucht und Brücke Dirschau.

3.) Im Westen kommt es darauf an, die Verantwortung für die Eröffnung von Feindseligkeiten eindeutig England und Frankreich zu überlassen. Geringfügigen Grenzverletzungen ist zunächst rein örtlich entgegen zu treten.

     Die von uns Holland, Belgien, Luxemburg und der Schweiz zugesicherte Neutralität ist peinlich zu achten.

- 2 -

- 2 -

Die deutsche Westgrenze ist zu Lande an keiner Stelle ohne meine ausdrückliche Genehmigung zu überschreiten. Zur See gilt das gleiche für alle kriegerischen oder als solche zu deutenden Handlungen.

Die defensiven Massnahmen der Luftwaffe sind zunächst auf die unbedingte Abwehr feindl. Luftangriffe an der Reichsgrenze zu beschränken, wobei so lange als möglich die Grenze der neutralen Staaten bei der Abwehr einzelner Flugzeuge und kleinerer Einheiten zu achten ist. Erst wenn beim Einsatz stärkerer franz. und engl. Angriffsverbände über die neutralen Staaten gegen deutsches Gebiet die Luftverteidigung im Westen nicht mehr gesichert ist, ist die Abwehr auch über diesem neutralen Gebiet freizugeben.

Schnellste Orientierung des OKW über jede Verletzung der Neutralität dritter Staaten durch die Westgegner ist besonders wichtig.

4.) Eröffnen England und Frankreich die Feindseligkeiten gegen Deutschland, so ist es Aufgabe der im Westen operierenden Teile der Wehrmacht, unter möglichster Schonung der Kräfte die Voraussetzungen für den siegreichen Abschluss der Operationen gegen Polen zu erhalten. Im Rahmen dieser Aufgabe sind die feindl. Streitkräfte und deren wehrwirtschaftl. Kraftquellen nach Kräften zu schädigen. Den Befehl zum Beginn von Angriffshandlungen behalte ich mir in jedem Fall vor.

- 3 -

- 3 -

Das Heer hält den Westwall und trifft Vorbereitungen, dessen Umfassung im Norden - unter Verletzung belg. oder holländ. Gebietes durch die Westmächte - zu verhindern. Rücken franz. Kräfte in Luxemburg ein, so bleibt die Sprengung der Grenzbrücken freigegeben.

Die Kriegsmarine führt Handelskrieg mit dem Schwerpunkt gegen England. Zur Verstärkung der Wirkung kann mit der Erklärung von Gefahrenzonen gerechnet werden. OKM meldet, in welchen Seegebieten und in welchem Umfang Gefahrenzonen für zweckmässig gehalten werden. Der Wortlaut für eine öffentl. Erklärung ist im Benehmen mit dem Ausw. Amte vorzubereiten und mir über OKW zur Genehmigung vorzulegen.

Die Ostsee ist gegen feindl. Einbruch zu sichern. Die Entscheidung, ob zu diesem Zwecke die Ostsee-Eingänge mit Minen gesperrt werden dürfen, bleibt vorbehalten.

Die Luftwaffe hat in erster Linie den Einsatz der franz. und engl. Luftwaffe gegen das deutsche Heer und den deutschen Lebensraum zu verhindern.

Bei der Kampfführung gegen England ist der Einsatz der Luftwaffe zur Störung der engl. Seezufuhr, der Rüstungsindustrie, der Truppentransporte nach Frankreich vorzubereiten. Günstige Gelegenheit zu einem wirkungsvollen Angriff gegen massierte engl. Flotteneinheiten, insbes. gegen Schlachtschiffe und Flugzeugträger ist auszunutzen. Angriffe gegen London bleiben meiner Entscheidung vorbehalten.

- 4 -

- 4 -

zunutzen. Angriffe gegen London bleiben meiner Entscheidung vorbehalten.

Die Angriffe gegen das engl. Mutterland sind unter den Gesichtspunkt vorzubereiten, dass unzureichender Erfolg mit Teilkräften unter allen Umständen zu vermeiden ist.

               A. Hitler

Verteiler:

OKH	1. Ausf.
OKM	2. "
R.d.L.u.Ob.d.L.	3. "
OKW:	
Chef WFA	4. "
L	5.-8. "

■ The Yellow Star

The yellow six-pointed Star of David with the word *"Jude"* (Jew) is universally known as a badge worn by Jews as part of their victimization by the Nazis. Although the persecution of Jews in Germany began as soon as Hitler came to power in 1933, they were not required to wear a badge or other sign marking them out from the rest of society. But yellow stars of David were painted on the windows of Jewish-owned stores as early as April 1, 1933, the date on which the Nazis declared a boycott on these premises. This offensive graffiti does not appear to have been officially organized, because the matter of special Jewish badges had not yet been a subject for discussion among Nazi leaders. More likely, ordinary rank-and-file Nazi party members and probably the SA (*Sturmabteilung*, or Stormtroopers) precipitated the paint-daubing ploy and the idea caught on, spreading quickly around Germany thanks to the media, especially the radio.

On November 7, 1938, Ernst vom Rath, Third Secretary at the German Embassy in Paris, was assassinated by Herschel Grynszpan, a Polish Jew. In retaliation, Reinhard Heydrich, Chief of the Sicherheitsdienst—Security Service (SD) —ordered the destruction of all places of Jewish worship in Germany and Austria. This action had long been prepared; the murder of vom Rath merely provided the excuse to begin the atrocity on the night of November 9. As well as demolishing 177 synagogues, bands of Nazis destroyed an estimated 7,500 Jewish stores. Streets in every town were covered in broken glass, and the event was named *Kristallnacht* (Crystal Night, or Night of Broken Glass). On November 12, at a meeting of Nazi leaders, Heydrich suggested a special badge for Jews. But no action was taken for nearly a year.

It was not until after the defeat of Poland in September 1939 that Jewish badges were introduced in the German-occupied sector (the Soviet Union occupied the eastern part of Poland). To begin with, there was no laid-down policy, and it was left to individual Nazi officials whether to issue orders that Jews in their area of jurisdiction were to wear badges. The designs varied from place to place. However, on November 23, 1939, Hans Frank, the German Governor General of Occupied Poland, ordered that all Jews above the age of ten were to wear a white armband with a yellow Star of David on their right arm. By December 1942, more than 85 percent of the Jewish people in Poland had been transported to extermination camps. This figure included Jews living in the former Soviet Polish territory, as by now the Soviets had been pushed out following Hitler's invasion of the Soviet Union in June 1941.

An instruction published on September 1, 1941 had ordered all Jews in Germany and Poland to wear the yellow Star of David with *"Jude"* inscribed on it, on the left side of the chest. This order was then extended to include Jews in most occupied territories and countries. There is a legend that when Jews in Denmark were ordered to wear the star, King Christian X wore one and his example was followed by the whole population, Jew and Gentile, causing the Germans to rescind the order. In fact, the Germans never required Danish Jews to wear the star. What is not legend is the reaction by the Danes to discovering that 7,500 Danish Jews were about to be deported to death camps. Most of these Jews were hidden by their neighbors, and many were subsequently smuggled out to Sweden.

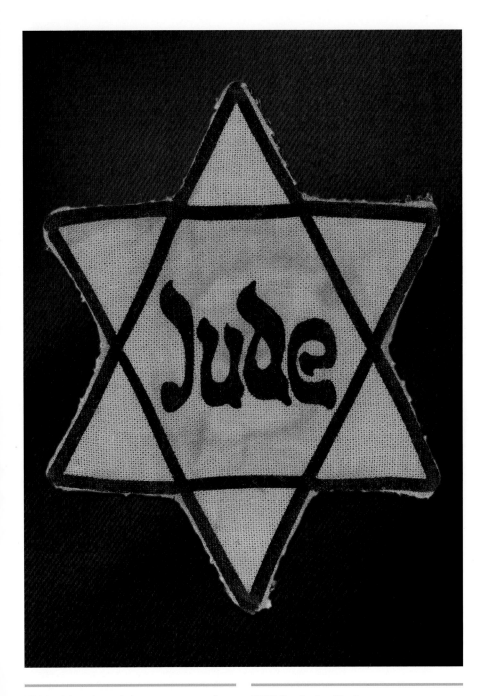

LEFT: French Jews photographed in a transit camp at Drancy northeast of Paris in July 1942. From here they were taken by train to extermination camps in the east.

ABOVE: The yellow Star of David.

■4 The Enigma Machine

Enigma is the codeword for a cipher machine based on a design by Dutchman, H. A. Koch. His ideas were developed by a Berlin engineer, Dr. Arthur Scherbius, who first marketed it in 1923. By 1929 both the German army and navy had purchased different versions of it. Later it was bought by the Luftwaffe, the SS (*Schutzstaffel* or Protection Squadron), the *Abwehr* (the German secret service), and the *Reichsbahn* (German state railways). The machine consisted of a set of three rotating disks, called rotors, connected to a keyboard and a series of electrically powered lights. When a key was pressed the rotor would turn, and a display lamp would illuminate a letter.

To encrypt a message, the operator would press the alphabetical key for the initial letter of the message, (for example, B), and the X lamp might light up. In earlier versions of Enigma, the operator copied down the resulting series of letters on to a message pad. Eventually the message would consist of an apparently meaningless jumble of letters, which in turn were transmitted by radio. The enigma operator at the receiving end would adjust his machine to the settings of the day and decrypt the message in the same way.

Throughout World War II, the Germans believed that the Enigma was unbreakable because for every signal sent there were millions of possible solutions. Every day the rotor settings were changed, and possessing a machine was only part way to breaking the code; you had to know what the

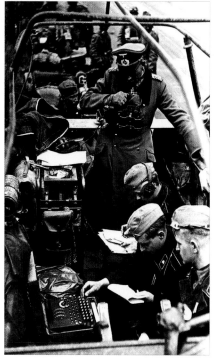

day's setting was. The limitations to Enigma were that there are only 26 letters in the alphabet, that no letter could stand for itself, and that there were no numeral keys, so figures had to be spelled out.

The Poles acquired an Enigma machine and started reading some German signal traffic as early as 1932. They passed on the information to the French in 1939, and the British in 1940. The British Government Code and Cypher School at Bletchley Park began to break the Luftwaffe Enigma codes during the Norwegian and French campaigns of 1940, but took longer to read the German navy traffic. During the Battle of Britain, most Luftwaffe traffic was sent over landlines, and consequently could not be read by Bletchley Park. The gravest crisis for the Allies arose during the Battle of the Atlantic when Admiral Dönitz's U-boat command began to use a fourth rotor on their Enigma machines, hugely multiplying the complexity of the enciphering of messages. The new German system was code-named "Shark." Brilliant work by Bletchley Park eventually resulted in the deciphering of much of the U-boat command signals, and eventually the breaking of "Shark," assisted by the fact that Dönitz controlled his U-boats so precisely that he transmitted a huge volume of radio traffic, believing "Shark" to be unbreakable.

A number of Enigma machines were captured during World War II, but these provided only a partial breakthrough in reading

German signal traffic. In March 1941, during a Commando raid on the Lofoten Islands off Norway, the German trawler *Krebs* was taken, with two Enigma machines and the current settings. In May 1941 and July 1941, the British captured two German weather ships, acquiring their codebooks for the following months. In May 1941, *U-110* was forced to the surface, and sailors from HMS *Bulldog* boarded and seized her Enigma machine and codes before she sank. In October 1942, HMS *Petard* depth-charged *U-559* to the surface and captured the latest codebooks. In June 1944, sailors from the USS *Pittsburgh* boarded the surfaced *U-505,* capturing her codebooks.

The work of Bletchley Park in breaking the German cyphers was greatly assisted by the invention of the "Bombe," an early form of computer.

■₅ The SS Insignia

Although there were a multiplicity of SS badges depending on the type of uniform worn and the unit, two themes were common: the double lightning flash and the death's head. The SS, short for *Schutzstaffel*, literally meaning "defense echelon," began its existence as the black-shirted personal guard for Hitler. Heinrich Himmler, a chicken farmer by trade who had never served as a soldier or heard a shot fired in action, was appointed by Hitler to command this guard. It was formed from the SA, the brown-shirt storm troopers of the Nazi party who had played a leading part in bringing Hitler to power. From small beginnings the SS was expanded into a very large force, an alternative army, whose main task in Himmler's eyes was to ensure the continuing existence of Nazi power.

The name *Schutzstaffel* was abbreviated to SS, depicted as a double lightning flash in imitation of ancient runic characters. This double flash was worn on a black collar patch, often just on one side of the collar. Although it became the insignia for all SS units, it was at first confined to members of Hitler's guard, the *Leibstandarte* Adolf Hitler, which after Hitler's accession to power moved from Munich to take over bodyguard duties from the Army Chancellery Guard in Berlin.

The other badge worn by the SS, usually on the front of their caps below the German eagle, was the death's head, the *Totenkopf*. This, with their black uniforms, was a copy of the outfit and headdress worn by the Life Guard Cavalry of the Prussian kings and German emperors, the "Death's Head" Hussars or *Leibhusaren*. In addition to collar and cap badges, the SS took to wearing cuff bands to denote their unit: the *Leibstandarte* Adolf Hitler wore one embroidered Adolf Hitler; the 2nd SS Panzer Division (*Das Reich*) wore a *Das Reich* cuff band, and so on.

From its original strength of 117 men, the *Leibstandarte* soon expanded into two battalions commanded by Sepp Dietrich, Hitler's personal bodyguard and chauffeur. On June 30, 1934, the *Liebstandarte* took part in the night of the "Long Knives" when Hitler ordered the elimination of Ernst Röhm, the Chief of Staff of the SA. The executioners led by Dietrich, and several *Liebstandarte* NCOs (non-commissioned officers) including the Drum Major, killed six SA men in Munich, and three in Berlin. One of the motives behind these murders was an unspoken agreement between Hitler and the army that the SA would not become a rival army. The SA did not, but the SS most certainly did.

During 1934–35 more SS units were formed into SS-*Verfugüngtruppe* (SS-VT), or Special Purpose Troops, including two new *Standarten* (regiments), the Germania and the Deutschland. A motorized battalion of the *Leibstandarte* led the German occupation force into Austria in March 1938. In July 1938, Hitler announced that all SS-VT *Standarten* would form part of the army in war. By 1943, the *Leibstandarte* had become the 1st SS Panzer Division *Leibstandarte*, and the *Deutschland* and *Der Führer* the 2nd SS Panzer Division *Das Reich*. Eventually there were almost a quarter of a million SS troops in 38 divisions of the Waffen SS, as the SS-VT came to be called. So much for Hitler's promise to the army. The Waffen SS acquired a reputation as fanatical and highly competent soldiers in World War II, but this should not obscure the fact that they carried out numerous atrocities against both soldiers and civilians, notably in Russia and France. The SS even had a slang word for it, *rabatz*, meaning "having fun killing everyone in sight."

Even more notorious for their atrocities were the concentration-camp guard units, the SS-*Totenkopfverbände* (SS-TV), a separate part of the SS from the Waffen although they did provide the manpower for the 3rd SS Panzer Division *Totenkopf*. Unlike the Waffen, the SS-TV wore a death's head insignia on their tunics. Under the direction of the murderous ex-chicken-farmer Himmler, they enslaved and murdered millions.

LEFT: The Nuremburg Rally 1933. The motto on the standards is "*Deutschland Erwache*" (Germany Awake).

ABOVE: An SS insignia in bronze, with silver-plated runes.

■₆ The Stuka

The Stuka Junkers 87 bomber was designed to provide close support for the German army. It was inspired by the experience of World War I when, by 1918, the German army was on the receiving end of fire delivered by the Royal Flying Corps and later the RAF in support of the British Army. The Germans further developed the techniques for this tactic, in stark contrast to the British. By 1939, the RAF was paying lip service to close air support of ground forces in the interests of pursuing an independent war strategy that disregarded the needs of the other two services. The German tactical doctrine of pushing their armor far ahead carried with it the risk that the tanks would outrun their artillery support. Tactical air support would fill the gap, especially the Stuka dive-bomber.

The Stuka's dive-bombing attack was especially effective in towns, and against vehicles on roads, when these were all lined up like ducks in a row. It was not so effective against infantry well spread out in open country, but it took a long time for troops to realize this. The psychological terror effect was enhanced by a wind-driven siren mounted on the fixed undercarriage, which gave out a loud wailing scream as it dived. The technique used by the Stuka pilots was to put the aircraft into a steep dive from about 6,000 feet (1,800 m), aiming the aircraft at the target using his ailerons to keep it aligned, while the dive brakes automatically kept the dive at the correct angle. As soon as the bombs were released, usually at about 900 feet (275 m), an automatic recovery system pulled the Stuka out of its near-vertical dive. The G-force on the aircrew was around force six. Stukas often dropped their bombs within a few yards of the target, and even achieved direct hits. This was something a conventional bomber could achieve only by sheer luck.

The Stuka was fitted with a twin-barreled rear-firing twin machine gun but, with a fixed undercarriage and gull wings, the aircraft was slow, and its rear gun gave little protection against well-flown modern fighters. The Stuka was especially vulnerable during the pull-up from its dive. The Spitfires and Hurricanes created such mayhem among the Stukas when they took part in the Battle of Britain that they were withdrawn from that particular contest.

The Stuka was used to great effect in Russia and in North Africa, in the role for which it was intended, destroying a significant number of tanks. The Stuka's successful time in North Africa came to an end when the RAF regained air superiority in early-to-mid-1942.

The Stuka also had a very long run of success at sea, especially in the Mediterranean, operating from airfields in Italy, the Greek Islands, and the North African coast. This was partially the result of the fact that the Royal Navy did not have a really effective carrier-borne fighter until it acquired American Grumman Hellcats in 1944. That in turn was because aircraft procurement for the Royal Navy in the interwar years was in the hands of the RAF, resulting in a run of poor-performance aircraft ordered by a service that had no interest in carrier warfare—unlike the situation prevailing in the U.S. and Japan.

Stukas inflicted heavy casualties, ship losses, and damage to British convoys transiting the Mediterranean, especially those supplying Malta. They were also responsible for much damage in Malta itself, as well as to ships in the dockyard there, notably the carrier HMS *Illustrious*, in for repair. Stukas were used extensively in Crete in 1941, both in support of the German airborne landings and against ships evacuating the British troops when the island fell.

LEFT: Stukas over Stalingrad during the German assault on the city, September–October 1942.

ABOVE TOP: A Stuka (JU-87) starts a half-roll before a nosedive.

ABOVE BOTTOM: The Stuka was at its best in close support of ground troops, and in the anti-ship role, especially in the first half of the war, before the Allies gained air superiority.

■7 The *Admiral Graf Spee*

The "pocket battleship" *Admiral Graf Spee* was the last of three *Deutschland* class cruisers, laid down before Adolf Hitler came to power, while Germany still observed the terms of the Treaty of Versailles of 1919. This treaty allowed Germany to build warships with a maximum displacement of 10,000 tons (11,200 short tons). In fact the class exceeded the displacement by 1,700 tons (1,900 short tons).

The *Admiral Graf Spee* and its sisters (*Deutschland* and *Admiral Scheer*) were not battleships, but heavily armed, thinly protected, long-range merchant raiders, stronger than any faster ship, and also faster than any other stronger vessels, except for the British battle cruisers *Hood*, *Renown*, and *Repulse*. They were potentially a very serious threat. If the Germans had built all eight of the class, as permitted by the Treaty, three British battle cruisers would have been insufficient to match them—and the Washington Naval Treaty (February 6, 1922) did not allow Britain to build any more battle cruisers.

On August 21 and 23, 1939, while diplomatic moves were being made to resolve the crisis over Danzig that eventually led to the outbreak of World War II, the *Admiral Graf Spee* and the *Deutschland* sailed from Wilhelmshaven for their intended areas of operations—the *Graf Spee* to the South Atlantic and the *Deutschland* to the North Atlantic. Their purpose: to strain British sea power by posing a constant threat to merchant-shipping routes. There were plenty of targets, because an average of 2,500 ships flying the Red Ensign were at sea on any given day. The two pocket battleships were permitted by Hitler to commence operations on September 24, following the failure of his "peace initiative" after he had crushed Poland.

The *Deutschland* sank only two merchantmen before being recalled to Germany and renamed *Lützow*; it would never do if the "Germany" were to be sunk. Eventually, after the *Graf Spee* under Captain Langsdorff had sunk nine ships, Commodore Harwood with the heavy cruiser *Exeter* and light cruisers *Ajax* and *Achilles* located her 150 miles (240 km) off the River Plate estuary in Uruguay, on December 12, 1939.

The *Graf Spee* was more heavily armored than the *Exeter*, and with six 28-cm (11-in) guns in two triple turrets, and secondary armament of eight 15-cm (5.9-in) guns, outgunned the heavy cruiser, let alone the light cruisers with their 15.2-cm (6-in) guns. *Graf Spee* had 54,000-horsepower diesel engines which gave her a radius of action of 10,000 miles (16,000 km) at cruising, even without refueling from her attendant supply ship—more than twice the radius of a steam-turbine ship. She had a catapult-launched seaplane and search radar to scan the sea for victims or enemy warships. At this time very few British ships were fitted with radar.

Notwithstanding the disparity in size and gun power, Commodore Harwood ordered his ships to engage *Graf Spee* on two sides. A running battle ensued, with *Graf Spee* in Harwood's words "wriggling like an eel behind smoke screens." His fire was very accurate. *Exeter* was so badly damaged she had to retire, but the two light cruisers kept

LEFT: The *Admiral Graf Spee* after being scuttled on the orders of her captain.

ABOVE: The "pocket battleship" *Admiral Graf Spee* off Montevideo with some of her crew over the side inspecting damage after the Battle of the River Plate.

up the fire. Soon they too were so damaged that Harwood ordered them to disengage. Instead of turning to crush the two light cruisers, Langsdorff kept heading for Montevideo in Uruguay. Admittedly he had suffered two flesh wounds and been temporarily knocked unconscious. Once in Montevideo, a clever deception scheme by the British persuaded Langsdorff that a large force had now assembled and was waiting for him to emerge. The plan included the British Ambassador in Montevideo making considerable efforts to delay the *Graf Spee*'s sailing, to gain time for British reinforcements to arrive in the shape of the carrier *Ark Royal* and the battle cruiser *Renown*.

Langsdorff came to the conclusion that to engage in battle would lead to the certain loss of his ship and pointless sacrifice of his crew. Admiral Raeder, the Commander-in-Chief (C-in-C) of

the German Navy, and Hitler both agreed that it was out of the question to accept internment of the *Graf Spee* by Uruguay.

On December 17, the *Graf Spee* with a skeleton crew weighed anchor and moved slowly into the estuary of the Plate. At 7:36 pm, her ensign was hauled down. Twenty minutes later her structure was shattered by explosive charges. Amid billowing smoke and flames, she settled on a sandbank. The *Ark Royal* and *Renown* were still 1,000 miles (1,600 km) away.

Three days later, Langsdorff wrapped himself up in the Imperial German Ensign (not the Swastika) and shot himself, having written in a final letter: "I alone bear the responsibility for scuttling the Panzerschiff *Admiral Graf Spee*. I am happy to pay with my life to prevent any possible reflection on the honor of the flag."

■8 Churchill's Cigar

Many photographs of Winston Churchill depict him with a cigar either in his mouth or in his hand. There is even one of him at the controls of the aircraft that flew him home from Washington in January 1942, with a large cigar jutting out into the cockpit.

In November 1895, just ten days short of his 21st birthday, Churchill—who had graduated from Sandhurst at the end of the previous year and was now a second lieutenant in the 4th Hussars—accompanied his friend Reginald Barnes to Cuba, where Spanish forces were attempting to crush a rebellion by the islanders. Before leaving he persuaded the *Daily Graphic* to publish his reports on the insurrection. He also went to see Field Marshal Lord Wolseley, Commander-in-Chief of the British Army, who gave him clearance to see the Director of Military Intelligence (DMI), General Chapman. The DMI gave him maps and intelligence, and asked him to garner as much information as he could on a number of military matters, including the effect of the new metal-jacket bullet.

Few second lieutenants, then or now, would have sufficient clout to gain direct access to such elevated folk. It was an indication of the influence that Churchill had by virtue of his family connections. As well as bringing back information, he wrote to his mother, Lady Randolph Churchill, "I shall bring back a great many Havana cigars, some of which can be laid down in the cellars of 35 Great Cumberland Place"—his mother's new London home.

Churchill spent about a month in Cuba, where he filed five despatches for the *Daily Graphic*, saw some fighting, and gained some sympathy for the rebel cause. On the soldierly qualities of Spanish troops, he told the *New York World*: "I make no reflections on their courage, but they are well versed in the art of retreat." During one attack, he was moving with General Valdez, who, as he later wrote to his mother, "drew

a great deal of fire on to us and I heard enough bullets whistle and hum to satisfy me for some time to come." Bullets sound, as he reported to the *Daily Graphic*, "sometimes like a sigh, sometimes like a whistle, and at others like the buzz of an offended hornet." Churchill was never to lose the taste for being near the action, of which he was to see a great deal during his life. King George VI had to write and forbid him to be present off the Normandy beaches on June 6, 1944.

The other lifelong habit he acquired in Cuba was smoking cigars: Cubans. He was as good as his word to his mother, and brought a large stock back with him. For the rest of his life he smoked between six and ten a day. He wore a cigar cutter on his watch chain, but never used it, preferring to pierce the end with a match. He was also careless with his ash, and his clothes and carpets had numerous burn marks on them.

During the Potsdam Conference (July 16–August 2, 1945) after the end of the War in Europe, Stalin told Churchill that he had taken to smoking cigars. Churchill replied that if a photograph of a cigar-smoking Stalin could be flashed across the world, it would cause an immense sensation. On Churchill's return to England after the Yalta Conference (February 4–11, 1945), he gave a banquet for King Ibn Saud of Saudi Arabia at Lake Fayyum in Egypt. He was told that the King, a strict Wahhabi Muslim, would not allow smoking in his presence. Churchill reported later: "I was the host and I said that if it was his religion that made him say such things, my religion prescribed as an absolute sacred ritual smoking cigars and drinking alcohol before, after and, if need be, during all meals and the intervals between them."

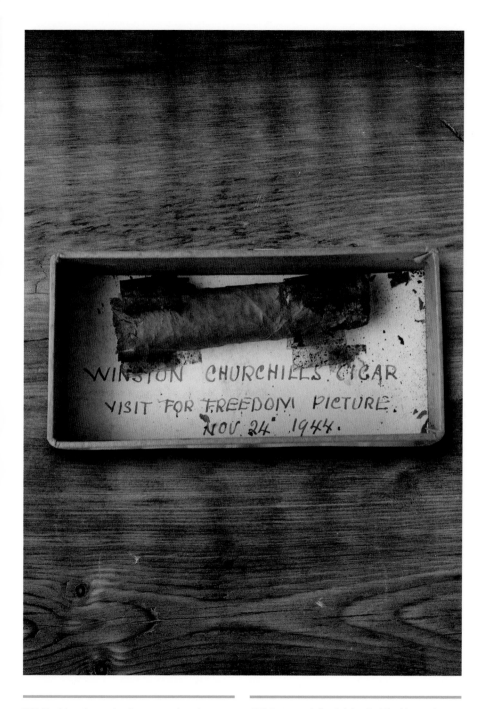

WINSTON CHURCHILLS CIGAR
VISIT FOR FREEDOM PICTURE.
NOV 24 1944.

LEFT: Churchill in a "siren suit" smoking a cigar in his study.

ABOVE: A cigar half-smoked by Churchill sold at Bonhams on January 17, 2011.

◼9 The U-boat

The terms of the 1919 Treaty of Versailles specifically forbade Germany from owning any submarines— *Unterseeboot* (hence known as U-boats). However, in 1922, the Germans set up a design bureau at The Hague in the Netherlands to ensure that they did not fall behind in submarine development. Using yards in Rotterdam and in Helsinki in Finland, they constructed submarines for export to Turkey, Spain, and Finland. A number of designs were prepared which would form the basis for future German submarines. The Germans also ran a secret submarine-crew-training program in Finnish boats. Thus, when Hitler came to power in Germany, and revoked the Treaty of Versailles, it was possible to begin the construction of submarines and expand the number of U-boat crews without delay.

In January 1935, construction of U-boats began at Bremen in Germany. The first boats, Type 1 A, were based on those built for Finland and Spain. On March 25, 1935, Germany announced her intention to re-arm. Ten Type VIIA boats, based on earlier designs, were built within ten months. These were the basis of the highly successful Type VII B and VII C boats that became the workhorse of the German navy, and operated in the Battle of the Atlantic from 1939 to 1943.

Like the submarines of any navy in World War II, U-boats dived only when necessary. They had good endurance and surface speed when using their diesel engines. Using electric batteries when it dived, a typical submarine could motor for about one hour at around eight knots, or for four days at two knots. But the air became foul after about a day submerged, despite oxygen supplies and CO_2 absorption equipment, which the Germans were the first to develop. When the batteries became too low to provide power, the submarine had to surface to start diesels and recharge. The surface range of large submarines motoring on diesels without refueling was many times that of any destroyer. The big German Type VII C had a range of 12,600 nautical miles (23,300 km), and 32,000 nautical miles (59,300 km) for the even bigger IX D. The Germans used large Type XIV *Milchkuh*, or "Milch Cow," submarines as tankers to extend the range of their boats in the South Atlantic and Mediterranean.

By mid-1942, the Allied development of centimetric airborne radar, carried in very-long-range aircraft covering large areas of the Atlantic, made surfacing at night very hazardous for all U-boats, including "Milch Cows." The Germans, searching for a solution, remembered that they had found the answer on Dutch submarines captured when they overran Holland in 1940. This consisted of a pipe that could reach the surface from a dived submarine at periscope depth. A valve at the top closed the pipe automatically when the submarine dived or an unexpectedly large wave covered the top, just as the ball in a recreational diver's snorkel does today. By mid-1944 about half the U-boat fleet had been fitted with these *Schnorchels*. But there were problems with *Schnorchel*-fitted boats: the boat could not exceed about six knots, or the *Schnorchel* would break off; and sometimes the valve would stick in the closed position, so the diesels sucked air from inside the boat until the engine shut down for lack of oxygen, meanwhile causing a vacuum in the boat resulting in very painful eardrums and even deafness among the crew; and finally, the noise of the running diesels blanked out the boat's sound-detection that warned of approaching enemy escorts.

The Germans constantly sought improvements to their boats in order to frustrate the Allies' increasingly effective anti-submarine measures. The Type XXI Electro boat, with greatly increased battery capacity, had a top submerged speed of 17.2 knots, and a range at five knots of 365 nautical miles (676 km) without using its *Schnorchel* except to refresh air in the boat. Luckily for the Allies, this type arrived too late to take part in active operations. Even more fortunately, so did another German invention: a boat with a turbine propulsion system supplied with oxygen and steam from the chemical reaction of hydrogen peroxide. It needed no air from outside the boat, and was the forerunner of the nuclear boats of today.

LEFT: A German U-boat captain tracking his target through the periscope.

ABOVE: The *U-505* in the Atlantic west of Africa after its capture on June 4, 1944, by a U.S. Navy Task Force consisting of the escort carrier U.S.S. *Guadalcanal* and escorts.

⬛10 The Maginot Line

At the outbreak of World War II, the French relied heavily on the Maginot Line, either to deter Germany from invading or to frustrate any attempts to do so. It was named after the War Minister from 1929 to 1932, who as Sergeant Maginot had been wounded at Verdun during World War I. Loss of some of the forts defending Verdun had nearly cost the French the battle. Their experiences there and during other battles in World War I, and the terrible losses they suffered, persuaded the French that fortresses and artillery were the answer in any future war. They fell into the age-old trap of planning to fight the next war on the basis of the previous one.

Constructed between 1930 and 1935, and extending from Luxembourg to the Swiss border, the Maginot Line was not really a line but a string of concrete forts built about 3 miles (5 km) apart and interspersed with smaller casemates. Both types were well buried, with only observation cupolas and gun turrets visible, and even these in many cases could be lowered flush with the roof. Advanced-

warning posts, antitank obstacles, wire, and mines screened the forts. The garrisons varied from about 12 to 30 men in each casemate, and from 200 to 1,200 in the forts. The latter were like underground villages, with barracks, kitchens, generators, magazines, and even electric railroads to transport men and ammunition from barrack and magazine to the gun positions. Casemates contained machine guns and one 1.85-inch (47-mm) antitank gun, with heavy artillery in the forts.

Belgium was still an ally of France when the Maginot Line was being built, and so extending the line to cover the 250 miles (400 km) of the Franco–Belgian border was considered tactless, as it would send a signal of no confidence in Belgium's capability to resist invasion and would isolate her on the "wrong side" of the line. An added disincentive to extending the line

was cost. The 87 miles (139 km) completed by 1935 had cost 4,000 million francs, an overspend of 3,000 million francs. Finally, an extension of the line would run through the heavily industrialized region of Lille-Valenciennes, causing major disruption to French industry. To avoid losing this region, as they had in World War I, the French decided that they would have to stop the invader before he crossed the French frontier. So when Belgium naively decided to opt for a policy of strict neutrality, the French planned to enter Belgian territory from the west the moment the Germans invaded from the east, with or without Belgian permission. When Belgian neutrality did not spare the country from invasion in May 1940, the French were allowed in, but instead of fighting from behind the concrete and steel of the Maginot line on which so much treasure had been spent, they were forced to engage in a mobile battle of encounter in open country, a contest for which they were neither mentally prepared nor organized.

This would have been unsettling enough, but the German armored advance through the supposedly "impassable to armored vehicles" Ardennes, which sliced the French armies in half, was the final straw that broke the French. They had deployed their best formations into Belgium, and thus deprived themselves of the means to form a reserve. When Winston Churchill flew to Paris to find out what was happening, he asked General Maurice Gamelin, commander of all French land forces, "Où est la masse de manoeuvre?" (Where is your strategic reserve?), to which Gamelin replied, "Aucune" (There isn't one). The soldiers who might have formed a reserve were sitting uselessly on the Maginot Line. Although at the last minute some troops were pulled out of the line, they possessed neither the training nor the equipment in the shape of armor or mobile artillery to fight as a strategic reserve against a highly mobile enemy.

LEFT: A drawing of the Maginot Line that appeared in a British illustrated magazine in January 1940. It was a piece of propaganda aimed at reassuring the British public by depicitng the impregnable Maginot Line with its stocks of food, medical supplies, and underground hospital. The internal railroad was actually of a much more modest size.

ABOVE: In the foreground, a steel gun or observation cupola, which could be lowered flush with the ground during a heavy artillery bombardment. In the background a concrete casemate housing heavier artillery.

BELOW: French officers show visiting British officers the Maginot Line.

◼️11️⃣ Civilian Gas Masks

Both well before and during the first two years of World War II, it was believed that any attack on the United Kingdom would include gas. This was because it had been used frequently during the fighting in World War I against troops in the field, although never against civilians. Furthermore, proponents of air power, such as the Italian General Giulio Douhet, had forecast the use of gas against cities. He and others were responsible for most of the predictions that aerial bombing would cause the rapid collapse of any populations subjected to it. In the event, these predictions proved wildly exaggerated, but among those who believed them were Britain's political leaders. Their fears were fed by the RAF's insistence that the bomber would always get through, a claim that helped in the battle with the other services for funding. Along with Douhet, they proved to be wrong.

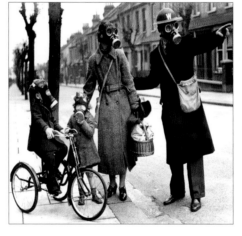

In September 1939, the only power to have an offensive gas capability was the Soviet Union. The Germans had about 3,250 tons of gas but no means of delivering it, as Hitler had banned its use. As the war progressed, they also developed a variety of lethal nerve gases, but never used them. Despite these facts, the British believed that such weapons would be used against their civilian population, and perception was everything. British gas protection, detection, and decontamination equipment were rated the best in the world. By 1938, gas masks for the civilian population were being manufactured in such quantities that by September 1939 some 38 million gas masks had been issued to households all over the country.

Everyone was required to carry their gas mask in its cardboard container with them at all times. Posters exhorting them to do so were widespread, as were instructions on how to don the mask. There were special masks for children and for babies. Wardens carried wooden gas rattles that would warn of an impending gas attack. A bell would signal the All Clear.

Civilians were not issued with protective clothing of any kind, so had mustard gas, for example, been used, their exposed skin would have been badly blistered. Thus, despite the universal issue of masks, and penalties for not carrying them, the protection measures instituted in Britain were not as effective as they might at first sight seem.

As the war progressed, people stopped carrying their gas masks, and soldiers, who in 1940 were never seen without them, stopped carrying them too. Paradoxically, this was just as the Germans were starting to develop the nerve agent Tabun, and by the end of the war an even more deadly gas, Sarin, was ready for production, with the deadliest of them all, Soman, under development. Neither the civilian population nor the armed forces of any Allied nation had clothing capable of giving protection against nerve gas.

In the event, the gas masks issued to the civilian population of Britain were never needed, and fear of retaliation prevented the Germans from using nerve gas.

ABOVE: An air raid warden gives directions to a mother and two children during a gas drill in Southend.

LEFT: A poster reminding people to carry their gas masks at all times and showing the correct way to hold it before pulling it on.

BELOW: A gas mask of the type issued to the civilian population of Britain.

◼12 The Mitsubishi A6M Zero

The Mitsubishi Zero, the most famous of all Japanese aircraft of World War II, was the first carrier-based aircraft to outperform contemporary land-based fighters. Its appearance when Japan attacked Pearl Harbor, and during the next year of the war, came as a great shock to the Americans and British, who had failed to note its performance in China in late 1940 and ignored reports by the U.S. General Claire Lee Chennault, commander of the Flying Tigers operating in support of Chinese forces, a year before America came into the war.

The A6M Zero was built by Mitsubishi in response to the Japanese navy's demand for a fighter with a top speed of 311 miles per hour (500 km/h) and fitted with two cannons and two machine guns. It was put into production in 1940, the Japanese year 2600, so it became popularly known as the Zero-Sen (Type 0 fighter). To its enemies it was the "Zero," although its official Allied code name was "Zeke." It first flew operationally in China in mid-1940 and in the first year of the war the Zero swept away Allied fighter opposition so completely that the Japanese began to believe it was invincible.

The Zero was light and maneuverable and had exceptionally long range. Its maximum speed at 350 miles per hour (563 km/h) exceeded the original specification and it had a range of 1,900 miles (3,060 km) with a drop tank. The American equivalent carrier fighter had a range of 1,750 miles (2,820 km). The Zero was able to operate from island bases if a carrier was not available; for example, during the Guadalcanal Campaign (August 7, 1942–February 9, 1943), Zeros were able to fly from islands 650 miles (1,050 km) away from the combat area. At low speeds, the lightly built Zero could easily out-turn its heavier American opponents.

At the beginning of the war it could climb twice as fast as its rivals. It was one of the most agile fighters ever built and in the hands of its well-trained navy pilots it was deadly, able to match any fighter in the world. This led the Americans to adopt the saying, "Never get into a dogfight with a Zero."

It had one drawback: in order to achieve this performance, and carry heavier guns than its rival U.S. and British fighters, it sacrificed protection. The Zero pilot was not protected by armor, nor did the aircraft have self-sealing fuel tanks. By the end of 1943, when the Zero was starting to lose its edge over American fighters, notably the Grumman F6F Hellcat, the

Japanese produced the A6M5c Zero. Improvements included a large canvas flotation bag in the rear end of the fuselage in case the aircraft ditched, mainly for use on takeoff or landing in the vicinity of the carrier. It had an 0.8-inch (20-mm) cannon and 0.5-inch (13.2-mm) heavy machine gun on each wing, as well as a heavy machine gun over the engine, which fired through the propeller. But other than armored glass in the cockpit, it still had no armor or self-sealing fuel tanks. The improvements made to the Zero were not enough to enable it to take on the Hellcat with any great chance of success.

As the tide turned against Japan, this great fighter aircraft was mainly used in the suicide Kamikaze role.

◼13 The 88-mm Gun

The German 88-mm gun, the antitank weapon most feared by the Allies in World War II, was originally produced as an antiaircraft, or *flak* gun—*flak* being German slang for *Fliegerabwehrkanone,* or antiaircraft gun. In its antiaircraft version, thousands of 88s were produced during the war. It had a very high muzzle velocity and ceiling (the distance up in the sky to which it could shoot). Although not as powerful as the nearest British equivalent, the 3.7-inch (94-mm) heavy antiaircraft gun, the 88's high muzzle velocity and hence flat trajectory was what made it such a formidable antitank gun.

The Germans first realized the potential of the 88 as an antitank weapon during the Spanish Civil War (1936–39) when the German Condor Legion employed it against armored vehicles. During the 1940 Battle for France, the British and French faced this weapon for the first time, as the German army order of battle in France and Flanders included *flak* battalions. The Germans found

that their 37-mm anti-tank guns could not penetrate the frontal armor of the British Matilda MkII and French Char B tanks, whereas the 88-mm shell could. Perhaps the most dramatic demonstration of this occurred during the British counter-stroke at Arras on May 21, 1940, where the British met Erwin Rommel for the first time in the war, when he was a major-general commanding the 7th Panzer Division. Rommel personally ordered his antiaircraft guns to fire on the British tanks attacking Wailly, southwest of Arras, bringing the British advance to a dead stop.

The British were slow to learn. The Germans repeatedly used the 88 in North Africa to devastating effect, a favorite ploy being to pull their armor back through a shield of well-concealed 88s, which then shattered the British tanks following as if they were hunting a fox. By now the antitank version of

the 88 had been officially designated *Panzerabwehrkanone,* or PAK for short, meaning anti-armor gun.

In Russia, the 88 proved to be the only antitank gun able to penetrate armor of the Soviet T34; except at very close range, shells from German 37-mm and 50-mm antitank guns bounced off. The flat terrain of Russia suited the characteristics of the 88 perfectly, as did the desert. It was less effective in the *bocage* in Normandy or the mountains of Italy, although still greatly feared.

The versatility of the 88 was never better demonstrated than during the battle code-named Goodwood, July 18–20, 1944, during the Normandy campaign. This operation was an attempt by three British armored divisions to break out into open country east of Caen. The rolling country, interspersed with small woods and villages, was very different to the *bocage* farther west. After making good progress, the British 11th Armoured Division was approaching the village of Cagny, when mayhem ensued. Cagny was occupied by four 88-mm *flak* guns of the 16th Luftwaffe Field Division. Also in the village was Colonel Hans von Luck, a battle group commander of 21st Panzer Division. He ordered the Luftwaffe officer in command to engage the approaching British armor. When the Luftwaffe officer demurred, von Luck prodded him in the stomach with his pistol, saying, "You can either die now, or later winning a medal." The 88s were duly switched from pointing at the sky and re-laid on the approaching tanks. The 11th Armoured Division lost a total of 126 tanks that day, many of them to the 88s.

The 88-mm was arguably the best antitank gun on either side in World War II. It was also mounted in several types of armored fighting vehicle, notably the Nashom, Ferdinand, and Jagdpanther tank destroyers and the Tiger tank.

LEFT: An 88 on an antiaircraft mount, a *flak* 36 cruciform, engages armor in Russia.

ABOVE: An 88 gun on wheeled mount, easy to tow and quicker to deploy than on antiaircraft mount; especially useful in the antitank role.

◾14 The Little Ships

The role of the "little ships" in the evacuation of the British Expeditionary Force (BEF) from Dunkirk between May 26 and June 4, 1940, is perhaps the thing that most people remember about the event.

In 1940, Dunkirk was the biggest harbor on the Channel coast. It had seven deep-water basins, four dry docks, and 5 miles (8 km) of quays. When the decision was made to evacuate the BEF, the port was under almost continuous attack by the Luftwaffe and fires and extensive damage made the quays unusable. A plan was therefore put forward to take the troops off the 10 miles (16 km) of beach east of Dunkirk. These shelved gently, so even small craft could get no nearer to the waterline than about a hundred yards/meters, and soldiers had to wade out to them. There were no jetties, fishing harbors, or piers. Large vessels had to anchor well offshore, and craft ferrying troops to them had a long turnaround time. Clearly the more small craft, the quicker the job would be done.

The officer responsible for organizing the evacuation (Operation Dynamo) was Vice Admiral Bertram Ramsay, the Flag Officer Dover. He arranged for the Admiralty Small Boat Pool to gather at Ramsgate as many small craft as could be found: tugs, trawlers, dredgers, fishing boats (some still under sail), cockle boats, yachts, and small motor cruisers whose owners loved "messing about in boats." Here their skippers, mostly their owners, were issued with charts, many of them with the course to Dunkirk already laid out for them. Many skippers had never crossed the Channel before and their knowledge of navigation was sparse; some had never even left the Thames. Navigation was made more challenging by the fact that the direct course for Dunkirk ran near Calais, which was occupied by the Germans, who shelled any vessel that came within range, making an alternative "dog leg" course necessary. British minefields laid in the Channel were an additional hazard, and it was necessary to keep to the swept route.

Admiral Ramsay's representative ashore at Dunkirk was Captain W. G. Tennant, with a beach party of 12 officers and 150 ratings. His arrival on May 27 coincided with repeated German air raids. By the end of that day it was apparent that evacuation from the beaches was desperately slow. By midnight on May 27/28, only 7,669 men had arrived in England, and about two-thirds of these had loaded in Dunkirk harbor before its use was suspended. But Tennant spotted that the 1,600-yard (1,460 m) long East Mole protecting Dunkirk harbor was connected to the beaches by a narrow causeway, and that evening he ordered a destroyer to come alongside the mole, followed by six more. The gamble succeeded, and this became the principal means of evacuation. Late on the afternoon of May 28, the first "little ships" appeared off the beaches. The evacuation gained momentum. Nevertheless, May 30 was the only day on which more men were lifted from the beaches (29,512) than from the harbor (24,311), and the day's total was the largest so far. The job of the "little ships" was to ferry troops out to waiting ships offshore. The courage displayed by civilian crews plowing back and forth hour after hour, day after day, in the face of bombing was unquestionable.

At 2:23 pm on June 4, the Admiralty gave the signal ending Operation Dynamo. Originally it was thought that some 45,000 soldiers might be rescued; in the end a total of 338,226 was reached. That the contribution of the "little ships" to the successful evacuation from the Dunkirk beaches was significant is without doubt, but their role has become the enduring myth of the operation to the extent of obliterating the contribution of the Royal and Merchant Navies. This can be understood in the context of the time—to boost national morale and cohesion, the story of the "little ships" was milked as hard as possible. The facts are that over two-and-a-half times as many troops were taken from Dunkirk harbor than from the beaches, and of those taken off the beaches, the majority were transported in destroyers or other ships, albeit in many cases ferried out to these larger vessels, either by "little ships" or ships' boats. The actual number of men taken directly from the beaches to England by the "little ships" was small.

LEFT: Low tide on the beaches between Dunkirk and La Panne; British troops await evacuation.

ABOVE: One of the Dunkirk "little ships," moored in Rye harbor.

OVERLEAF: A river motor cruiser gets a tow from a trawler, both laden with troops from the Dunkirk beaches.

■15 The Spitfire

The Supermarine Spitfire is the most famous British aircraft ever built. It was among the fastest and most maneuverable fighters of World War II and served in every theater of that war. One of the most beautiful aircraft ever produced, it was designed by R. J. Mitchell, the chief designer at Supermarine Aviation Works (part of Vickers Armstrong Aviation) in response to a British Air Ministry specification to produce a fighter capable of 251 miles per hour (404 km/h). He was not satisfied with his initial designs, and it was not until March 1936 that the first successful prototype took off from Eastleigh Airport (now Southampton Airport) piloted by Joseph "Mutt" Summers, Chief Test Pilot for Vickers. In June 1936, the Air Ministry placed the first order for 310 Spitfires. Although Mitchell

died the following year as a result of cancer, he lived long enough to see his prototype fly.

Mitchell's design, the Spitfire MK1A, the first all-metal stressed-skin fighter to go into production in Britain, was an eight-gunned aircraft with elliptical wings powered by a Rolls Royce Merlin engine. Spitfires were hand-built and took three times as long to assemble as their main rival, the German Messerschmitt Bf 109E. But it was produced in sufficient numbers to play a key role in the Battle of Britain (July–October 1940). With a top speed in level flight of 360 miles per hour (570 km/h), it was comparable to the Messerschmitt BF109E, but more maneuverable in a tight turn, provided the pilot could withstand the G forces on his body. The bulged canopy gave the pilot a better all-around view than the Bf 109E, but the latter was faster

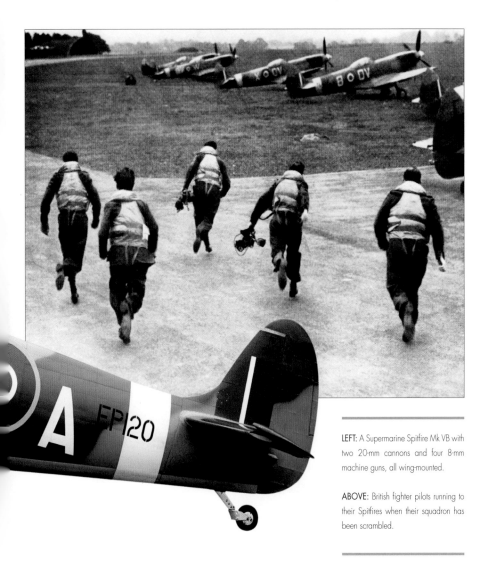

LEFT: A Supermarine Spitfire Mk VB with two 20-mm cannons and four 8-mm machine guns, all wing-mounted.

ABOVE: British fighter pilots running to their Spitfires when their squadron has been scrambled.

in a dive than the Spitfire MK1A, and had a higher ceiling, thanks to its fuel-injected engine. The Bf 109E's 20-mm cannon gave it a significant range and hitting power advantage over the Spitfire MK1A. In 1941, Spitfires came into service with two similar-sized cannon and four machine guns. The engine was constantly modified during the war, and in the later versions the Rolls Royce Griffon had twice the power of the original Merlin.

Eventually, 22,890 Spitfires of 19 different marks were built between 1936 and 1947. Although it was used as a fighter until the end of the war, its main role became high-level photo-reconnaissance. The United States Army Air Force flew more than 600 Spitfires during World War II.

The Spitfire was modified to operate off carriers, and the Seafire, as it was called, played a significant part in air battles fought by the Royal Navy's Fleet Air Arm, especially in the Mediterranean during the North African campaign in 1942–43. The last of the 2,556 Seafires produced flew in the Korean War (1950–53) with considerable success.

The last mark of Spitfire produced during World War II was the MkXIX reconnaissance version, with a pressurized cockpit and wing tanks to give it a 1,800-mile (2,896 km) range compared with the Mk1A's range of 395 miles (635 km). In April 1954 the MkXIX flew the last-ever RAF Spitfire sortie over Malaya.

■16 The Messerschmitt Bf 109

First produced in January 1937, long before any production Hurricanes or Spitfires, and thanks to its participation in the Spanish Civil War (1936–39), the Messerschmitt Bf 109 was a thoroughly combat-proven aircraft by the time of the Munich crisis in September 1938. Earlier versions were the 109 B, C, and D (the original prototype being Type A), but by the outbreak of World War II the 109E was available in ever increasing numbers. Nicknamed the "Emil" by its pilots, the 109E outclassed all other fighters except the Spitfire during the first couple of years of the war.

It was a small aircraft, cheap to produce and very maneuverable, with a fast rate of climb and dive, and high acceleration. It was normally fitted with two, or sometimes three, 20-mm cannon as well as two machine guns, which gave the 109 greater range and hitting power than fighters

carrying eight machine guns, notably the earlier Marks of Spitfires and Hurricanes. As the war progressed, the 109E and succeeding models were fitted with a variety of weapons, including rockets and bombs. It had very narrow landing gear, specifically designed to enable wings to be removed for repair or replacement without having to place the fuselage on jacks; and to enable maintenance to be carried out on forward airstrips with minimal facilities. The narrow landing gear resulted in a pronounced swing on takeoff and landing, which in the hands of an inexperienced pilot sometimes ended in a crash.

The cockpit was narrow with a poor forward view through armored glass, and some pilots complained about the cramped conditions. One 109 ace, Adolf Galland, designed a higher cockpit hood, which was named after him and fitted in the K series 109s.

The 109E, with a top speed of 354 miles per hour (569

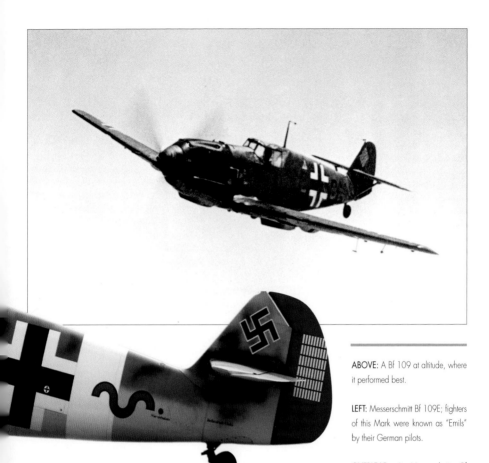

ABOVE: A Bf 109 at altitude, where it performed best.

LEFT: Messerschmitt Bf 109E; fighters of this Mark were known as "Emils" by their German pilots.

OVERLEAF: A Messerschmitt Bf 109E on the ground in 1941.

km/h), was marginally slower than the Spitfire Mk 1A at some altitudes, but faster in a dive and at very high altitude thanks to its two-stage engine supercharger. The Spitfire could turn more tightly than the 109E. The climb rate of the 109E was impressive: 3,300 feet (1,005 m) per minute, compared with the Spitfire Mk 1A at 2,530 feet (771 m) per minute and Hurricane at 2,260 feet (668 m) per minute. The 109-E outclassed the Hurricane under all conditions.

Although the 109 had control of the skies over Poland and France in the first year of the war, certain aspects of the Battle of Britain combined to limit its effectiveness. If allowed to cross the Channel at around 30,000 feet (9,100 m) and engage the Spitfires and Hurricanes on their own, the 109s proved superior. But the RAF turned the Hurricanes on the German bombers, dealing death and destruction at small loss to themselves. This forced the Luftwaffe to change tactics

and order the 109s to escort the bomber stream if they were not to take unacceptable losses in their bomber force. Tied to the bombers, the 109s, without drop tanks (which were introduced later), could spend only 30 minutes over England, and were unable to fly high and use their superior diving and climbing speed to advantage. Their two-stage supercharger made the 109 far more effective at high altitude than their rivals. Had the Battle of Britain been fought at 30,000 feet (9,100 m), it is possible that the RAF would have lost.

Radar also gave the British an overpowering advantage by giving ample warning of the approach of raids, which the Germans had totally discounted in their strategic calculations. To engage the RAF, the German aircrew had long flights over water and a similar return trip. All these factors limited the effectiveness of the ME 109. The happy days of almost uncontested skies over Poland and France were gone.

17 The Fairey Swordfish

The Swordfish was obsolete before it entered service. It was an open cockpit, fabric and wire-braced biplane, looking like a survivor from the First World War rather than an aircraft of the Second. But it did great work throughout World War II in a variety of roles. It was designed as a torpedo attacking aircraft and carried one 18-inch (46 cm) torpedo. Its maximum speed was a mere 138 miles per hour (222 km/h), but it had a respectable range of 1,028 miles (1,694 km) and could carry as good a weapon load as the Japanese carrier-borne bomber, the B5N Kate, and a far better one than the American Douglas Devastator. The latter was more advanced, but far less effective than the Swordfish, which was the most successful British torpedo bomber of the war, sinking more ships than all the Royal Navy's battleships added together.

The Swordfish usually had a crew of three: pilot, observer (navigator in RAF parlance), and a radio operator/air gunner. His single Vickers K .303-inch machine gun was no match for a modern fighter. The pilot communicated with his crew through a voice pipe, known as a Gosport tube. The Swordfish was nicknamed the "Stringbag" because, like the household shopping bag of the time, it seemed to be able to carry anything and was infinitely flexible and indestructible. It could be patched up much more quickly than more sophisticated aircraft.

On November 11, 1940, 21 Swordfish were launched from the carrier Illustrious 180 miles (285 km) from the Italian fleet main base at Taranto. They attacked in two waves, an hour apart. Surprise was complete; one new and two old battleships were torpedoed, a cruiser was hit, and the dockyard damaged. Two Swordfish were lost, but the balance of maritime power in the Mediterranean tilted in favor of the Royal Navy. The Commander-in-Chief Mediterranean Fleet, Admiral Andrew Cunningham, wrote:

The 11th and 12th November 1940 will be remembered

for ever as having shown once and for all that in the Fleet Air Arm the Navy has a devastating weapon. In a total flying time of about six and a half hours carrier to carrier, twenty aircraft inflicted more damage upon the Italian Fleet than was inflicted on the German High Seas Fleet in the daylight action of Jutland. (Engage the Enemy More Closely: The Royal Navy in the Second World War, by Correlli Barnett, Hodder & Stoughton, 1991, page 249)

One outcome of the attack was not so welcome. The Japanese took note that battleships could be attacked in harbor by torpedo-carrying aircraft, and duly put this into effect a year later at Pearl Harbor.

Six months after Taranto, the Swordfish struck another devastating blow. The German battleship Bismarck, having sunk the British battle cruiser Hood in the Denmark Strait on May 24, 1941, was heading for Brest to repair damage inflicted in the battle. A Swordfish strike launched from the Victorious early on May 25 failed to damage the Bismarck further. As the Bismarck neared Brest, and Luftwaffe fighter cover, the Home Fleet battleships pursuing her in heavy seas were running short of fuel and lagging 130 miles (210 km) behind. But the Ark Royal in Admiral James Somerville's Force H was about 40 miles (65 km) northeast of the Bismarck. A Swordfish strike was launched and one torpedo hit the Bismarck's rudder, crippling her. The Home Fleet battleships caught up and sank her.

Swordfish were also extensively employed in the anti-submarine role, carrying a radar set and rockets. The aircraft could carry depth charges, mines, and bombs, and its long endurance enabled it to remain on patrol over convoys for hours. A total of 2,391 Swordfishes were built between 1934 and 1944. The last front-line Swordfish squadron was disbanded on May 21, 1945, two weeks after VE Day. The "Stringbag" had outlasted many of its more modern rivals.

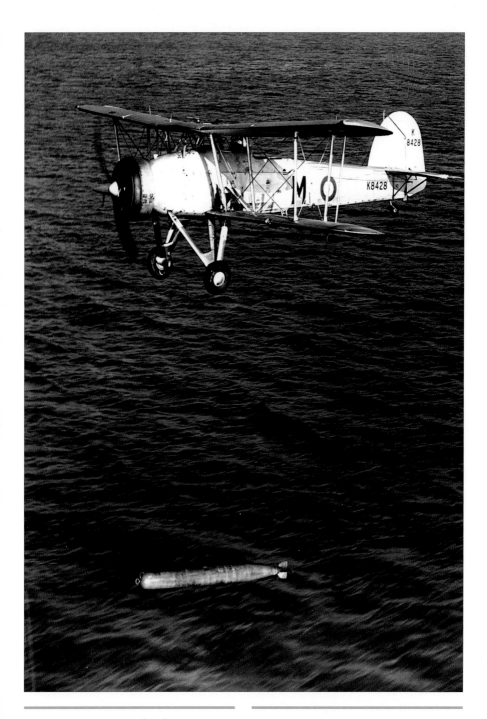

LEFT: Royal Navy Fleet Air Arm Swordfish in formation.

ABOVE: Despite its antiquated appearance, the Swordfish could deliver a torpedo to devastating effect, as it could bombs or depth charges.

■18 An Air Raid Shelter

In 1937, government officials predicted that in any future war with Germany, bombing raids on the civilian population would cause massive casualties. The German air raids on the United Kingdom in the 1914–18 war had killed 1,413 people; next time, it was estimated, Germany would bomb the United Kingdom immediately when war broke out and continue the assault for 60 days. Each ton of explosive dropped would kill or wound 50 people, a total of almost two million casualties. The fact that these statistics flew in the face of reason, not least because the Germans would be incapable of mounting an air assault of these proportions, was not material: they galvanized the government into taking a number of precautions. In 1938, the Munich crisis led to the digging of trenches in public parks and by the outbreak of war, enough covered trenches were available to shelter half a million people. At the same time, Anderson shelters were issued.

This was intended to be erected in a town or suburban back garden and to accommodate six people. It was designed by William Paterson, and named after the Lord Privy Seal, John Anderson, who was responsible for British civil defense. The Anderson shelter consisted of 14 panels of corrugated galvanized steel: six curved panels formed the roof, six straight ones the walls, and two straight panels were erected at each end, one fitted with a door. The resulting upside-down U-shaped structure was 6 feet (1.8 m) high, 4 feet 6 inches (1.37 m) wide, and 6 feet 6 inches (2 m) long, and

internal fitting out was left to individual householders. It was buried 4 feet (1.2 m) deep and the roof was covered with about 15 inches (0.4 m) of soil; the earth roof and walls were often planted as gardens.

Anderson shelters were issued free to householders who earned below a certain income; anyone with a higher income could buy one. Up to the outbreak of war, some 1.5 million shelters were distributed, and a further 2 million after that. The Anderson shelter did provide good protection except against a direct hit by a bomb, but as the war progressed and all-night alerts became more frequent, it was found that, particularly in winter, many people were reluctant to go to a damp, cold hole in the ground which often flooded.

Because many houses lacked cellars, Herbert Morrison, the Minister of Home Security, decided that there was a need for an effective indoor shelter. The result was the Morrison shelter, devised by John Baker. It was issued in kit form to be bolted together inside the house, and consisted of a cage 6 feet 6 inches (2 m) long, 4 feet (1.2 m) wide, and 2 feet 6 inches (0.75 m) high, with a steel top, wire mesh sides, and a steel floor. The shelter was designed to protect people against the upper floor of a typical two-story house falling on them if the house collapsed through blast, but it was unlikely to save their lives if the house received a direct hit. A family could sleep in the cage at night, and use it as a dining table on other occasions. Over half a million Morrison shelters

LEFT: Damage caused by the first night raid on London on August 24/25, 1940; the house has been destroyed, along with the Anderson shelter in the garden.

ABOVE: A family uses its Morrison shelter as a dining table, as envisaged by its designer, John Baker.

RIGHT: A German photograph of two Dornier Do 217 bombers over the Silvertown area of London in 1940. Fires have started in the gas plant at Beckton. West Ham greyhound track is in the center of the picture.

were issued in the course of the war and they were highly effective, saving many lives.

Some householders built their own brick and concrete shelters in their gardens. In addition to the small shelters intended for household use, larger shelters of concrete were built in some communities to provide protection for local inhabitants who lacked alternative means of taking cover from bombing.

Before the outbreak of war, and until the night raids on London in September 1940, taking cover in Tube (subway) stations in London was banned on health grounds, the main justification for this being the spread of disease through lack of sanitary facilities. However, on the night of September 19/20 thousands of Londoners took the matter into their own hands and went to the Tube stations for shelter. The government recognized defeat and took steps to make the use of Tube stations as efficient as possible, including closing off short spur sections of the railway and concreting over the tracks there, and fitting 79 stations with bunks and chemical toilets.

ABOVE: Londoners asleep on the platform at Piccadilly Tube station during an air raid.

RIGHT: A row of houses in Stepney, London, gutted by bombs dropped in a night raid.

◼19 The Parachute X-Type

Britain's first parachute troops started training in the summer of 1940 in response to Winston Churchill's directive of June 22, which asked for "a corps of at least five thousand parachute troops." To begin with, jumpers were trained using the RAF parachute designed for emergency use, operated by pulling a ripcord after leaving the aircraft. The person jumping had to estimate when to do so and have his hands free to operate it. This method was, however, soon found to be unsuitable for army parachute troops, who would be required to jump in groups from the lowest height consistent with safety while carrying heavy equipment. The parachute school at Ringway therefore changed to a parachute of American design, the statichute.

After 135 descents, one man was killed when he became entangled in the rigging lines of his parachute. The American statichute, which their airborne forces used in a modified form throughout the War, was designed so that as the parachutist jumped and fell, the static line connected to the aircraft pulled the canopy out of the bag on his back, followed by the rigging lines, the cords connecting the canopy to the harness. If the jumper made a bad exit, twisting and tumbling before the lazy cord—the final tie connecting the canopy to the static line—broke, he risked being entangled in his own rigging lines. At best, he would then descend hanging by one or both feet and would land on his back or his head. At worst, he would get wrapped up so badly that the parachute would not deploy at all. British parachute soldiers did not jump with reserve chutes in World War II, so if this happened he would die. Even if all went well, the jumper always experienced a bit of a shock as he was brought up with a jerk at the end of his rigging lines.

Raymond Quilter of the GQ Parachute Company found the remedy. Working with Irvin's Parachute Company, he produced the combination of an Irvin parachute in a GQ

packing bag. This X-type parachute, which was to be the standard parachute until the 1960s, worked using a different sequence of opening. As the man jumped, the parachute pack itself broke away from his back, remaining attached to the static line and the aircraft. As the man continued to fall, his weight pulled first his lift webs—the canvas straps attaching the rigging lines to the harness—and then the rigging lines out of the bag. Finally, at the end of the taut and extended rigging lines with the jumper 20 feet (6 m) below the bag, the canopy pulled out of the bag, the final tie which held the apex of the canopy to the pack broke, and the parachute was fully extended, leaving pack and static line attached to the aircraft. The opening shock was negligible and the danger of becoming entangled greatly reduced. The next 24,000 drops were made without a single accident.

The number of parachute soldiers requiring training increased and so, despite the success of the X-type, a team from the Airborne Forces Experimental Establishment and the Royal Aircraft Establishment monitored the procedures followed at the Parachute Training School. As a result, it was decided that twisting and somersaulting in the slipstream could be reduced if a new design of pack was introduced, in which the strap that connected the parachutist to the static line in the aircraft pulled out of the pack at the level of his neck, rather than at waist level. Some accidents still occurred because canopies made of silk sometimes failed to open properly when the material adhered to itself through static electricity. This problem was solved by changing to canopies made of nylon.

The X-type parachute was the standard type used by British airborne forces throughout World War II. Of a total of more than half a million descents made in training at No. 1 Parachute Training School with this statichute up to August 1948, only 42 fatal accidents occurred: a ratio of one in 12,000.

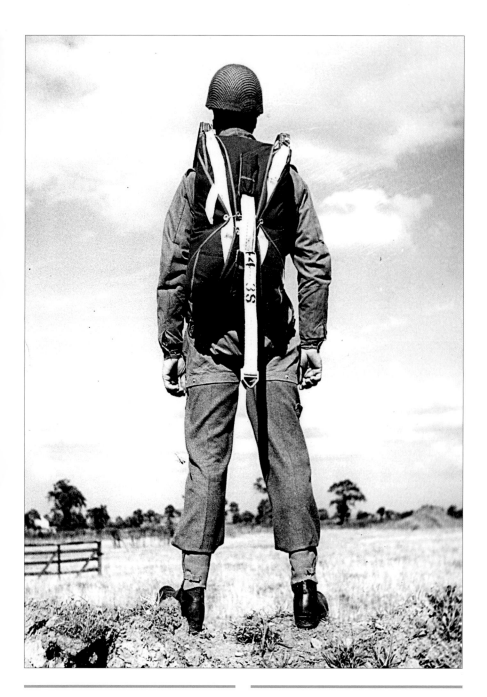

LEFT: A parachutist at the moment of landing. His feet are not together, risking a broken ankle and a reprimand.

ABOVE: Back view of a parachutist in a steel helmet, wearing an X-type parachute. The "D" ring at the end of the strap is to connect it to the static line in the aircraft.

20 The Sten Gun

During the 1940 campaign leading up to the fall of France, the British Expeditionary Force (BEF) encountered an enemy armed with submachine guns, principally the German MP28. A British soldier armed with a bolt-action rifle, especially at close quarters, was at a disadvantage against a German equipped with a submachine gun with automatic fire; officers and specialists such as despatch riders armed only with a revolver, even more so.

Following the evacuation of the BEF, there was a pressing need to manufacture small arms to make up losses incurred in the campaign, as well as to equip a rapidly enlarging army. The British bought as many Thompson submachine guns (Tommy guns) from the United States as could be spared from America's own program to re-equip their expanding armed forces, but this made up only part of the shortfall. The Royal Small Arms Factory at Enfield was therefore charged with producing a British submachine gun. The design selected was the Sten, an acronym formed from the first letter of the surnames of the designers (Major Reginald V. Shepherd and Mr Harold J. Turpin) and the first two letters of Enfield.

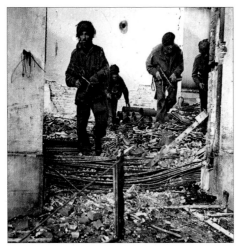

The Sten was cheap and easy to manufacture and could be turned out in small workshops by relatively unskilled labor. Eventually there were eight marks, including models with suppressers or silencers. The Mark III, which was the cheapest and simplest, consisted of only 47 parts and took five man-hours to assemble.

The magazine was side-mounted, copying the German MP28, but this made the gun awkward to hold and fire, especially from the waist, as the firer had to either curve his left wrist under the magazine to grip the fore end or hold the magazine. The latter was discouraged, as the vibration caused by automatic firing against the lever effect of the hand holding the magazine could distort the poorly manufactured magazine catch, altering the angle of the magazine and so causing the round to misfeed and jam. It was not unknown for the magazine to be wrenched out of its socket, leaving the firer holding the gun in one hand and the magazine in the other—embarrassing if not fatal. Despite this being well understood, there are numerous photographs of troops taken in World War II holding their Stens by the magazine.

The Sten worked on the blowback principle: the explosion that sent the bullet up the barrel also blew back the bolt, so only half the energy of the explosion was used to send the round on its way. This, combined with the type of $1/3$-inch (9-mm) ammunition used, meant that the Sten had poor penetrating power. Earlier marks had no safety catch and as a consequence the Sten was sometimes more dangerous to its owner and to friends standing around than to the enemy—wounds and fatalities from accidental discharges were commonplace. Even if the weapon was not cocked, banging it hard on the butt or dropping it butt-down could cause the bolt to drive back sufficiently far for it to pick up a round from the magazine when the spring reasserted itself and pushed the bolt forward. Once the round was seated in the breech, the fixed firing pin on the bolt fired the round, blowing back the bolt to repeat the process until the magazine was empty. To prevent this from happening, later marks had a hole drilled in the casing to take the cocking handle.

Despite these imperfections, millions of Stens were produced during World War II, and on the whole it was a successful weapon in the right circumstances. It was suitable for close-quarter battle, but ineffective at ranges above about 100 yards (90 m), and therefore useless in open country.

LEFT: A posed photograph of British Paratroops at Oosterbeek, Holland, September 1944, in the battle for Arnhem. Shown here holding their Sten guns by the magazine.

ABOVE: A Mark III Sten with skeleton butt.

21 The T-34 Tank

The T-34 was the most significant Soviet tank of World War II. Its inventor, Mikhail Koshkin, named it the T-34 because he first conceived the basics of its design in 1934. Some 40,000 were built during World War II, and it was the most advanced design of its time anywhere in the world. Prototypes were completed in early 1940, and production started immediately, stimulated by the German invasion of France and the Low Countries, even though the Soviet Union was not at war at the time. The T-34 was fast and had fully sloped armor which was thicker than that of any contemporary German, British, or American tanks, with a low silhouette. Its main armament as the vehicle developed was the formidable 76.2-mm L40 gun. Its wide tracks and Christie suspension (with wheels connected to springs) gave it a low ground pressure and hence good terrain-crossing ability, even in mud and snow. This was critical in Russia, and in this respect it was far superior to any German tank. Its V12 diesel engine was also less flammable than the gas engines in German tanks.

Simple to maintain and operate, the T-34 looks more modern than any other tank of its day. Right up to the end of World War II, the Germans and the British, and to some extent the Americans, were building tanks with flat front glacis plates and front turret plates. A flat surface at 90 degrees to the trajectory of an incoming round is more easily penetrated by armor-piercing shot, which ricochets off fully sloped armor like that of the T-34.

As with any armored vehicle, you achieve a combination of thick armor, a big gun, and high speed only with a trade-off. In the case of the T-34, it was size and crew space—the tank was very cramped. Until the improved T-34-85 came into service in early 1944, there was room for only two men in the turret: the commander and the loader. Most tanks in other armies had a three-man turret crew: commander, gunner, and loader. A T-34 commander had to aim and fire the gun while attempting to command his tank, and in the case of platoon commanders, command his subunit at the same time. The commander's problems were not made any easier by the fact that few Soviet tanks were fitted with radios. Only company commanders and upward had radios, while the rest had flags. Therefore a company commander could speak only to fellow company commanders and his battalion commander; he had to give orders to his company using flags.

The Germans remained ignorant about the T-34 in the first few months after they invaded the Soviet Union, as few T-34s were deployed when Operation Barbarossa was launched in June 1941. To begin with, the Germans had a field day destroying several thousand Soviet tanks, but in September 1941 they met the T-34 in large numbers, and it soon demonstrated that it could outshoot, outrun, and outlast any German tank. The effect was to make all German tanks obsolete. The Panzer divisions that had hitherto swept all before them in Poland, France, the Low Countries, and North Africa were no longer kings of the battlefield. Field Marshal Ewald von Kleist called the T-34 "the finest tank in the world." Major General Friedrich von Mellenthin wrote later, "We had nothing comparable." But the Germans continued to inflict defeats on the Red Army until late 1942, and occasionally beyond, because until that time Soviet tactics were faulty; their command and control and operational techniques were nothing like as good as the Germans'—lack of radios being a factor—and they deployed their armor badly. An additional contributor to German continued success for a while was the introduction of new tanks, notably the Tiger heavy gun tank and the medium Panther. The T-34 remained the backbone of Soviet tank divisions to the end of World War II.

■22 The Atlantic Charter

Even before the United States became an official belligerent in World War II, President Franklin D. Roosevelt worried about the common war aims of the United States, Great Britain, and the Soviet Union. By covenant and inference Roosevelt, Churchill, and Stalin had agreed to the defeat of Nazi Germany as a common war aim. For their nations to survive and prosper, Germany would be forced to disarm, reform, and submit to an international treaty regime that would forever restrict its power for imperialistic expansion and political coercion through the threat of war.

In the face of domestic opposition to entering the war or forming an alliance with Great Britain and the Soviet Union, Roosevelt, a wiser and older Wilsonian (i.e. committed to the idea of collective international security), wanted a general statement of war aims that would appeal to idealistic, internationalist Americans, the sort of people who wrote and read magazine and newspaper articles on foreign policy. Since Churchill and Stalin had reputations as imperialists, Roosevelt knew they had few admirers in the United States beyond Anglophiles and dedicated Communists, but FDR could at least improve Churchill's image as a firm ally and internationalist.

Between August 9 and 12, 1941, Roosevelt and Churchill met aboard warships in Placentia Bay, Newfoundland to discuss their current strategic relationship and their future plans if and when the United States became a belligerent. They also wanted to reassure Stalin they would aid him in his defense of the Soviet Union, largely by threatening Japan and saving Stalin from a two-front war. Part of FDR's bargain in aiding Great Britain with surplus U.S. Navy destroyers and Lend-Lease supplies was to convince Churchill to sign the Atlantic Charter.

The document was a promissory pact between the United States and Great Britain, supposed to reassure their own people and potential allies that they did not seek imperial gains in territory or economic advantage, and that they believed in national self-determination and freedom of the seas.

The document also contained a hope for the future, which embodied FDR's "Four Freedoms." They were: freedom from fear, freedom from want, freedom to worship, and freedom of speech, announced by FDR in a speech in January 1941. Churchill, who at that point in the war would, by his own admission, have made a pact with the devil, agreed that these goals were admirable statements of principle. He did not comment on their likelihood of realization. Sharing Churchill's desperation, Stalin agreed to accept the Atlantic Charter later in the year.

Neither FDR nor Churchill actually signed an Atlantic Charter document; instead they made it a press release. However idealistic and expedient, the provisions of the Atlantic Charter eventually took on life in the Charter of the United Nations.

ABOVE: American president Franklin Delano Roosevelt with British prime minister Winston Churchill on board HMS *Prince of Wales* in Placentia Bay, Newfoundland in August 1941.

RIGHT: The final draft of the Atlantic Charter with Winston Churchill's corrections marked.

OVERLEAF: The declaration of the United Nations, signed by 26 nations, agreeing to the principles of the Atlantic Charter.

Prime Minister's meeting with President Roosevelt — Aug. 1941
Draft of Joint Declaration —

COPY NO: ___1___

M O S T   S E C R E T

NOTE: This document should not be left lying about and, if it
is unnecessary to retain, should be returned to the
Private Office.

P R O P O S E D   D E C L A R A T I O N

B. ALTERNATIVE VERSION - i.e. VERSION "A"
INCORPORATING NEW PARAGRAPH PROPOSED BY
CABINET IN ABBEY TELEGRAM NUMBER:- 31.

The President of the United States of America and the
Prime Minister, Mr. Churchill, representing His Majesty's
Government in the United Kingdom, being met together, deem it
right to make known certain common principles in the national
policies of their respective countries on which they base their
hopes for a better future for the world.

First, their countries seek no aggrandisement,
territorial or other;

Second, they desire to see no territorial changes
that do not accord with the freely expressed wishes of the
peoples concerned.

Third, they respect the right of all peoples to choose
the form of government under which they will live; and they
wish to see self-government restored to those from whom it
has been forcibly removed.

Fourth, they will endeavour, with due respect to their
existing obligations, to further the enjoyment by all peoples
of access, on equal terms, to the trade and to the raw
materials of the world which are needed for their economic
prosperity.

Fifth, they support fullest collaboration between
Nations in economic field with object of securing for all
peoples freedom from want, improved labour standards, economic
advancement and social security.

Sixth, they hope to see established a peace, after the
final destruction of the Nazi tyranny, which will afford to
all nations the means of dwelling in security within their own
boundaries, and which will afford assurance to all peoples
that they may live out their lives in freedom from fear.

Seventh, they desire such a peace to establish for all nations
safety on the high seas and oceans.

Eighth, they believe that all of the nations of the
world must be guided in spirit to the abandonment of the use
of force. Because no future peace can be maintained if land,
sea or air armaments continue to be employed by nations which
threaten, or may threaten, aggression outside of their
frontiers, they believe that the disarmament of such nations
is essential pending the establishment of a wider and more
permanent system of general security. They will further the
adoption of all other practicable measures which will lighten
for peace-loving peoples the crushing burden of armaments.

Private Office.
August 12, 1941

DECLARATION BY

DECLARATION BY UNITED NATIONS:

A JOINT DECLARATION BY THE UNITED STATES OF AMERICA,
THE UNITED KINGDOM OF GREAT BRITAIN AND NORTHERN
IRELAND, THE UNION OF SOVIET SOCIALIST REPUBLICS,
CHINA, AUSTRALIA, BELGIUM, CANADA, COSTA RICA, CUBA,
CZECHOSLOVAKIA, DOMINICAN REPUBLIC, EL SALVADOR,
GREECE, GUATEMALA, HAITI, HONDURAS, INDIA, LUXEMBOURG,
NETHERLANDS, NEW ZEALAND, NICARAGUA, NORWAY, PANAMA,
POLAND, SOUTH AFRICA, YUGOSLAVIA.

The Governments signatory hereto,

Having subscribed to a common program of purposes
and principles embodied in the Joint Declaration of
the President of the United States of America and the
Prime Minister of the United Kingdom of Great Britain
and Northern Ireland dated August 14, 1941, known as
the Atlantic Charter.

Being convinced that complete victory over their
enemies is essential to defend life, liberty, independence
and religious freedom, and to preserve human rights and
justice in their own lands as well as in other lands,
and that they are now engaged in a common struggle
against savage and brutal forces seeking to subjugate
the world, DECLARE:

(1) Each Government pledges itself to employ its
full resources, military or economic, against those
members of the Tripartite Pact and its adherents with
which such government is at war.

(2) Each Government
with the Governments sign
a separate armistice or p

The foregoing declare
other nations which are,
material assistance and c
for victory over Hitleris

Done at Washington
January First 1942

The Un
a No
by Un

on b
of the
Egada

National

The Co
by

The King
by
Canad
by

60

NITED NATIONS

The Republic of Costa Rica
by *[signature]*

The Republic of Cuba
by *[signature]*

Czechoslovak Republic
by *[signature]*

the Dominican Republic
by *[signature]*

The Republic of El Salvador
by *[signature]*

The Kingdom of Greece
by *[signature]*

The Republic of Guatemala
by *[signature]*

La République d'Haïti
par *[signature]*

The Republic of Honduras
by *[signature]*

India by
[signature]

The Grand Duchy of Luxembourg
by *[signature]*

The Kingdom of the Netherlands
by *[signature]*
Signed on behalf of
the Government of the Dominion
of New Zealand
by *[signature]*

The Republic of Nicaragua
by *[signature]*

The Kingdom of Norway
by *[signature]*

The Republic of Panamá
by *[signature]*

The Republic of Poland
by *[signature]*

The Union of South Africa
by *[signature]*

The Kingdom of Yugoslavia
by *[signature]*

61

▪ 23 The Mosin-Nagant Rifle

The Mosin-Nagant rifle was in service for over 100 years, first with the Imperial Russian Army, then the Red Army, and finally the Northern Alliance forces in Afghanistan in 2001. Experience in the Russo–Turkish war of 1877–78, where the Turks were using Winchester repeaters and the Russians single-shot rifles, persuaded the Imperial Army that modernization of their small arms was overdue. Captain Sergei Ivanovich Mosin submitted a design for a $1/_3$-inch (7.62-mm) magazine-fed rifle, in competition with a rifle designed by a Belgian, Léon Nagant. After some deliberation, the commission formed to decide which rifle should be adopted by the Imperial Army chose Mosin's design, but as the final production model of 1891 incorporated some features of Nagant's design, the rifle was designated the Mosin-Nagant M1891. Production was started both in Russia and in France. By the outbreak of the Russo–Japanese War in 1904, about 3.8 million Mosin-Nagants had been delivered to the Imperial Army, but few were actually used, as scarcely any soldiers had been trained to use them.

Because of the poor state of Russian industry at the outbreak of World War I, a shortage of Mosin-Nagants forced the government to place orders for M1891s with two companies in the USA: Remington and Westinghouse. The first consignment arrived just as the 1917 October Revolution broke out, followed by the Russians signing the Treaty of Brest-Litovsk with Germany and its allies, which took Russia out of the war for a while. To avoid the risk that the next consignment would fall into the hands of the Germans or

Austrians, the U.S. Army bought the remaining quarter of a million Mosin-Nagants. These rifles were used to equip the British and U.S. forces sent to northern Russia in the anti-Bolshevik campaign of 1918–19.

The Mosin-Nagant was used by both sides in the Russian Civil War of 1918–24, and by the Finns in the "Winter War" of 1939–40 against the Red Army. The Mosin-Nagant was the standard-issue weapon for the Red Army when Hitler invaded Russia in 1941. By the end of World War II about 17.4 million M1891s had been produced. The Mosin-Nagant was highly popular, and easy to maintain; Russian soldiers called it just the Mosin, or "Mosinka." It was also modified as a sniper rifle and used by the famous Red Army snipers, notably at Stalingrad (1942–43) but in all other battles too. The Finns also used the sniper model against the Red Army: one Finnish sniper claimed over 500 kills with a Mosin-Nagant.

After World War II, the Soviet Union ceased producing Mosin-Nagants, progressively replacing them with the AK series of assault rifles. However, the M1891 was used in many of the campaigns that followed World War II: Korea (1950–53), Vietnam (1955–75), and Afghanistan (2001–present). Every country or insurgent group that received military aid from the Soviet Union used some Mosin-Nagants, including Egypt, Syria, Iraq, and Palestinian terrorist groups.

Through its long service life, eight models of Mosin-Nagant were produced. In addition several countries, including Finland, Czechoslovakia, China, Hungary, Romania, and Poland, manufactured variants.

ABOVE LEFT: The Mosin-Nagant rifle.

ABOVE: Red Army infantry with Mosin-Nagant rifles jump down from a T-34 in December 1942.

▣ The Boeing B-17

At the heart of Allied strategy for the defeat of Nazi Germany, the Combined Bomber Offensive, code-named Pointblank, required the Royal Air Force and U.S. Army Air Forces (USAAF) to destroy Germany's industrial heartland. The aircraft for this mission could not be developed overnight, and it was decisions made in the 1930s by the Ministry of Air and the U.S. War Department that dictated the bomber types the RAF and USAAF used to strike Germany.

After underfunded, incremental bomber development following World War I, the U.S. Army Air Corps asked Boeing Aircraft in 1934 to develop a multi-engine bomber that could carry one ton of bombs a minimum of 1,000 miles (1,600 km) and return to base. It gave Boeing no advance payment, but the company would be paid if its bomber became the USAAC's choice. Boeing's Model 229 or XB-17 flew for the first time in July 1935, but crashed four months later. The accident, which

happened at takeoff, killed much of the design and testing team, but the USAAC ordered 13 more aircraft because this bomber had become its highest priority.

The development of the B-17 focused on over-water flight and the bombing of an enemy invasion fleet. While such a mission seemed far-fetched for the protection of the Atlantic Coast, it was relevant to the defense of the Commonwealth of the Philippines, the Territory of Hawaii, and the Panama Canal Zone. Although USAAC planners in 1939 foresaw the need for bombers to reach Germany and Japan in the future, the coastal defense mission was the only one that convinced Congress to fund the XB-17 project.

As more models received testing between 1936 and 1941, the basic character of the wartime B-17 (E and F models) took shape. The four-engine bomber (four Pratt & Whitney 1,200 hp supercharged radial piston engines)

ABOVE: A B-17 bomber circa 1941.

OVERLEAF: The "Flying Fortress" being built in a Boeing factory during World War II.

could drive a 65,000-pound (29,000-kg) aircraft almost 2,000 miles (3,200 km) at speeds up to 287 miles per hour (462 km/h) and at altitudes up to 35,000 feet (10,700 m). The aircraft would be a "Flying Fortress" with a crew of ten, eight of whom could man an assortment of 13 turret-mounted or swinging machine guns. The bomb load for missions might run as high as 17,000 pounds (7,700 kg). The bombsight, the Norden type developed by Sperry-Rand, enabled the bombardier to fly the plane for greater accuracy, and made automatic corrections for altitude, wind, and drifting.

Although USAAC (U.S. Army Air Forces after June 1941) ordered B-17s for operational deployment, the number of B-17s (models B-E) numbered fewer than 600 by December 1941, and did little to slow the Japanese campaign of 1941–42. Some of these models had been sent to RAF Coastal Command to attack U-boat bases. The models E and F (almost 4,000 aircraft) went to British bases in 1942 to begin the daylight bombing of Germany, but German air defenses brought long distance raids to a halt in December 1943. Actual combat experience brought changes to the models G and H, principally improvements to the engine and armoring, and the addition of a chin turret to meet head-on fighter attacks. By war's end, Boeing and two other contractors had built 12,677 B-17s. Enemy air defenses destroyed about 5,000 of them across all theaters of war, and hundreds more crashed in operational accidents.

■ 25 Oboe

During World War II the Germans, British, and Americans introduced electronic navigation systems to assist their bombers in finding the correct target at night or in bad weather. Early in the war, both sides discovered that bombing a well-defended country by day in good weather without heavy fighter escort was extremely costly. The RAF was the first to learn that its doctrine that "the bomber will always get through," so assiduously proclaimed before World War II, was spurious. The losses sustained by the RAF in the first months of the war persuaded the Air Staff that the only way a strategic bombing campaign against Germany could be sustained was by bombing at night. The Americans in their turn discovered that daylight bombing without using fighter protection when over heavily defended occupied Europe was unsustainable. Their solution was to provide plenty of long-range fighter escorts.

The main problem when night bombing was locating the target. The Germans, turning to night bombing of Britain

after their defeat in the Battle of Britain, were the first to light on a solution. They used a system of radio beams, initially Knickebein, but superseded by X-Gerät (X-Apparatus), and Y-Gerät. Despite these the German results were mediocre, not least because the system could be jammed. Meanwhile, the RAF's performance, without any navigational aids, was abysmal. Only one in three RAF crews placed their bombs within 5 miles (8 km) of the aiming point; some were tens of miles off target.

In early 1942, the RAF introduced a radio system called Gee. It was not so accurate as Knickebein, but it did improve bombing accuracy until the Germans started jamming it. The

RAF's answer, in early 1943, was Oboe, so called because its radar pulses sounded like the woodwind instrument. The system used two ground stations in England. One tracked the aircraft as it flew along an arc of constant range running through the target, and passed correction signals if it deviated from the arc. The second station measured the range along the arc, and when the aircraft reached the previously computed bomb release point, a signal was broadcast. Mosquito pathfinder aircraft were fitted to receive the signals, and they marked the target with flares for the main force to bomb.

Oboe was very accurate and difficult to jam. Its one drawback was that the curvature of the earth reduced its range to about 280 miles (450 km) from the ground stations. Pathfinder Mosquitoes flew as high as they could so that they were still "visible" to the radar beams as far out as possible. After sufficient French territory had been liberated in 1944, ground stations could be set up much nearer Germany and could thus cover more of the country east of the Ruhr, which had been only just within the range of Oboe stations based in England.

The installation in mid-1943 of H2S radar sets in RAF bombers, which gave a "picture" of the ground on a screen, enabled sorties to be carried out beyond the range of Oboe, although bombing accuracy depended on the quality of the radar echo. Coastal targets showed up clearly; targets inland, especially in broken terrain, were more difficult to find.

The Americans installed electronic navigation systems similar to Oboe in their bombers, to enable them to find and attack daylight targets through cloud and haze.

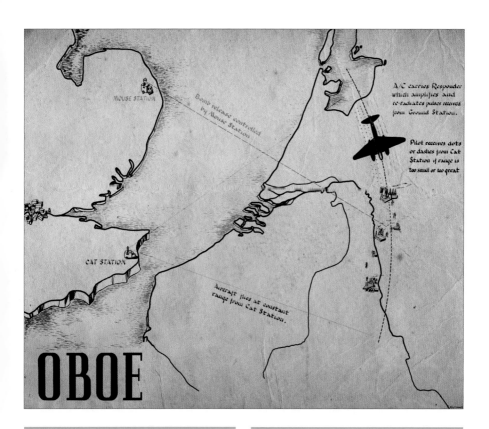

A/C carries Responder which amplifies and re-radiates pulses received from Ground Station.

Pilot receives dots or dashes from Cat Station if range is too small or too great

MOUSE STATION

Bomb release controlled by Mouse Station

CAT STATION

Aircraft flies at constant range from Cat Station.

OBOE

LEFT: A Mosquito B MkXVI fitted with a ventral raydome testing an H2S radar. This aircraft was also used to test Oboe.

ABOVE: A diagram showing the principle on which Oboe worked, with two ground stations in England tracking the Mosquito marker aircraft as it flies along the arc.

◾26 The Human Torpedo

The Italians were the first to use human torpedoes in World War II, and were swiftly copied by the British, Germans, and Japanese. The Italian Maiale ("pig") was 22 feet (6.7 m) long, with a detachable explosive nose. It had a two-man crew who sat astride the torpedo wearing rubber suits and oxygen cylinders and masks.

On December 19, 1941, two Italian frogmen were caught sitting on the bow buoy of the British battleship *Valiant* in Alexandria harbor. Under interrogation they said that they had got into difficulties outside the harbor and had had to abandon their equipment and swim. A few minutes later there was an explosion under the stern of the tanker *Sagonia*. The Italians told the captain of the *Valiant* to bring everyone on deck, as there would shortly be an explosion under his ship. He did so, and minutes later a massive explosion caused extensive damage to the *Valiant*. Soon after, another explosion severely damaged the battleship *Queen Elizabeth*. Three pairs of Italians on human torpedoes, brought to Alexandria by submarine, had immobilized the only two battleships in the Mediterranean Fleet and put them out of action for many months, though there were no casualties. The Italians also used human torpedoes to attack Allied shipping in Gibraltar, Malta, and Algiers Bay later in the war.

Copying the Italian example, the British developed the Chariot, based on a 25-foot (7.6-m) torpedo, specifically to attack the German battleship *Tirpitz* at Trondheim in Norway. On the night of October 30/31, 1942, two Chariots were taken into the Trondheimfjord slung under a fishing boat, but on the approach while still about ten miles (15 km) from the *Tirpitz*, the Chariots broke loose and sank. The Chariot crews, however, made their way to Sweden as planned.

On October 28, 1944, a successful attack was made by a pair of Chariots on two ships at Phuket in Siam (Thailand). The crew were taken to the target area by the submarine *Trenchant*, motored in on their Chariots, and clamped the explosive heads to the bilges of the two target merchant ships, the *Sumatra* and the *Volpi*. Having returned to the *Trenchant*, two explosions were heard, and both ships were out of action for the rest of the war. It was the last and only completely successful Chariot operation, out of a total of eight, in the whole war.

The German one-man Neger, sometimes called the Mohr after its inventor Richard Mohr, consisted of two torpedoes clamped together on top of each other. The upper one had a small plexiglass-covered cockpit instead of a warhead. It was slow and could not dive, motoring with the cockpit above the water. It had to be released close to the target, and was easily seen in daylight, often with sunlight flashing off the cockpit. Negers were used against Allied shipping at Anzio in January 1944 and again in Normandy in June. They damaged two minesweepers and a light cruiser off the Normandy beaches, but large numbers of Negers were lost. The successor to the Neger, the Marder ("pine marten") was no more successful.

The Japanese Kaiten was a converted Long Lance torpedo, which included a compartment for the crewman and a conning tower. The Long Lance was a huge torpedo, 30 feet (9 m) long, with half a ton of explosive in the warhead, and capable of 49 knots (91 km/h). It was usually driven straight at the target as a suicide weapon. They were first used at Ulithi atoll, the U.S. fleet anchorage, in November 1944, sinking a tanker for the loss of eight Kaiten pilots. At Iwo Jima, Okinawa, and at other beachheads in the Pacific, they sank four U.S. vessels (the largest being the destroyer U.S.S. *Underhill*). The Japanese loss rate was huge. Of the 18 submarines converted to carry Kaitens, eight were sunk either before or after launching the human torpedoes; others were forced to abort their missions. About 80 Kaitens were also lost.

The Italian human torpedo attacks were the most successful in terms of "return on investment" — the result balanced against the cost in the lives of extremely brave men, the time, expense, and effort in developing the weapon, and taking it to the target. The return on investment by the British, Germans, and Japanese on human torpedoes was negligible; but this is not in any way to denigrate the courage of the men who rode the torpedoes.

ABOVE: The Italian human torpedo, known as the Maiale ("pig").

RIGHT: The controls of the "pig."

OVERLEAF: A damaged Italian human torpedo captured with the mother ship *Otterra*, a converted merchant ship that was used to mount attacks against Allied shipping in Gibraltar in 1942 and 1943. After the ship was surrendered to the British in 1943, the torpedo was found in a secret compartment.

◪ Japanese Headgear

The two most familiar forms of headgear worn by the Japanese armed forces were the pot-shaped steel helmet, and the cloth field cap with its short, cloth, occasionally leather, peak. A star for the Imperial Japanese Army (IJA) and an anchor for the Imperial Japanese Navy (IJN) was welded onto the front of the helmet, and sewn on to the front of the cap.

The comfortable and practical field cap was worn with more formal uniforms, as shown in the photograph of Japanese officers attending the surrender ceremony aboard the U.S.S. *Missouri*, and as worn by General Tomoyuki Yamashita at his trial by the War Crimes Commission in Manila in October 1945. The cap was the same pattern for all ranks.

The steel helmet was often covered in a net into which foliage and grass camouflage could be inserted. Even in the equivalent of service dress, Japanese officers of all ranks often wore a tunic open at the neck, over a white shirt without a tie.

The ubiquitous field cap was symptomatic of the practical approach to kit and equipment on the part of the Japanese, especially in the IJA. For example, their soldiers were equipped with a very efficient grenade launcher which

threw a 1 pound 12 ounce (0.8 kg) shell out to around 700 yards (640 m), accurately and effectively—far better than anything possessed by the Allies.

The Japanese were trained to fight with their 15-inch (38-cm) bayonet fixed to a .256-inch (6.5-mm) caliber rifle at all times to instill fear into their enemy. Their infantry especially was recruited from the rural population, whose tough farmers made excellent soldiers. It would be wrong to imagine them as uneducated peasants, for the standard of schooling in Japan was high. They were indoctrinated to believe that they were the toughest race in the world, and that death was to be expected, not feared.

In addition to the field cap in blue cloth, Japanese seamen wore a round white hat, like those issued in the British Navy, when in white uniform, and a blue one with their blue, winter uniform. Both types of round hat had what the Royal Navy called a cap "tally" around the brow part of the cap with the name of the wearer's ship in Japanese characters. Officers and petty officers of the IJN wore blue or white peaked caps, according to the time of year. These caps were similar to those worn in most navies. Japanese sailors in working dress wore either the field cap or, when working with aircraft on carrier flight decks, a cotton flying helmet.

ABOVE: A Japanese soldier in Bataan in the Philippines after it fell.

RIGHT: An example of the typical Japanese cloth field cap.

∎ 28 The Secret Radio

Inserting spies, agents, and saboteurs into enemy territory was usually only the first phase of a clandestine operation. If they could not communicate, they were probably useless. Among other things, they needed to receive instructions from base and likewise pass information back; ask for airdrops of equipment; request extraction, either for themselves or others; and vector and talk to the dropping or pick-up aircraft. The only efficient and speedy way to achieve this was by radio, or wireless as the British called it, so special radio sets had to be devised for use by agents which had to meet several important criteria.

First, the set had to be rugged and able to stand up to rough treatment. It also needed to be as small as possible in order to be easily portable, and if possible fit into a suitcase or some other innocuous container for concealment. It had to be capable of transmitting and receiving over long ranges. Ideally it needed to be able to work on batteries, electricity, or a hand or pedal generator.

Some of these requirements conflicted. The technology of the time usually demanded a big radio set with plenty of power to transmit over long ranges. The transistor had not been invented at that time and all radios worked using valves, which were easily broken. Meanwhile, long-range communications normally required big antennae, which was out of the question for clandestine operations.

These problems were addressed mainly by the Special Operations Executive (SOE) in Britain, and the Office for Strategic Services (OSS) in the United States, and by early 1942 sets that fulfilled the key criteria were being produced. The smallest radio for agents was the Paraset Clandestine Radio designed for SOE and the Secret Intelligence Service (MI6), weighing about 5 pounds (2.3 kg). But more reliable, and seen in many a movie, was the SOE Type A, Mk III suitcase radio weighing about 13 pounds (6 kg), which had a range of 500 miles (800

km). The U.S. equivalent was the AN/PRC-1 suitcase design, weighing about 30 pounds (13.5 kg).

The radios in existence at the time were insecure; they could not automatically "scramble" their messages to prevent anyone listening in from deciphering the text. Today clandestine radios use burst transmission to send a long text message over the air in micro-seconds, giving an enemy direction-finding station too little time to fix the transmitting radio's location. The sets in the 1940s could not do this.

The high-frequency radios used by agents were unable to send and receive voice messages over long distances, so Morse code was the communicating method. Messages were enciphered using one-time pads: the sender and receiver had identical pads of tear-off sheets containing the information for enciphering and deciphering a signal, the sender transmitting the sheet number. Once the message had been sent and deciphered at the other end, both operators destroyed their copy. No other copies existed. This method was unbreakable but slow, and tapping out a long message exposed the sender to the danger of being picked up by hostile direction-finding equipment, of which the Germans had numerous high-quality sets. Many operators were caught this way.

The agent communicated with supply aircraft over an S-phone using voice transmission—radio telephone in the jargon of the day. The aircraft carried the master set while the agent carried the "ground set" which weighed around 15 pounds (7 kg), fitted in a suitcase or pack on the agent's back. The theoretical range when used as a radio telephone to an aircraft at 10,000 feet (3,000 m) was about 40 miles (65 km), down to 6 miles (10 km) at 500 feet (150 m). Ground detectors more than a mile away could not pick up transmissions to an aircraft. The signal from the set could also be used to aid in vectoring the aircraft to the dropping zone from about 80 miles (130 km) away.

LEFT: Members of the French Resistance operating a radio.

ABOVE: The radio set used in training by Yvonne Baseden an F Section SOE radio operator. Aged 22, she was parachuted into France to join the SCHOLAR circuit operating near Dijon. Following participation in the largest daylight drop of supplies to the Resistance up to that time, she was captured on June 26, 1944, interrogated by the Gestapo, sent to Ravensbruck Concentration Camp, and liberated in April 1945. She was awarded the MBE (Military), Legion d'Honneur, and the Croix de Guerre with Palm.

29 Roosevelt's Wheelchair

America's greatest wartime leader in World War II rode a wheelchair, not a tank. Almost completely paralyzed below the waist by poliomyelitis in 1921, President Franklin Delano Roosevelt (1882–1945) turned the personal strength he developed in coping with his condition into his indomitable wartime leadership of the United States. Under his command, the United States was the only Allied power that played a critical part in defeating both Germany and Japan.

Before his paralysis, Roosevelt (FDR) lived a life of privilege and limited accomplishment. Born into an aristocracy of inherited wealth, FDR toyed with education, the law, and business, but found in politics an outlet for his energy and restless intellect. After three years of New York Democratic politics, he took his first national office in 1913 as Assistant Secretary of the Navy, serving through a program of naval modernization and World War I. He learned a great deal about waging global war as well as party politics. Not yet 40, he became his party's nominee for vice president in 1920. Although the Democrats lost the election, FDR's career did not suffer. Then polio struck.

Despite his heroic and painful struggles to walk again, FDR never managed to take more than a few steps in leg braces with canes. He spent long hours in his wheelchair and endured physical therapy of limited effect. With the encouragement of his wife Eleanor, mother of his five children, FDR reentered politics as a protégé of Governor Alfred E. Smith and succeeded him as governor of New York in 1929. Reelected in 1930, FDR became a natural candidate for President in 1932. He won the election and took office in 1933.

FDR designed his own wheelchair and had four made by local Hyde Park craftsmen. He despised the conventional high-back wicker wheelchair with high armrests which he purchased in the 1920s. To stress mobility, comfort, and freedom, FDR had a standard wooden table chair without arms attached to a rolling metal frame with large bicycle wheels forward and two small, pivoting wheels aft. FDR could move the chair himself with the large wheels. He designed a personal attachment, an ashtray on a wooden extension from the chair. The frame also had a wooden footrest. The wheelchair could be disassembled for travel.

Multiple copies of the chair enabled FDR's staff to station chairs at Hyde Park, the White House, and the Little White House at the polio rehabilitation clinic at Warm Springs, Georgia.

Throughout his presidency, FDR avoided public appearances in his wheelchair. With some reason, he feared it would frighten the faithful and embolden his foes. Washington insiders, of course, knew of FDR's condition, but even the President's Republican media critics did not raise the issue in that era of shared elitist protocols in national politics. When he had to stand to give a speech, Roosevelt hooked himself to the podium. He conducted most of his public business in front of photographers in a chair behind his desk. Outside, he appeared most often in an open car or seated with a blanket covering his braced legs. No one saw photos or newsreels of people carrying him to and from his chair. Only a few personal photographs of Roosevelt in his wheelchair survive. When FDR died suddenly in April 1945, he was doing physical therapy at Warm Spring at the center he had established for polio victims.

FDR's struggle with polio reshaped his character by adding determination and faith to his natural optimism. His wheelchair is a symbol of triumph, not defeat.

LEFT: President Roosevelt greets another polio victim at Warm Springs, Georgia.

ABOVE: One of FDR's four homemade wheelchairs, Hyde Park, New York.

30 The Bombe and Colossus

The Bombe, spelled with an "e," was precursor to the first ever computer, Colossus. It was an electro-mechanical machine invented to break coded messages transmitted by the Germans. These messages were usually enciphered on an Enigma machine before being transmitted. Invented in 1923, the Enigma was used by the German Army and Navy, the Luftwaffe, the SS, the Military Intelligence Service (Abwehr), and the German State Railways (Reichsbahn). Originally it consisted of three rotors and a keyboard linked by an electric circuit, arranged in such a way that pressing a lettered key would light up a different letter on a display on the machine. Having been given the text of a message in clear, the operator would rewrite it substituting the original letters for those displayed by Enigma. The rotor settings were changed daily. Even in its simplest form, there were hundreds of millions of possible solutions for every letter. As the war progressed, an additional rotor was added, hugely increasing the number of steps that anyone deciphering the message had to get right before the message made sense. Throughout the war the Germans believed that Enigma was unbreakable.

Although a number of Enigma machines fell into British hands during the war, knowing how it worked was only the beginning, and the British already possessed a similar machine known as Typex. The trick was to know the daily rotor settings. The British, recognizing that Enigma could be "broken," installed a group of university mathematicians at the Government Code and Cypher School at Bletchley Park, north of London. To begin with, the deciphering of messages was partly achieved by the application of mathematical formulae based on the facts that a) there are only 26 letters in the alphabet, b) no letter could stand for itself, and c) without number keys, figures had to be spelled out. To assist in this process, a type of machine devised by Polish code breakers, and greatly improved by a brilliant mathematician, Alan Turing, was installed at Bletchley. Nicknamed the Bombe, these machines were continually upgraded throughout the war, and eventually there were five types in use, not all at Bletchley. However it was there that the first Enigma codes were broken mechanically by the Bombe on August 1, 1940.

The Colossus, the world's first ever true computer which was devised to break the Lorenz enciphering machine code, was installed at Bletchley in December 1943. The Lorenz had 12 rotors instead of the improved Enigma's four. Eventually five Colossus machines were installed at Bletchley, some of which were used to decipher Japanese codes. The breaking of these codes provided an unexpected bonus in the form of intelligence for Allied planning for the landings in Normandy in June 1944. Early in 1944, the Japanese Military Attaché in Berlin was given a comprehensive tour of the part of the Atlantic Wall defending among other places, the beaches selected for the Allied assault. On return to his embassy, he sent a series of long messages back to Army HQ in Tokyo giving a highly detailed description of what he had seen in the minutest detail. His messages were intercepted by one of the British listening stations in England, and deciphered. The information they contained proved invaluable when read in conjunction with air photographic reconnaissance in establishing the number and caliber of guns, down to machine gun nests, defending the beaches.

ABOVE LEFT: One of the priority teams at work at Bletchley Park, handling the high priority coded radio traffic, such as signals that affected key operations, including the Normandy landings.

LEFT: A Bombe code breaking machine of the type that broke the Enigma codes mechanically for the first time on August 1, 1940.

TOP: A rare picture of the Colossus with its Wren operators. The Mark I was powered by 1,500 valves, the Mark II by 2,500.

ABOVE RIGHT: A Bombe unit room at Eastcote in Middlesex. This was similar to the Bombe room at Bletchley. As the workload on the Bombe machines increased during the war, units were established at more than eight other locations in addition to Bletchley Park. By 1944, there were at least 200 machines in operation at their various sites.

31 Medal of Honor

The Medal of Honor, awarded in the name of the Congress of the United States, is the highest military decoration the nation presents to military personnel who perform an act or acts conspicuous "by gallantry and intrepidity at the risk of his life, above and beyond the call of duty ..." The use of "his" now can be "her," although no woman has yet won the Medal for combat action.

The criteria for the awarding of the Medal of Honor, informal and official, varied until World War II. The major changes limited the award to acts of valor in action against the enemy (not just dangerous flight) and allowed posthumous awards. Established by legislation in 1861 and 1862, the Medal of Honor had been awarded without much formal guidance until the period 1898–1916, when several reviews by the War Department set more stringent criteria and revoked 911 of the 2,625 Medals awarded since 1862 to American soldiers (and some civilians). Within the statutory criteria, based on legislation in 1918 and 1942, the Medal goes to service members who rescue or protect the wounded and lose their lives by doing so, or who perform individual acts of unusual heroism in combat under fire, usually when wounded, often fatally. The acts must be witnessed and recorded. The action must be valorous well beyond the normal expectations for the service member's rank, experience, and military specialty.

During and after World War II, the U.S. armed forces awarded 464 members the Medal of Honor for heroism "above and beyond the call of duty" in that war. The awards went to 287 soldiers, 37 members of the U.S. Army Air Forces, 57 naval officers and sailors, 82 Marines, and one Coast Guardsman. Fifty-seven percent (266 Medals) of the awards were posthumous.

Even though the criteria for the Medal of Honor had become more focused by World War II, there were anomalous awards made to senior officers and fighter pilots early in the war that showed the Roosevelt administration's desire to create heroes and encourage public confidence. General Douglas MacArthur, U.S. Army, General Jonathan M. Wainwright, U.S. Army, and Major General A. A. Vandegrift, U.S. Marine Corps, received Medals for acts that justified a Distinguished Service Medal, but not the Medal of Honor. Admirals Isaac C. Kidd, Norman Scott, and Daniel J. Callahan received posthumous Medals for leadership that might have justified a DSM. The same applies to Brigadier General James H. Doolittle, USAAF, for leading the April 1942 raid on Tokyo. Later in the war, Brigadier General Theodore Roosevelt, Jr., received a "sympathy" Medal for heroism on D-Day, awarded after he died a month later of a heart attack. Medals of Honor were also awarded in unusual numbers to nine Navy and Marine Corps aviators for aerial combat in 1942 in the Pacific.

The largest change in Medals of Honor awarded for World War II heroism came in the 1990s after Congress passed laws that allowed recipients of the Distinguished Service Cross or Navy Cross to have their awards "upgraded" to the Medal of Honor if a review panel could find racial bias in awarding decorations. No African American and only one Asian American had received a Medal of Honor during the war. Upon review, seven African Americans and 22 Asian Americans received retroactive Medals for acts of valor while serving as soldiers.

LEFT: President Truman awards the Medal of Honor to General Jonathan Wainwright, a former POW, 1945.

ABOVE: The Medal of Honor (Army design).

32 The *Stars and Stripes*

Published as a newspaper for the soldiers of the American Expeditionary Forces in 1917–19, *Stars and Stripes* came to life again in 1942 in order to provide news of the Home Front and the global war effort to deployed GIs. The newspaper had the War Department's endorsement and financial support, but editorial control swung back and forth between on the one hand, the Army's commanders and senior public affairs officers, and on the other, the newspaper's editorial staff, most of whom were established journalists who wore uniforms but remained more loyal to the First Amendment than to the Articles of War.

Reporting news from the Home Front presented no special "freedom of speech" problems since *Stars and Stripes* relied on U.S. news services and national newspapers for domestic news. Sound coverage of government policies and domestic events, even unpleasant ones, offset rumors, the biased views of families, and enemy propaganda. *Stars and Stripes* could also give GIs a sense of the conduct of the war in other theaters, the contributions of the other services and the Allies, and the reasoning behind the Army's strategic and operational decisions as seen from the War Department. There were few revelations about operations that violated security. *Stars and Stripes* reporters followed the censorship rules on security which applied to all newsmen.

Where *Stars and Stripes* ran into trouble was among senior commanders, who saw the newspaper as a subversive influence that undermined their authority and encouraged indiscipline. The *Stars and Stripes* editorial staff, however, did not regard senior officers as infallible, or all Army policies as wise. Popular cartoonist Sergeant Bill Mauldin created his characters Willy and Joe, the iconic GIs of World War II, as a vehicle to criticize what he saw as the Army's tactical sophistry, and to expose the unjustified privileges for officers and rear area personnel. *Stars and Stripes* sought examples of commanders violating Army policies that advantaged enlisted men. This investigative reporting ferreted out examples of black-marketeering and misallocation of scarce supplies meant for combat units.

General Mark W. Clark continually hectored military reporters. General Douglas MacArthur, as senior military commander in the Pacific, banned *Stars and Stripes* in the area until 1945. However, *Stars and Stripes* reporters could attack command influence by leaking stories to their civilian war correspondent colleagues. General George S. Patton wanted Mauldin court-martialed; instead he received a Pulitzer Prize in 1945.

Stars and Stripes reached more than a million readers during World War II, and its reporting on the war with Germany remains an invaluable source of information about the war as fought by American enlisted men.

ABOVE: U.S. soldiers reading an issue of *Stars and Stripes*.

RIGHT: The special edition of *Stars and Stripes* published to mark V-E Day on May 9, 1945.

---

33 The Auster Light Aircraft

The Auster light aircraft was arguably the best airborne artillery spotter in World War II. It was designed by Taylorcraft in the USA for the expanding light private aircraft market, and in 1938 Taylorcraft Aeroplanes (England) was formed to build the aircraft under license. Several variants were produced and on the outbreak of World War II these were evaluated for use as airborne spotters for artillery. The Taylorcraft Plus C two seater was selected for military production and designated the Auster Mk I.

The design was so successful that it was developed into the Mk III version. It was fitted with a Gipsy Major I engine, and 470 of this type were built. The next progression was to the Mk IV, with an American Lycoming engine and a larger cabin to accommodate a third seat. The fully glazed cockpit of the Mk IV and subsequent models were a great improvement on the earlier variants, which did not afford good visibility to the side and rear. But the most common Auster found with British forces was the Mk V, which included blind-flying instruments. Around 800 of these were built.

The Auster could operate off short, rough strips, and could land on roads and tracks provided obstructions on either side were removed. It had a high mounted wing, which gave excellent lift, and provided an unobstructed view of the ground. Thanks to its large trailing edge wing flaps, the Auster could fly at very low speed without stalling, which was invaluable when observation over the ground was needed. This, combined with its large rudder giving it exceptional turning ability especially at low speed, made it surprisingly difficult for a fighter to shoot down. By twisting and turning in flight and suddenly applying full flap, a skilled Auster pilot could bring his aircraft almost to a stop momentarily, and a pursuing fighter would often overshoot. The Lysander developed by the RAF for air spotting was shot out of the sky when used in this role.

The Auster Mk V with a top speed of 130 miles per hour (209 km/h) was faster than the German equivalent, the Fieseler Fi 156C Storch whose top speed was 108 miles per hour (174 km/h), and the American O-49 Vigilant (122 miles

per hour/196 km/h). The Auster also had a greater range (250 miles/204 km) than the Storch (240 miles/286 km), although it was less than the Vigilant (280 miles/450 km). Thanks to its low takeoff weight (1,846 pounds/837 kg) the Auster could operate from smaller strips—forest clearings and the like—than either the Storch (2,915 pounds/1,322 kg) or the Vigilant (3,392 pounds/1.539 kg). This enabled the Auster to be deployed much closer to the front line and hence its reaction time to calls for support was usually quick.

The Auster was used for reconnaissance, often by senior commanders who wanted to see the terrain over which they were going to deploy their troops, in the way that a helicopter is used today. But by far the most common use of the aircraft was to put an artillery observer up in the air from where he could correct the fall of shot. Artillery officers were taught to fly and, together with RAF pilots, were formed into joint air observation post squadrons (Air OP for short). They were able to detect and engage targets out of sight of friendly artillery observers on the ground. As an added bonus, it was found that the presence of an artillery spotter aircraft often caused the opposing side's artillery to cease firing for fear of being spotted and having counter-battery fire brought down on it.

The Air OP did not fly directly over the target, but usually remained on his own side of the battlefield, while remaining high enough to see dead ground out of sight of OPs on the ground.

To begin with, the formation of the Air OP was resisted by the RAF, who were paranoid, as they are to this day, about any suggestion that the Army was forming a private air force and about any threat to the notion that only the RAF should fly every type of aircraft.

RIGHT: An Auster Mk III with a 130-hp Gipsy engine, the most widely produced of the early Auster variants.

34 Instructions for American Servicemen

Aware of the potential friction between American servicemen sent to the United Kingdom and uniformed British servicemen and uniformed women and civilians, the War Department established cultural education programs for the deploying GIs. One part of this sensitivity training was a little book, *Instructions for American Servicemen in Britain 1942.* The unidentified authors were former academics and media experts who had lived in the United Kingdom before the war. These cultural interpreters served in the Information and Education Division of the Special Services Division, Army Service Forces. The I&E Division authors produced similar books about Germany, France, Italy, Japan, North Africa, and Australia.

The U.S. Army's cultural affairs experts recognized that hostile incidents between GIs and the British would fuel Nazi propaganda and distract the Allies from the American military buildup in England and the 8th Air Force's bombing campaign on Germany. By 1944, the U.S. Army in the United Kingdom alone numbered two million officers and enlisted personnel.

The Instructions for American Servicemen stressed that the key to good interallied relations was GI appreciation of several basic facts. The United Kingdom had been at war since 1939 and its civilian population had been bombed by the Luftwaffe since 1940 and starved and deprived by the German U-boat campaign for four years. The country was a "war zone," where life had been reshaped by air

defense and shortages of all kinds of consumer goods. Natural British reserve toward foreigners—especially brash, young American men—had deepened under wartime stress. The Britons did not need reminding that their popular culture might appear peculiar to Americans at the best of times and inexplicable in wartime.

The GI guidebook stressed that British traditions of individual liberties, privacy, political democracy, the rule of law, and cultural diversity had much in common with American culture. GIs should not be distracted by British currency, warm beer, different words for the same things ("petrol" vs "gas"), an obsession with social form, commitment to unique sports like cricket, and traffic patterns. At their foundation British and American social values had much in common. The guidebook stressed the need for attitude adjustment: "The British don't know how to make a good cup of coffee. You don't know how to make a good cup of tea. It's an even swap."

The Instructions for American Servicemen warned against GI boasting, wasting food and gasoline, aggressive courting of British women, contempt for British military customs and battlefield performance, and impatience with time-consuming social forms. The stress of war had made the British "smaller" in outlook because they lived amid danger and deprivation unknown in the United States. The experience of a global empire that brought nonwhite immigrants to Great Britain, however, had not created the racially segregated access to public facilities common throughout much of the United States.

If anything, *Instructions* did not address the likely negative British reaction to the U.S. Army's racial segregation policies.

On balance, *Instructions* reflected the command policies of the U.S. Army in Great Britain. Commanders would not tolerate GI misbehavior and encouraged people-to-people contacts that shared American food, clothing, and surplus material with needy Britons. Military policemen would work with local British police officers to keep order in the pubs, theaters, and bus and rail stations. The Allied partners cooperated to curb black-marketeering, a phenomenon ignored in the *Instructions*. As a guide to adjusting to British culture, however, the book was relevant and wise.

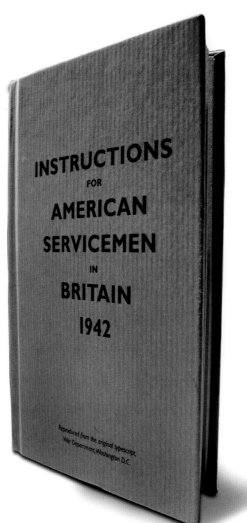

LEFT: A GI with his British girlfriend in Piccadilly Circus, London, January 27, 1945.

ABOVE: The guide to proper behavior in Great Britain amused GIs and their hosts.

35 The MG 42 German Machine Gun

By the end of World War I, machine guns consisted of two types: light and heavy. The latter, such as the Vickers, Maxim, and Browning, were almost all water-cooled. Although the .50-caliber Browning was invented toward the end of the war, it did not come into service with the U.S. army until 1922. The heavy machine gun, in some armies designated "medium," was designed to be used for long-range suppressive fire in support of attacks, and to be fired at all ranges in defense from fixed positions. It fired from a heavy tripod, or in some armies, an even heavier sled, and sometimes had a shield. The condenser can for the water-cooling system was cumbersome, and if all the water evaporated and no more was available, someone might have to urinate on the gun to cool it down. The ammunition was carried in a bulky box known in the British army as a "liner," containing one 250-round belt. The whole system—condenser can, ammunition liner, tripod, and gun—could not be carried by one man. Because of its bulk, such a machine gun was difficult to conceal; to have a good chance of surviving, it had to be sited in a pit dug for it, or in a fold in the ground.

Before World War I, the American Colonel Isaac Lewis designed a light machine gun, initially manufactured by the British Birmingham Small Arms Company. It saw much service with the British and U.S. armies in World War I, and was still used extensively in the Second. The Lewis, able to be carried by one man (although others carried extra ammunition for it) could be fired from a prone position, or, at a pinch, while standing; it was also easily concealed. The interwar years saw the introduction of improved light machine guns into armies: the U.S. Browning Automatic Rifle (BAR); the British Bren (actually a Czech design); and the French-designed Vickers-Berthier—

all magazine-fed weapons. Light machine guns were all air-cooled, so that when the barrel became too hot from prolonged firing, it could be replaced with a cool spare barrel.

Most armies fought throughout World War II with at least two types of machine-gun: light, medium, and in some cases heavy as well. The German Army, however, believed that having two varieties of machine gun for different tactical roles often resulted in the correct weapon not being available. They therefore designed the first general purpose machine gun, or GPMG. The basic weapon was the same, a belt-fed gun with an easily changed barrel, capable of being mounted on a tripod, and provided with long-range sights, but also with a bipod and shoulder butt. For long-range tasks the butt could be removed, the bipod unclipped, the gun quickly mounted on a tripod, and sights fitted that enabled indirect fire and night shooting on fixed lines. The advantage was that only one type of gun had to be manufactured.

The first of the type was the MG 34, designed in the early 1930s and adopted for service in 1934. It weighed 26 pounds 11 ounces (12.1 kg), fired 7.92-mm ammunition, and was belt- or magazine-fed, with a cyclic rate of 650 rounds per minute. It remained the German army's GPMG until 1942, when it was replaced by the more reliable and cheaper MG-42. This gun at 25 pounds 8 ounces (11.6 kg) weighed marginally less than the MG

34 and was belt-fed only, but had a cyclic rate of 1,200 rounds per minute, twice that of the 34. Incorrectly called the Spandau, because the original pre-World War I Maxim had been modified for use by the Imperial German Army at the Spandau arsenal, it was actually made by Mauser. The MG 42 was a greatly respected and feared weapon; its rate of fire was so fast, it sounded like a buzz saw. By contrast, British and U.S. medium and light machine guns had cyclic rates of between 450 and 550 rounds per minute. A British infantry platoon commander remembered: "When it came to a firefight between a German platoon and a British platoon, their MG 42 won hands down. I remember my first reaction to actual infantry warfare in July 1944 was one of amazement at the crushing fire-power of this very rapid-firing gun." (*18 Platoon* by Sydney Jary, published by Sydney Jary Ltd, 1987.)

Now most armies have a GPMG in their inventory.

ABOVE: An MG 42 German machine gun.

LEFT: German paratroopers fire MG 42s across the Arno River in Florence in mid-1944 during the Italian campaign.

🔳36 PLUTO

The acronym PLUTO stands for Pipeline Under The Ocean. As early as 1942, the problem was being considered of how to supply the huge quantities of fuel required by Allied forces invading and operating in Europe. Eventually there would be around two million soldiers and airmen ashore, with thousands of tanks, trucks, and aircraft all requiring fuel. Following successful trials of a pipeline laid across the floor of the Bristol Channel, the development of a system to be laid in the English Channel went ahead. The final design was a 3-inch (75-mm) diameter steel pipe welded into continuous lengths each of 30 miles (48 km), and rolled onto big floating drums—Conundrums—from which the pipe would be laid. The Conundrums looked like giant cotton reels, 90 feet (27.5 m) long and 50 feet (15 m) in diameter, and when carrying a full length of pipe, weighed as much as a destroyer.

Starting at the Isle of Wight, the Conundrums were towed across the Channel, laying four lengths of pipe to Cherbourg after its capture by the Americans. Pipes were also laid from Liverpool to the Isle of Wight, over land except for the section in the Solent. These enabled fuel to be landed at Liverpool and pumped to Cherbourg.

PLUTO was unable to provide fuel for the Battle of Normandy in 1944 and the breakout operations, a period of over three months, because the first four pipelines, code name Bambi, could not be deployed until enemy minefields around the port and in the Cotentin Peninsula had been cleared. Pumping operations began on September 18, by which time the Allied armies were hundreds of miles away on a line stretching from Holland and Belgium to the borders of Germany, and the Vosges.

Meanwhile fuel for the fighting was provided by Operation Tombola. This involved gas being pumped ashore from small tankers off the Normandy coast along buoyed pipelines, direct to storage tanks at the British pipehead at

Port-en-Bessin and the American one at Ste. Honorine. These pipelines had a daily capacity of 8,960 tons. Fuel packed in jerry cans was also shipped in huge quantities to the Normandy beachhead—by the end of August 202,700 tons of fuel had been delivered to the British alone by this means.

From Normandy, gas pipelines were linked up and extended to provide a through route from Cherbourg and Port-en-Bessin to Rouen. After October 3, piped gas was pumped into storage tanks at Darnetal, north of the Seine just outside Rouen.

By September 20, with Ostend in Belgium in Allied hands, tankers could dock there and discharge fuel directly ashore. In November 1944, three PLUTO pipes were laid from Dungeness to Boulogne, which had been captured by the Canadians on September 23. Another three were laid by December 1. These were set up just in time, as the Tombola pipes were put out of action by a storm that month. Pipeheads with a good storage capacity were established at Ghent and Boulogne for the British and near Paris and Lyons for the Americans. Pipelines for the southern group of U.S. armies were extended toward Metz and Dijon, while in the north separate pipelines for the British and Americans were laid from Antwerp to the east and southeast.

The appetite for fuel of mechanized armies supported by air forces is brought home when one considers that of the 3,920,000 million tons of supplies discharged at ports in France and Belgium in April 1945 alone, including ammunition, replacement tanks and vehicles of all kinds, railroad engines and trucks, some 1,008,000 tons was bulk gas. There were eventually 11 PLUTO pipes operating, pumping an average of 3,475 tons of fuel a day during March and April 1945; on the last day of the campaign 3,920 tons were delivered. PLUTO had played a major part in supplying what the French called "*le sang rouge de la guerre*" ("the red blood of war").

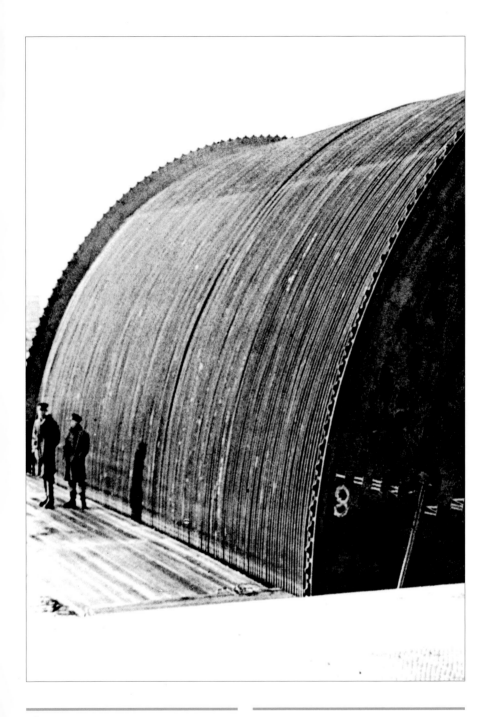

LEFT: The Pipeline Under the Ocean being reeled out over stern rollers from HMS *Sancroft* in June 1944.

ABOVE: A Conundrum ready to be towed across the Channel.

■37 Combat Boots

With a tradition of walking long distances carrying heavy loads of weapons and equipment, the U.S. Army took the issue of field footwear very seriously in World War II. The Marine Corps did, too, while the Navy, not noted for walking, was slightly less interested in the matter.

The common field shoe for the American forces from 1941 to 1945 was an ankle high half-boot, nicknamed the "boondocker." The standard issue "service shoe" of 1941 came with a smooth red-brown or russet upper with a toe cap and leather sole. Another version appeared the same year with a thicker, composite sole. The next model (1943) came with an all-rubber, durable sole. The leather was now "rough side out" and could be treated for flexibility and waterproofing. The Model 1943 remained standard in the Marine Corps for the entire war and the Navy ordered a black version of the Model 1941 for general issue.

As they had since the 1890s, all the services used cloth leggings to blouse service trousers. The blousing was supposed to prevent trousers from catching on foreign objects like barbed wire or jungle vines. The leggings, however, were hard to take on and off and became worn and unsightly in the field. In 1943, the Army redesigned the ankle field shoe by adding a two-buckle leather ankle strap above the top of the traditional field shoe, thus creating the

"combat boot." These boots entered field service to wide acclaim in 1944. The Marine Corps continued the half boot-leggings tradition for symbolic and financial reasons, while the Navy remained wedded to the black ankle boot.

In addition to the Model 1941 field shoe or Model 1943 combat boot, the Army issued other field footwear. Paratroopers wore the smooth leather, brown "Corcoran jump boot," laced tight and high. Jump boots became popular throughout the Army; officers could buy and wear them without the fear of open ridicule. Another variant was an experimental "jungle boot," a canvas-rubber high boot with laces with poor walking characteristics. The more serious challenge was finding footwear that would keep the GI's feet warm and dry and thus free of frostbite and trench foot. One solution was to wear rubber overshoes above the leather field boots. The other option was the Model 1944 "shoepac," which had thick rubber lowers and a leather upper, designed much like commercial hunting boots. Either option had adequate walking characteristics, but both caused overheating and held moisture. The only real barrier to foot problems remained fresh, dry socks and time for manual massage. Neither was easy in a rifle company, and in Europe's harsh winter of 1944–45, foot problems became a widespread issue for GI's that no footwear could cure.

ABOVE: GIs test several varieties of cold weather boots in Belgium, 1944.

RIGHT: The first version of U.S. Army combat boots, 1942.

◼38 The Jeep

The vehicle's official title was the MB 4x4 Truck, but everyone called it a Jeep, and everyone wanted one. Before World War II ended, American automobile manufacturers, primarily the Ford Motor Company and Willys-Overland, had made 640,000 Jeeps.

Although the U.S. Army had tried to standardize its family of motor vehicles into six different size classes in 1939, the field exercises of 1940 revealed a requirement for a small dual-drive wheeled vehicle that could carry a driver and three passengers in all sorts of terrain. The final model was powered by a four-cylinder inline engine of 60 hp and was capable of carrying 1,200 pounds (550 kg). Pulling a trailer added to its cargo capacity. It also had to have a removable canvas roof and side panels on a metal frame to deal with bad weather.

The War Department's request for a prototype went to 135 companies with a requirement to propose a design in 49 days. Only the American Bantam Car Company responded, submitting a design by Karl Probst, who drew up plans for the vehicle in two days. It was earlier design work by two Army officers for Bantam that made this response possible.

Because the American Bantam Car Company did not have the plant capacity or workforce to make the new vehicle, the Jeep contract went to Ford and Willys using the Probst-American Bantam Car design under a royalties agreement.

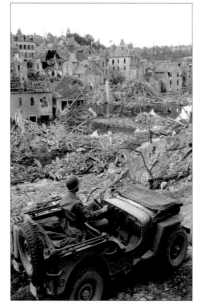

The unloaded vehicle weighed 2,400 pounds (1,090 kg), which meant it could be pushed and pulled by soldiers if necessary. Its four-cylinder engine, 60 hp motor enabled it to creep up steep inclines, yet it could speed along good roads at 55 miles per hour (89 km/h). Its range was 280 miles (450 km). It could be adapted to carry radios and stretchers, as well as a mount for a .30-caliber or a .50-caliber machine gun for combat zone missions. It could even pull light anti-tank guns and small howitzers.

Stuck with the name "Jeep"—whose origin is uncertain, but popular theories are that it came from "GP" meaning "general purpose," or was derived from the go-anywhere character Eugene the Jeep in *Popeye* cartoons—the vehicle became common in every Allied army in various models and modes, or was duplicated in some variants, as in the Red Army. American divisions normally rated around 1,350 service support motor vehicles, and of these, 612 would have been Jeeps. Every infantry company had one Jeep and trailer; enterprising units found more than one. Since seven out of every ten GIs came from families that had a car, a truck, or a tractor, maintenance and minor repairs could be performed at the unit level. The simplicity of the Jeep's motor made this possible. Its utility in rough terrain made it popular in World War II, a popularity that explains the presence of Jeeps in a variety of models all over the world, even today.

ABOVE: A U.S. soldier looks over the destroyed city of Saint-Lô from his Jeep.

RIGHT: Finished Jeeps stand in rows having been mass-produced for the Allied invasion of Nazi-Europe.

■39 V-mail

A long with generous and edible rations, American service personnel valued prompt mail service, no matter how far from home they were deployed. Unit commanders encouraged regular correspondence with friends and families because it built morale (most of the time) and improved discipline through maintaining a sense of community accountability. The biggest challenge, however, was transporting tons of letters by aircraft and shipping when cargo space was at a premium.

The V-mail or "Victory" system, pioneered by the postal department of the U.S. Army Service Forces, helped reduce the mail tonnage shipped abroad. Using a British system already in use, the ASF microfilmed letters to overseas personnel, then reconstituted the letters at one-fourth their original size for delivery.

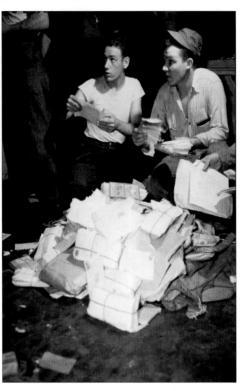

The letters had to be written on special paper that could be folded and sealed as an envelope. This photographic paper also required special ink. A V-mail kit cost $1.00 and could be purchased at U.S. Postal Service Stations. When a service member received a V-mail letter, it had been reduced to a 5 × 4 inch (12.5 × 10 cm) black and white copy. It could have no enclosures, which meant that photographs had to be sent in normal mailing envelopes.

Service members encouraged their correspondents to use V-mail on the promise that these miniaturized letters would arrive more rapidly and in better condition. Deployed service members could use the V-mail system to write home, too. The savings in space and weight was dramatic. A total of 150,000 regular-sized first class letters filled 37 mail bags and weighed more than a ton. The same number of letters in V-mail form filled only one mailbag and weighed 45 pounds (20.5 kg).

Between June 1942 and August 1945, the ASF postal system processed 1.2 billion V-mail letters to and from service personnel abroad. Most of the correspondence traveled during the June 1942– May 1944 period. From the Normandy and Marianas campaigns until the war's end, V-mail postings declined to 14 million because space available on transport aircraft increased dramatically for regular first class mail. Various estimates put regular mailings at a 4:1 ratio over V-mail after May 1944. In 1942–43, however, the V-mail system saved valuable space as the U.S. armed forces deployed abroad.

ABOVE: U.S. Navy postal clerks sort out conventional mail.

RIGHT: An American wife sends family news by V-mail.

▪️40 The Panzerfaust

The Panzerfaust ("armor fist") was a German shoulder-launched antitank weapon. It was the second generation of its type, the first being the Panzerschreck. The Americans had been first to produce a shoulder-launched antitank rocket fired from a 2.36-inch (60-mm) tube: the Bazooka. Although a prewar idea, it was not effective until the invention of the shaped or hollow charge, which could defeat armor. The principle was to mold the explosive around a cone, which increased its power by up to 15 times.

Until then, armor-piercing weapons relied solely on firing a projectile made of very hard steel, which "drilled" its way through the armor by virtue of its kinetic energy; some anti-armor weapons rely on this characteristic to this day. To produce the necessary muzzle velocity requires a large and powerful gun, which cannot be carried around by an infantry soldier. As the war progressed and tanks with heavier armor appeared on the battlefield, antitank guns became correspondingly bigger. The British army, for example, developed from the useless Boyes antitank rifle and 25-mm Hotchkiss in 1939 to the very effective 17-pounder in 1943. Antitank guns had to be towed or fitted in vehicles, and were difficult to conceal because of the dust and flame of their muzzle blast.

The hollow charge changed this. It works by projecting a stream of super-hot molten metal through the armor, which sprays the interior of the vehicle, killing the crew and setting fire to ammunition and fuel. This often causes a massive explosion, on occasions big enough to blow the turret off a tank. A hollow charge does not have to be especially large to achieve a "kill" against an armored vehicle. With the addition of an aerodynamic nose cone, it can be fixed to a rocket, and this, with the launcher, is light enough to be carried by an infantry soldier.

The American Bazooka was sent in considerable numbers to Russia, where several fell into German hands. The Germans copied it and produced the Panzerschreck, which fired an electrically ignited 88-mm rocket grenade. It was operated by two men, one to carry and fire it, the other to carry spare rockets and load the tube. It had a range of 150 yards (135 m), and could penetrate 8.25 inches (21 cm) of armor. The tube could be reloaded, and, like a Bazooka, fired as often as there were rockets available.

The Panzerfaust also fired a hollow-charge bomb, but from a disposable tube. It was light, and could be carried and fired by one man. It first appeared in late 1942, had a range of up to 100 yards (90 meters), and could penetrate 7.8 inches (19.8 cm) of armor. It was cheap, and over six million were manufactured during the war. It was widely used by the German army and, towards the end of the war, by the *Volkssturm*.

In built-up areas and thick country such as the Normandy Bocage, it was extremely effective. Small bodies of infantry could hide in ambush and, having allowed a tank to pass them, could fire a Panzerfaust into the side or rear of the tank, where the armor was usually thinner. For this reason the Panzerfaust was feared by Allied tank crews, especially when fighting in towns or villages, around agricultural buildings, and in terrain consisting of woods and thick hedgerows.

LEFT: A soldier of the Waffen SS with a Panzerfaust in the Ukraine on the Eastern Front in January 1944.

ABOVE: The Panzerfaust.

OVERLEAF: German infantry carrying Panzerschreck rocket launchers with blast shields. This weapon preceded the Panzerfaust.

▪41 Welding Torch

The industrial effort of the United States provided the Allies with quantities of weapons the Axis could not match. An aircraft industry that could build only 6,000 aircraft in 1939 produced 96,000 planes in 1944. The tonnage of new merchant ships built climbed from one million tons (1941) to 19 million tons in 1943.

The development of new manufacturing techniques became essential to aircraft, ship, and armored vehicle production. The use of rivets to join sections of structural steel became less common than using high temperature acetylene torches and welding compounds to fuse metal sections. A Liberty ship, for example, required cutting and joining 3,500 tons of steel plating. Replacing riveting with welding required skilled, patient workers who would accept greater risks in order to speed manufacturing. Women war workers filled this need. Between 30 to 40 percent of welders were female. "Rosie the Riveter" gave way to the "Arc Welding Queen," an actual annual competition.

Stark necessity opened the industrial workforce to women. By war's end, six million were working in manufacturing assembly-line jobs. In shipyards, where women had not been hired before 1940, 10 percent of the wartime work force of 1.5 million was female. When the aircraft and shipbuilding industries requested 80,000 women for training programs in 1941–42, 750,000 women volunteered. They faced serious barriers in the work force: employers seldom paid women the same wages as male workers. The average differential was 40 percent, which could be narrowed only by working overtime (more than 40 hours in a six-day work week) and taking grueling, demanding jobs like welding. Fifty percent of working women supported families, which led to high absentee rates, used by employers to excuse low wages.

On balance, however, women proved to be more trainable and skilled than the males who escaped military service because of occupational and dependency deferments and age. Employers admitted that young women showed unappreciated physical stamina and surprising innovativeness. Additionally, by the end of the war, the percentage of black women in the work force had climbed 11.3 percent. Working wives often made more money than their servicemen husbands and women moved to industrial centers far from the rural midlands of America. An Army photographer discovered one photogenic young woman working in a Burbank, California, aircraft factory. Her name was Norma Jeane Baker, which changed with her postwar employment to Marilyn Monroe.

The entry of women into dangerous work like welding created a greater interest in workplace safety. The mixture of oxygen and acetylene gases could produce a narrow flame of 6,300°F (3,500°C) or twice the temperature needed to make metal molten and thus ready for fusing. Women workers demanded and received special masks and clothing for protection and those working in shell factories demanded more rigorous safety standards. Although many women quit the industrial work force after 1945, they left their factories a better place to work than they found them.

ABOVE: No rivets needed here: a young woman masters the welding torch.

RIGHT: Women and minority workers weld ship plates in California, 1944.

42 The Midget Submarine

The British, Germans, Italians, and Japanese all built midget submarines in World War II. They were usually used to attack warships in harbors which conventional submarines would find difficult to penetrate. British midget submarines, X-craft, carried two one-ton high explosive charges on either side of the hull which could be dropped on the seabed below the target, or fixed to the enemy ship's hull by magnetic clamps—the latter required a diver to exit from the X-craft. Axis midget submarines, on the other hand, fired torpedoes.

British X-craft carried out one of the most successful attacks of World War II on September 22, 1943, the target being the German battleship *Tirpitz* in Kaafjord, Norway. Of the six X-craft, each with a crew of four, that were towed across the North Sea by six submarines, four actually entered Kaafjord as two were lost en route, though the crew of one of them survived. *X7*, under Lieutenant Godfrey Place, was for a time caught in anti-submarine nets, but after freeing his boat Place went on to drop his two charges under the *Tirpitz*. *X6* (Lieutenant Commander Donald Cameron) was sighted by the *Tirpitz* and engaged by small-arms fire, but Cameron surfaced alongside the battleship, dropped his charges, and scuttled his boat. He and his crew were, however, taken prisoner.

When all four charges detonated, *X7* was temporarily trapped in another net on her way out, and with her controls damaged by the explosions, she shot to the surface, where she was sunk by enemy gunfire. Place and another officer survived, and were taken prisoner. One of *X7*'s charges exploded right under the *Tirpitz*'s engine room, putting the battleship out of action for six months and thereby altering the balance of sea power in the North Atlantic in the Allies' favor.

X5 was never seen again, and *X10*, which had been sent to attack the *Scharnhorst*, thought to be nearby but actually at sea, returned to her parent submarine, only to sink on the homeward trip. Cameron and Place were both awarded the Victoria Cross.

The following April, Lieutenant Commander Max Shean in *X24* went in to attack a large floating dock in Bergen, Norway. A mistake in identifying the target resulted in the mines being placed under a large German merchantman, sinking it. Shean and his crew managed to return to the parent submarine.

Two X-craft were used to mark the approaches to the British beaches for the Normandy landings of June 6, 1944. Two of the later types, XE-class vessels, sank the Japanese heavy cruiser *Takao* off Singapore and both captains were awarded the VC. On the same day, two other XE-craft managed to cut the telegraph cables off Saigon and Hong Kong.

The Germans developed a number of types of midget submarine late in the war to counter Allied amphibious operations, and these were used in open waters off beaches rather than in harbors, though for little gain. The most successful class was the Seehund (Seal) operating against Allied sea lines of communication in the English Channel. In 142 sorties, eight ships were sunk for the loss of 35 *Seehunds*.

The Japanese built 50 midget submarines, but most attacks were unsuccessful. Five were used and lost at Pearl Harbor on December 7, 1941. An attack on Sydney harbor on May 31, 1942, by three midget submarines resulted in the sinking of the depot ship HMAS *Kuttabul*, killing 21 sailors for the loss of all the submarines. The day before, on May 30, 1942, two midget submarines entered Diego Suarez harbor in Madagascar: one of them damaged the old British battleship *Ramillies* while the other sank a tanker. One submarine was subsequently lost at sea; the crew of the other landed to find food and were killed in an encounter with Allied troops. Japanese midget submarine attacks around Guadalcanal, Okinawa, and the Philippines were largely failures.

The Italians completed only four midget submarines in World War II. They deployed to the Black Sea during the German siege and blockade of Sevastopol in 1942, but without success.

ABOVE: A German *Seehund* (Seal) midget submarine in a U-boat shelter.

LEFT: Leading Seaman Rhodes at the diving controls of a British XE4, the same type of midget submarine that sank the Japanese heavy cruiser *Takao*.

RIGHT: Another shot clearly showing the controls of the XE4.

OVERLEAF: A damaged Japanese dry dock at Kure with Japanese midget submarines. Taken after the Japanese surrender.

43 The Avro Lancaster Bomber

One of the greatest aircraft in the history of air warfare, the Avro Lancaster was produced because of a design flaw in its immediate predecessor, the Manchester. The RAF specification in 1939 was for a twin-engined bomber of an exceptional—for those days—size. The first Manchester flew on July 26, 1939, and 209 were delivered to operational squadrons. But its poor performance and unreliable engines resulted in its being withdrawn from service and all surviving aircraft were scrapped. It was decided to base its replacement on the Manchester design, but to build it with a longer span and four Rolls-Royce Merlin engines. The first Lancaster, called the Manchester III, flew at the beginning of 1941. It was so successful that the type went into immediate full-scale production. It was one of the few warplanes in history that was close to perfect from the start, and only minor changes were made to the

design throughout its production history. In early 1942 the first operational squadron, number 44, received its Lancasters. From then until the end of World War II, 59 RAF squadrons flew Lancasters on 150,000 sorties in Europe, dropping 679,400 tons of bombs.

The Lancaster carried a heavier load and bigger bombs than any other aircraft in the European theater, over twice that of the B-17 Flying Fortress. The normal bomb load for a Lancaster was 13,970 pounds (6336 kg) which gave it a range of 1,674 miles (2,694 km), but it could carry the massive

ABOVE: An RAF Lancaster bomber.

FAR LEFT: Ground crews load anti-ship mines on to a Lancaster Bomber. Mining operations, code name Gardening, attracted little publicity but were flown on almost every night of the war by RAF Bomber Command, inflicting heavy losses on German shipping and submarines. It was highly dangerous, the dropping height was around 11,000 feet (3,352 m) over the relatively few deep-water channels off the North Sea and Baltic coasts: obvious targets. The mining aircraft flew in small groups, and were easily detected by German radar and attacked often by fighters.

"Grand Slam" at 21,954 pounds (9,958 kg) over a shorter range—1,000 pounds (450 kg), more than even a B-29 Super Fortress's capability. The B-17 Flying Fortress had the potential to carry almost as big a bomb load as the Lancaster, but the USAAF preferred to carry more and heavier guns together with much more armor, in line with their tactic of the self-defending bomber force attacking in daylight. The Lancaster's six .303-inch (7mm) machine guns were far less effective than the B-17's 13 0.5-inch (12.7-mm) heavy machine guns. Unlike the B-17, the Lancaster did not have a ball turret in the belly of the fuselage, and had no waist gunners. This made the Lancaster very vulnerable from below, the favorite attack position of the German night fighters. One Lancaster was built with a belly ball turret, but no more were produced thereafter.

The sortie that made the Lancaster famous to the British public was the Dams Raid on May 17, 1943, but the Lancaster was the "workhorse" of the RAF's bombing offensive over Germany and took part in every major night attack. They dropped 148 tons of bombs for every Lancaster lost, compared with 96 for the Halifax and 46 for the Stirling (the other two British four-engined bombers flown by the RAF). The German battleship *Tirpitz* was eventually sunk by a Lancaster dropping a 12,000-pound (5,450-kg) bomb on November 12, 1944. Lancasters were also used in support of ground offensives in Europe, perhaps most notably and controversially several times in and around Caen in Normandy, and most famously before Operation Goodwood in July 1944. After which the abrasive Commander of Bomber Command, Air Chief Marshal Sir Arthur Harris remarked, "Unfortunately the army did not exploit its opportunities."

The Lancaster remains the symbol of the RAF's strategic bombing effort and, although it was not yet in use at the time, one still flies today with the Battle of Britain Memorial Flight.

▪44 U.S. Airborne Divisional Insignia

Of the 89 divisions the U.S. Army organized in World War II, five were designated airborne divisions. This title meant that their soldiers had been trained to go into action by parachuting from a transport plane or riding to the ground in a piloted glider that had been towed to the landing zone by a transport plane. Three U.S. airborne divisions fought the Germans: the 17th, 82nd, and 101st. One, the 11th Airborne Division, fought the Japanese in the Philippines. The fifth, the 13th Airborne Division, went to Europe but did not see combat. During the course of the war, independent parachute infantry regiments also entered combat. One such unit, the First Special Service Force, was an American-Canadian parachute regiment that fought in Italy and southern France. The Army also organized an African-American airborne unit, the 555th Parachute Infantry Battalion, but it did not deploy overseas.

It was German use of airborne troops that encouraged the U.S. Army to convert a parachute-training battalion to a fully fledged 501st Parachute Infantry Regiment in early 1942, followed three months later by the re-designation of the 82nd Infantry Division to airborne status, and the creation of the 101st Airborne Division in August 1942. The three most famous members of the Army's "Airborne mafia," Matthew B. Ridgway, Maxwell D. Taylor, and James M. Gavin, were part of these organizational creations.

During the formation of the two pioneer airborne divisions, Army planners debated their mission. One potential use was to land deep behind enemy lines by parachute and glider, and seize an airfield for follow-on forces delivered by transports. This "strategic" use looked too vulnerable to enemy air and armored counterattacks. Instead, the "operational" mission won approval: using parachute and glider forces to give depth

to an amphibious operation in which conventional forces of infantry, artillery, and armor would join up with the airborne forces in 24–28 hours and thus spare them annihilation. This concept, tested in North Africa in November 1942 and Sicily in July 1943, led to larger operations in Italy (September 1943), France (June and August 1944), Holland (September 1944), and Germany (March 1945), with mixed results.

The basic problem was that unreinforced airborne units were left in combat too long to function because of mounting casualties, especially to troop leaders. The lack of adequate numbers and types of transports and gliders also shaped planning. Close air support in airborne operations never reached its potential.

By 1944, the organization of airborne divisions reflected the planners' assumption that they would fight violent but short-lived battles with a confused enemy. A division had three parachute infantry regiments: a glider infantry regiment, a four-battalion artillery regiment (75-mm and short 105-mm howitzers), and airborne engineer, antiair, and antitank battalions. Division strength climbed from 8,400 to 13,000 in an effort to increase firepower and infantry sustainability.

To the GI with physical confidence and an adventurous spirit, joining an airborne division became irresistible. A paratrooper received extra pay, wore jump wings and a special cap patch, and walked about in glistening jump boots below bloused trousers. He also wore a distinctive jump suit in combat and carried special infantry weapons designed for parachuting. A paratrooper could count on elite infantry comrades in his "band of brothers." High casualties also ensured rapid promotion for the survivors. The U.S. Army never lacked for airborne volunteers.

LEFT: American paratroopers of either the 82nd or 101st Division preparing to jump during the invasion of Normandy, June 6, 1944.

ABOVE: (Top) The insignia for the 82nd Airborne Division. (Below) The insignia for the 101st Airborne Division.

OVERLEAF: Paratroopers of the 17th Airborne Division jump into Germany on March 24, 1945, as part of Operation Varsity. The Division was part of XVIII Airborne Corps, First Allied Airborne Army, and secured bridges over the Essel River for the U.S. 12th Army Group's ground divisions in the final offensive on Germany.

⬛45 The Desert Rats Insignia

The term "Desert Rats" is often incorrectly used to include everyone who fought on the British side in the North African desert in World War II. It is sometimes confused with the name bestowed by the traitor Lord Haw Haw, when broadcasting on German radio, on the Australian defenders of Tobruk—"the rats of Tobruk." In fact, the Desert Rats was the name given to the British 7th Armoured Division from 1940 to 1945.

In March 1938, the British formed a Mobile Force on the coast of Egypt at Mersa Matruh, 120 miles (195 km) west of Alexandria. Its aim was to protect the Egyptian frontier should the Italians, garrisoned in their colony of Libya, attack the British base in Egypt and the Suez Canal. The Mobile Force consisted of four armored regiments: the 7th, 8th, and 11th Hussars, and 1st Royal Tank Regiment supported by the 3rd Regiment Royal Horse Artillery (RHA). Their equipment was obsolescent: Rolls Royce armored cars of World War I vintage, old light tanks, 15-cwt trucks, and 3.7-inch howitzers.

These units were soon joined by 1st Battalion the King's Royal Rifle Corps (KRRC), commanded by a man who was to become a legend in the Western Desert,

Lieutenant Colonel William "Strafer" Gott. Many soldiers in Egypt regarded the Mobile Force as a joke, calling it the "Mobile Farce." Fortunately, in September 1938 it was taken over by Major General Percy Hobart. He took it out into the desert for weeks of vigorous, realistic training, and welded it into a first-class formation comprising a mobile division of three brigades. On the outbreak of war, this Mobile Division moved to the Egyptian/Libyan frontier but soon afterward Hobart, who fell out with the British Commander in Egypt, was sacked, much to his soldiers' dismay. He returned to England and became a corporal in the Home Guard, and eventually formed and commanded the 79th Armoured Division.

On February 16, 1940, the Mobile Division became the 7th Armoured Division. The wife of the divisional commander, Major General Michael O'Moore Creagh, visited the Cairo Zoo, where she sketched a jerboa, and this became the basis for the divisional sign.

The 7th Armoured Division began its long years of fighting by defeating the Italians at the Battle of Sidi Barrani on December 9, 1940. After the British took Tobruk on January 22, 1941, the Desert Rats were sent in a daring cross-desert thrust to Beda Fomm, where they inflicted a crushing defeat on the Italian 10th Army. Thereafter, the Division took part in most of the major engagements of the Desert War, including Operations Battleaxe (June 15–17, 1941) and Crusader (November 18–December 30, 1941), and the Battles of Gazala (May 26–June 21, 1942) and the Cauldron (May 27–June 13, 1942), Alam Halfa (August 30–September 5, 1942) and the Second Battle of El Alamein (October 23–November 4, 1942). From Alamein they participated in the fighting advance to Tripoli, ending the North African campaign in Tunis in May 1943.

By now they had been on the go for two-and-a-half years. But there would be no respite: from September to November 1943 the division was in action in Italy, before being sent back to England to prepare for the campaign in northwest Europe. Many in the Division thought it was time that some of the formations that had been training in the UK since Dunkirk did some fighting, and there was considerable unhappiness. A senior officer, watching units of the Division on their way to embark for France in June 1944, remarked in shock, "they were the Desert Rats, the most famous division in the British Army, and they were fed up and irresponsible." (Brigadier later General Sir Otway Herbert, quoted in Monty: Master of the Battlefield 1942–1944 by Nigel Hamilton, Hamish Hamilton, 1984.)

Following some early setbacks in Normandy and a change of divisional commander, the Division regained its confidence and style. On May 3, 1945, the 11th Hussars led the 7th Armoured Division into Hamburg; except for taking part in the Victory Parade in Berlin on July 21, 1945, the long march of the Division was over. A sign on the outskirts of Berlin erected by the Division records the route from Alamein to the heart of Germany, omitting the first two-and-a-half years in the life of one of the most famous divisions in the history of the British Army.

LEFT: Lee Grant tanks of 22nd Armoured Brigade of the 7th Armoured Division in the Western Desert in July 1942.

ABOVE, TOP: The Desert Rat insignia based on the design by the wife of the first commander of the division, Major General Creagh, after a visit to Cairo Zoo, where she sketched a jerboa. This is the modified version worn by 7th Armoured Brigade.

ABOVE, BOTTOM LEFT: After being sent to Burma in early 1942, the 7th Armoured Brigade returned to its parent formation, the 7th Armoured Division, but modified its badge to a green "jungle" rat.

ABOVE, BOTTOM RIGHT: An early-pattern desert version of the Desert Rat insignia.

▪46 MacArthur's Dress Hat

General of the Army Douglas MacArthur (1880–1964) always found some flamboyant way to alter his uniform and add to his theatrical public image. As the youngest general (age 38) in the American Expeditionary Forces (AEF) in World War I, he sported a short field coat of non-regulation design and a sweeping wool muffler. He often looked as if he flew a Spad biplane rather than commanding an infantry brigade and a division. By World War II, the MacArthur trademark had become a highly embroidered officer's dress hat (tan or khaki hat cover with a grommet) and a corncob pipe of several designs. Aviator's sunglasses enhanced the general's aura of invincibility.

MacArthur's hat dates from his service as field marshal of the army of the Commonwealth of the Philippines, 1936–41. Having served as Chief of Staff, U.S. Army, 1930–35, MacArthur chose to retire and take up new employment rather than return to his permanent rank of major-general. The rank of field marshal did not exist in the American service, so MacArthur could invent his own uniform. Except for the hat, he followed U.S. Army convention. American generals at the time wore the same unadorned hat as junior officers. MacArthur, however, added gold embroidered oak leaves and acorns to the brim and the circular band of the hat cover that fits over the hat frame. The effect is dazzling and certainly identifies the wearer as a very senior general. The gold or silver adornments, now common to senior officer hats in the American services, are known as "scrambled eggs." MacArthur retained the traditional American eagle of the national seal as his hat's centerplate.

When MacArthur returned to American service in July 1941, he did not change hats. Throughout World War II, the occupation of Japan, and the Korean War, the MacArthur hat went everywhere with "El Supremo." MacArthur did not like helmets and never wore one. He did not favor the convenient "fore and aft" overseas cap, probably for esthetic reasons. The hat did not surrender for cleaning, or so it appeared. In his meeting with MacArthur at Wake Island in October 1950, President Harry S. Truman remarked that the famous hat needed a clean and repairing. As an AEF veteran, Truman disliked flamboyant generals, even those who flaunted austerity as MacArthur did in his plain, unadorned khaki uniform without a tie.

The hat came close to becoming a casualty in two wars. Thoroughly soaked in the PT boat ride from Corregidor to Mindanao during MacArthur's escape to Australia in 1942, the hat shrank. "El Supremo" vowed to return to the Philippines wearing his white dress hat until his aides stretched the "real" hat back to wearable dimensions. The next crisis came in October 1950, when Truman and the press noted that the hat had become worn, ragged, and soiled, perhaps hidden commentary about the wearer. Mrs. MacArthur used some borrowed time when the general was ill to have the hat refurbished in Tokyo.

When Truman relieved MacArthur in April 1951 for making a public effort to widen the Korean War to China, the general and the hat came home together. Today they both rest in the MacArthur Memorial Museum, Norfolk, Virginia.

LEFT: General MacArthur and his staff wade ashore at Leyte, the Philippines, 1944.

ABOVE: General of the Army Douglas MacArthur and his famous hat, 1945.

▪47 Australian Divisional Badges

When the Second Australian Imperial Force (AIF) was formed at the start of World War II, the newly raised divisions chose typically Australian animals to appear on their identifying badges. The 7th Division had a kookaburra, and the 9th Division a platypus, while the 6th Division's badge featured a kangaroo and that of the 8th Division was an emu. All of the animals were generally shown on top of another Australian icon, a boomerang. A variant of the badges was used in white on black as a unit vehicle identifier. The 6th, 7th, 8th, and 9th Divisions were the only ones to experience active service as complete divisions in World War II.

The 6th Division was the first to see action, in January 1941 at the Battle of Bardia, a stronghold held by the Italians just inside Libya which was then an Italian colony. After two days' fighting, the division captured 44,400 prisoners, 260 guns, and 130 tanks for the loss of 130 Australian dead and 320 wounded. During the second night of the battle, some Italians came in to surrender and were told by an Australian officer that they didn't have time to deal with them, and to come back in the morning. The division went on to capture Tobruk on January 22, 1941, and to participate in the crushing defeat of the Italian 10th Army at Beda Fomm. Further service in Greece and Crete was followed by fighting against the Japanese in New Guinea.

One brigade of the 7th Division took part in the defense of Tobruk with the 9th Division, while the remainder of the 7th took part in the invasion of Vichy French Syria in June–July 1941. After this, the division fought in New Guinea and Borneo between August 1942 and August 1945.

The 8th Division fought in Malaya and Singapore, where the bulk of the division was taken prisoner following the surrender to the Japanese in February 1942.

The 9th Division spent more time fighting in World War II than any other Australian division. The Division was the mainstay of the defense of Tobruk during the first part of the siege from April to October 1941 at a cost of 3,164 Australian casualties, and took part in both Battles of El Alamein (July 1–27, 1942, and October 23–November 4, 1942). In the Second Battle, under Montgomery's command, the 9th were given the tough task of smashing through the Italian Trento Division and the German 164th Division in the north of the battlefield. Their success drew German reinforcements northward, fulfilling Montgomery's hopes and enabling him to execute Operation Supercharge, which clinched the battle. Over a period of four months of fighting in the Alamein sector, the Division suffered another 5,809 casualties. The high regard in which the 9th was held is exemplified by the remark made by General Montgomery's Chief of Staff on the morning of the Normandy invasion: "My God, I wish we had 9th Australian Division with us this morning" (*The Australian Army in World War II* by Mark Johnston, Osprey, 2007). But the 9th had been sent to fight in New Guinea and Borneo.

The 9th Australian Division was the most highly decorated of the four AIF divisions in World War II, including seven Victoria Cross winners, six of them posthumous.

ABOVE: Soldiers of the 9th Australian Division during the Second Battle of Alamein, November 1942.

RIGHT, TOP: The badge of the 7th Australian Division, a Kookaburra perched on a boomerang.

RIGHT, BOTTOM: The 9th Australian Division adopted the duck-billed platypus above a boomerang after leaving the Middle East to serve in New Guinea.

BELOW: Australian infantry displaying the Anzac spirit during house-to-house fighting in Bardia, Libya, in 1941.

▪ 48 The U.S.S. *Enterprise*

At the time of the Japanese attack on Pearl Harbor on December 7, 1941, the U.S. Navy had six large fleet carriers. The U.S.S. *Enterprise* (CV-6) was one of two to survive the Pacific War. Ordered with one other similar carrier in 1933, *Enterprise* was built by the Newport News (Virginia) Shipbuilding Corporation and commissioned in May 1938. She was nicknamed "the Big E," and earned the most battle honors of any U.S.N. warship in the war with Japan.

Designed from the keel up as an aircraft carrier, *Enterprise* had a standard displacement of 19,800 tons and was 810 feet (247 m) long by 83 feet (25 m) abeam, with a normal cruising speed of around 20 knots (37 km/h). She could carry an air group of up to 80 aircraft plus six utility aircraft, together with a crew and air-group personnel of 2,500. Her defense armament included eight 5-inch/38-caliber guns and assorted 1.6-inch (40-mm) and 0.8-inch (20-mm) rapid-fire antiaircraft guns. She also had a special communications suite that enabled her to be the flagship of a task force or carrier group.

After the attack on Pearl Harbor, the *Enterprise* won the first of her 20 battle stars by participating in carrier raids on the Marshall Islands and providing air cover for the U.S.S. *Hornet* when it brought USAAF B-25s close enough to Japan to bomb Tokyo in April 1942. The carrier next engaged the Imperial Japanese Navy in the battle of Midway (June 4–7, 1942) as the flagship of Task Force 16 (Rear Admiral Raymond A. Spruance), where its dive-bombers helped sink two Japanese carriers.

The *Enterprise* faced its greatest challenge in the Solomons campaign. In the battle of the Eastern Solomons on August 24, 1942, the carrier absorbed three bomb hits that killed or wounded 168 crewmen. After repairs in Hawaii, the ship returned to the Solomon Islands in time for the Battle of the Santa Cruz Islands on October 26–27, 1942 where once more, two Japanese bombs caused serious damage, but the *Enterprise*, repaired enough for sea duty, returned to action in November. Some of her air group operated from Guadalcanal when she again had to go to Noumea for repairs. She then returned to the United States for an overhaul, bearer of a coveted Presidential Unit Citation. The Japanese had by now twice reported that the carrier had been sunk.

Returning to the Pacific War in November 1943, the *Enterprise* participated in the Gilbert and Marshall Islands campaign, and her air group played important roles in the Battles of the Philippine Sea and Leyte Gulf in August and October 1944. She continued to mount air attacks on China and Formosa in 1944–45, but it was off Okinawa on May 14, 1945, that a kamikaze struck her forward flight deck and elevator, which forced her to sail back to the United States for more yard works. For the third time, the Imperial Japanese Navy reported the *Enterprise* sunk.

Replaced by larger, modern carriers, the *Enterprise* finally left the fleet in February 1947 and she was scrapped in 1958. A newer nuclear carrier now bears her name.

LEFT: Shrapnel and fires pepper the *Enterprise* as a result of an antiaircraft shell from another ship helping her ward off a kamikaze attack off the coast of Japan.

ABOVE: Aerial shot of U.S.S *Enterprise* underway, with aircraft on deck; April 12, 1939.

▪ 49 The Long Range Desert Group Vehicle

The Long Range Desert Group (LRDG) was founded in June 1940 by Major Ralph A. Bagnold, an officer on the staff of General Sir Archibald Wavell, Commander-in-Chief Middle East Command. When Italy came into the war on the side of the Germans, the large Italian garrison in Libya posed a threat to the British bases in Egypt and the Suez Canal. Bagnold suggested to Wavell that a reconnaissance force be formed to penetrate behind enemy lines to see what the Italians were up to. According to the Imperial War Museum Sound Archive, when Wavell asked, "What if the Italians are doing nothing?" Bagnold replied, "How about some piracy on the high desert?" Wavell was delighted and immediately gave Bagnold permission to raise a force from volunteers among the British and New Zealand troops in Egypt.

Bagnold had spent several years in Egypt before World War II, and had pioneered the art of driving and navigating in the desert. The selection of vehicles was made by Bagnold; he was looking for a total of 33. Nothing the British motor industry produced at the time was suitable, so he tested a variety of American vehicles, and selected the commercial two-wheeled drive Chevrolet 30-cwt. He could find only 14, so he had to beg the remaining 19 from the Egyptian Army, plus some sun compasses.

A magnetic compass was unreliable because there was so much metal in a truck. If you wanted to take a bearing you had to stop and walk some distance off, and the delays caused by such frequent stops were unacceptable over a long journey. The sun shone all day and every day, so Bagnold

chose a sun compass, a modified sundial. You drove the truck keeping the shadow from the dial's central spike on the requisite pointer. The compass was mounted in front of the navigator, who sat beside the driver in the lead truck. Distance traveled was measured with the help of the speedometer. On a twisting journey of 100 miles (150 km), avoiding obstacles, going around the bigger dunes and so forth, the LRDG were very put out if their dead reckoning was out by more than a fraction. The positions were checked by taking sun shots by day and star shots by night using a theodolite, in the same way that a sailor at sea uses a sextant.

To reduce wastage of water when the radiator boiled, a pipe was led from the overflow down in to a can half-full of water, strapped to the side of the vehicle. The steam then condensed in the can. If the contents of the can began to boil it would spurt boiling water over the driver, who would stop, turn the vehicle into the wind, and wait for perhaps a minute. There would be a gurgling sound, and the water would be sucked back into the radiator, refilling it.

The vehicles carried metal sand channels, which could be placed under the wheels when the truck was stuck in soft sand. To begin with, the front gunner was armed with an Italian Breda machine gun, and the rear gunner manned a Lewis gun of World War I vintage. But as time went on, a variety of weapons were carried, including Boyes antitank rifles, Vickers .303-inch (7.7-mm) medium machine guns, 0.5-inch (2.7-mm) heavy machine guns, and Bofors 37-mm antitank guns.

Initially, a patrol consisted of ten Chevrolets, each able to carry up to three tons of load, and two or three

LEFT: Chevrolet trucks of the Long Range Desert Group.

ABOVE: The Bagnold Sun Compass.

men. They were capable of traveling a distance of up to 1,800 miles (2,900 km), and existing for six weeks on the rations, gas, and water each carried. Communication back to base was by radio, or wireless as it was then known. Eventually the patrols were cut down to five vehicles each in order to cover more terrain. The Chevrolets were replaced in mid-1941 by four-wheel-drive Fords, which carried the same load but were not so maneuverable. In mid-1942, these were in turn replaced by Canadian 30-cwt Chevrolets.

The LRDG must rate as the most cost-effective special force in history. Between December 26, 1940, its first long patrol, and April 10, 1943, there were only 15 days when there were no LRDG patrols out in the desert.

▣50 M1 Helmet

The helmet worn by U.S. service personnel in World War II survived that war by 40 years and remains a fond memory for those who wore it—and used it as a wash basin. Designed to replace the shallow "tin hat" of World War I, the new helmet provided the wearer with greater protection from both bullets and fragments. The M1 helmet saved American lives in World War II, Korea, and Vietnam until it was replaced before the Gulf War (1990–91) by the Kevlar helmet, which provided even more protection, but could not be used for other purposes.

Approved for mass production in June 1941, the M1 helmet, made of tempered Hadfield steel, provided protection to the GI's whole head and neck. The helmet weighed 2.3 pounds (1 kg) and its liner 0.7 pounds (0.3 kg). Its basic color was Shade No. 7 of dull olive green paint, thickened with sand to reduce any telltale glare. The M1 was a two-piece system, with an outer steel shell and an inner liner of plastic-fabric material. The steel outer helmet came with a green woven chin strap, actually worn below the jaw, which featured a hook-and-ball device to join the two straps. Many GIs wore the fabric chin strap joined at the helmet's rear and used the liner's leather chin strap to anchor the helmet to the liner. The key to a good fit was the suspension system within the liner, which kept the head free of the liner. It had a soft leather circular headband that could be easily adjusted.

Paratroopers wore a different helmet, the M1C, which featured a special chinstrap. Like the liner's suspension

system, the M1C chinstrap duplicated the new football helmet of the 1940s because it featured a double strap system across both the wearer's cheeks that ended in a tight padded chinstrap. The M1C chinstrap, pulled tight, ensured that a paratrooper still had a helmet when his parachute snapped open. The outer helmet also had to be secured to the liner using the conventional chinstraps. The helmet then had three layers. More than one bullet or fragment pierced the steel outer helmet, but deflected by the liner, gave the wearer only a bad headache.

By 1943, the Army and Marine Corps began to issue helmet covers that might break the distinctive shape of the helmet when adorned with foliage. The Army helmet cover was made of netting; the Marine Corps cover of solid camouflage cloth, "green side" or "brown side" to match the terrain. The Army also issued a solid burlap-like helmet cover by war's end. The Army netting cover enabled GIs to identify officers and NCOs by a white vertical bar (officers) or white horizontal bar (sergeants) painted on the rear of the helmet. Wearing rank insignia on the helmet's front only encouraged snipers.

The outer steel helmet had many other functions besides protection. It became a wash basin and emergency toilet on many occasions. Officers discouraged its use as a cooking pot since heat reduced the tempered steel's protective qualities. Although awkward to handle, the helmet could be used as an entrenching tool in soft soil. In all, the American helmet served its wearers well.

LEFT: A GI poses with his camouflaged helmet.

ABOVE: The M-1 Helmet, a lifesaver and wash basin.

■51 The Purple Heart

The Purple Heart is a decoration awarded to American military personnel for wounds received in combat. It may be awarded to the same person for multiple wounds if suffered on different occasions. It is also awarded to service members who are killed in action, who die of wounds, or who are missing in action and presumed dead from combat action. Estimates of the number of Purple Hearts awarded during World War II and afterward range between 800,000 and over a million.

Created by the War Department in 1932, the Purple Heart drew its inspiration from a Badge of Military Merit in the form of a purple heart with the word "merit" embroidered on it. This award was established by George Washington in 1782 for combat heroism and distinguished service, and records show that Washington made only three such awards to members of the Continental Army.

The U.S. Army had no official medals or other distinguishing badges to recognize wounds until World War I, when the War Department created a wound chevron to be worn above the cuff of the right sleeve of the service and dress uniform. This award required the authorization of the Commanding General, American Expeditionary Forces, based on the records of the AEF Medical Department. The wound stripe could be awarded for earlier combat actions. The 1932 regulations dictated that the Purple Heart would replace the wound chevrons, which might be confused with overseas service stripes, also worn on a uniform sleeve. The new model could also be awarded after 1932 to a member of the U.S. Army who had performed an act or acts of merit that reflected "extraordinary fidelity" or provided "essential service."

In 1942 by Executive Order 9277, President Franklin D. Roosevelt extended eligibility of the award to all the armed forces, and even to American citizens serving in a civilian capacity in the armed forces, such as a Red Cross worker or war correspondent. The order ended awards of the Purple Heart for anything other than combat wounds, although earlier recipients could exchange their Purple Hearts for other distinguished service medals like the Legion of Merit.

The Purple Heart bears the profile of George Washington to honor the award's founder. The profile is superimposed on a metallic heart attached to a purple ribbon edged in white. Multiple awards are designated either by an oak leaf device (Army and Air Force) or a gold star (Navy and Marine Corps).

To be eligible for a Purple Heart, a service member must be wounded by enemy action and treated for that wound in a medical facility that records that treatment. Many people who might qualify for an award refuse treatment and evacuation and thus have no record of being "officially" wounded; this condition has plagued veterans ever since World War II since it may affect current treatment and disability payments.

ABOVE: Five Marines having just received the Purple Heart. From left: Lieutenant Colonel George Mays, Corporal James W. Powell Jr., Corporal Arthur John Madden, Corporal Jack Warrens, and Corporal Clifford Heinson. Also shown are Private First Class James B. Rutledge and Samuel Boyd, who also received the citation.

RIGHT: The Purple Heart medal.

52 Kamikaze

Kamikaze is Japanese for "divine wind," named after the typhoons that destroyed Mongolian invasion fleets in 1274 and 1281. In the Pacific campaign (December 7, 1941–August 12, 1945) of World War II, the word Kamikaze was applied to aircraft that were deliberately crashed on to the target, sacrificing the aircraft and the life of the pilot.

By October 1944 the air ascendancy that Japan had enjoyed since December 1941 had been reversed. Many experienced pilots had been lost, and the United States was producing aircraft that outfought the once-dominant Zero. At Midway on June 4, 1942, the Japanese lost as many aircrew in one day as their training system produced in one year. The inexorable advance of the U.S. Navy across the Pacific toward the Japanese homeland, backed by the massively superior American industrial power, led to the decision to employ Kamikaze.

Early in the war, Japanese pilots had occasionally deliberately crashed on Allied warships, but on October 19, 1944, Vice Admiral Onishi Takijino suggested forming a Kamikaze force to attack American carriers supporting the landings at Leyte in the Philippines. The suggestion was eagerly received and implemented. Commander

Asaiki Tamai formed the first Special Attack Force from a group of volunteer student pilots he had trained, and Lieutenant Yuio Seki was asked to command the force. The first Kamikaze attack in the Philippines campaign is thought to have been on the Australian cruiser *Australia* in Leyte Bay on October 21, 1944, killing the captain, seven officers, and 23 sailors, and wounding 61 of the ship's company in the area of the bridge and superstructure. However, this attack was not carried out by the Special Attack Force, but by a Mitsubishi of the Japanese Army Air Force; the Special Attack Force was part of the Japanese Navy Air Arm, and flew Zeros.

On October 25, 1944, the Special Attack Force attacked five escort carriers, but succeeded only in damaging one so badly that the bomb magazine exploded, sinking the ship. Subsequent Kamikaze waves totaling 55 aircraft were more successful. Seven carriers were hit, along with 40 other ships, sinking five and damaging 35, including 23 heavily.

Kamikaze sorties were not confined to ship attack. When the USAAF's B-29 strategic bombing offensive began to pulverize the Japanese mainland, the Japanese Army Air Force formed the Shinten Special Unit to defend Tokyo, flying Nakajima Ki-44 Shoki "Tojo" interceptors to ram the U.S. B-29s. Armed with a mix of heavy and medium cannon, the Tojo was a formidable interceptor, but ramming a fast, maneuverable target like a B-29 was far more challenging than crashing on a ship. Furthermore, the B-29, with a total of 11 0.5-inch (13-mm) and 0.8-inch (20-mm) cannon, was a fearsome adversary. An attack on a B-29 demanded a high degree of airmanship, whereas the concept of the Kamikaze was to use poorly trained and hence expendable pilots. Attacking Allied shipping was a much more profitable tactic and continued right up to the last day of the Pacific campaign.

The most damage inflicted by Kamikaze attacks was during the invasion of Okinawa in April 1945, when massed onslaughts sank 36 ships and landing craft, and damaged 368. It is thought that nearly 1,500 Kamikaze pilots died in these attacks alone. While carriers were the prize target, none were sunk in these attacks, although many were badly damaged. The U.S. carriers with wooden decks were especially easy to damage. One Kamikaze attack on the U.S.S. *Bunker Hill* on May 11, 1945, killed 389 men, hugely exceeding the total deaths inflicted on all six Royal Navy armored-deck carriers by all types of attack throughout the war. During the Pacific campaign five Royal Navy carriers were hit by a total of eight Kamikazes, killing 20 sailors. A Kamikaze hit on a U.S. carrier usually resulted in a long time spent in dock for extensive repair, whereas on a British armored-deck carrier it was, in the words of a U.S. Navy officer serving on one of these ships, a case of "sweepers, man your brooms," push the wreckage over the side, and carry on.

The last Kamikaze attack of the war was on August 15, 1945 against Allied ships at Okinawa.

LEFT: A Japanese Kamikaze being shot down while attacking the U.S.S. *Hornet* off Santa Cruz Island during the Guadalcanal campaign in the Pacific (August 7, 1942–February 9, 1943).

ABOVE: Kamikaze pilots with the ribbons showing that they are about to go on a suicide mission.

ABOVE: A Zero Kamikaze aircraft about to plunge into the sea after being hit by American antiaircraft fire.

RIGHT: The U.S.S. *Bunker Hill* burns after being hit by two Kamikaze Zeros on May 11, 1945, while supporting the invasion of Okinawa.

■53 U.S. Navy Fleet Oiler

The Allied victory over Japan required mastery of the Pacific Ocean and the elimination of Japanese air and naval bases and the forces defending them. The advance across the Pacific in 1942–45 enabled American air and submarine forces to starve and bombard Japan into surrender. The essential element in this conquest of the Japanese oceanic defense system was the U.S. Navy's Pacific Fleet, divided into task forces of battleships, aircraft carriers, cruisers, destroyers, submarines, and many other vessel types. Except for submerged submarines, all these ships ran on steam engines whose steam-producing boilers were fueled with oil. A carrier task force of 20 warships had an insatiable thirst for it. Steaming at 15 knots, such a force consumed 50 tons of fuel per hour or an estimated 1,200 tons a day in routine operations. No oil, no movement.

The presence of fleet oilers in the Pacific Fleet Service Force enabled the warships to keep their engines operating. The fleet oiler looked much like its commercial counterpart, the oil tanker, which sailed from oil wells in the Caribbean basin to refineries in the United States. The difference explained a distinct U.S. Navy capacity, the ability to transfer oil while still underway. Oil replenishment did not require a quiet harbor or a secure

lagoon, and only high waves prevented a fleet oiler from rigging hoses above the water to deliver oil or aviation gasoline. As ships sailed a parallel course, only 20–40 yards (18–36 m) apart, the fleet oiler's crew pumped fuel to the thirsty warships. The same techniques enabled battleships and aircraft carriers to refuel their escorts.

Of the 107 fleet oilers assigned to Service Force missions, 72 served the fleet and survived the war. Three ships were canceled, 22 converted to other roles, and five scrapped as too old, too small, and too slow. The Japanese sank only five oilers. The fleet oilers came in two main types, the MC (Maritime Commission) Type T3-S2-A1 (two screws, 24,000 tons, six million gallon capacity) and the MC Type T2-SE-A1 (single screw, about the same capability). The Navy gave fleet oilers Native American or Hispanic names. The names of the five oilers that sank make the point: *Kanawha* (1943), *Nueces* (1942), *Pecos* (1942), *Neosho* (1942), and *Mississinewa* (1944).

Fleet commanders understood the value of their fleet oilers and provided them with anti-submarine escorts and combat air patrols from small escort carriers. After the early stages of the Pacific naval war, the Navy lost only one Fleet Oiler to Japanese attack.

ABOVE: A fleet oiler services an aircraft carrier underway in the Pacific.

RIGHT: The U.S. Navy Fleet oiler (AO) gave the Pacific Fleet great mobility.

54 Penicillin

One of the paradoxes of warfare is that it has often led to significant advances in technology and medicine, which have proved to be of great advantage to humans, and in some cases animals as well. One of the outstanding examples of this is the development of penicillin during World War II. Until the early 1940s, bacterial infections resulting from injury and disease were usually treated with sulphonamide drugs. These were effective for the treatment of some conditions, but not in the case of streptococcal infections. Research was therefore carried out into the development of new drugs that acted on the principle that some microbes might destroy others. In 1939, Professor William Florey and Ernst Chain (a Jewish refugee from Nazi Germany), both at the School of Pathology in Oxford, began investigating the antibacterial properties of assorted organic matter including *Penicillium notatum*, first noted by Alexander Fleming ten years earlier.

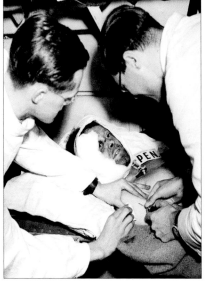

As a captain in the Royal Army Medical Corps, Fleming had seen many soldiers in World War I die of infected wounds. He maintained that antiseptics killed the patient's natural defenses more effectively than they killed the bacteria, especially in deep wounds. After the war he returned to St. Mary's Hospital, London, where in 1928 he became Professor of Bacteriology. Here, as he was to later recount, he discovered antibiotics, or bacteria-killers, by mistake. On return from holiday he noticed that among the cultures of staphylococci on his workbench, one culture was contaminated by a fungus that had killed the staphylococci. He identified the mold as being from the *Penicillium* genus. At first he called it "mold juice," but he named it penicillin on March 7, 1929. Fleming published his discovery in the same year, but his article attracted little attention.

In May 1940, the results obtained by Florey, Chain, and their assistants on the effect of penicillin on streptococcal infections were sufficiently encouraging to lead on to the next stage: clinical trials. These showed that even the most severe bacterial infections could be controlled by penicillin without dangerous side effects. Unfortunately, in a laboratory penicillin could be produced in only infinitesimal amounts, whereas one case of sepsis alone might need around 440 gallons (660 L) of the organism to be produced. The only way to produce sufficient quantities of the drug would be to do so using the resources of industry, but by now the industrial capacity of Britain was at full stretch meeting the demands of wartime production of medicines and drugs. Fortunately, an approach to the Rockefeller Foundation in the United States led to a suitable manufacturer being found. By 1942, penicillin was in full production in America, and it was first used in field conditions in North Africa in 1943.

The use of penicillin had an important effect on field surgical procedures as World War II progressed. In some theaters, because of the terrain (Burma, for example) and distances involved, or the speed at which the battle moved back and forth, as in North Africa, it was difficult to operate on the wounded until they had been evacuated to base hospitals. In Burma, this might be by light aircraft, and bad weather or enemy action might impose long delays before the wounded man reached hospital. The requirement was to carry out sufficient surgery to stabilize the patient so that he could survive the journey to hospital. Antibiotics kept the wound free from infection while the patient was awaiting evacuation and during the journey back.

Alexander Fleming and Howard Florey were awarded the Nobel Prize in Physiology for Medicine in 1945, which they shared with Ernst Chain.

LEFT: A soldier being injected with Penicillin while being transported in a hospital train. His label marked "Penicillin" is to avoid him being overdosed in error.

ABOVE: A penicillin bottle and ampoule.

⬛55 Browning M2HB .50 Caliber Heavy Machine Gun

One of three machine gun types invented by John M. Browning and adopted by the U.S. Army just after World War I, the .50-caliber heavy machine gun has reached almost a century of service. In World War II, "the Fifty" added firepower to ground forces, aircraft, and naval vessels of all types. It often replaced the Browning water-cooled or air-cooled .30-caliber machine guns when it could be mounted on a vehicle, because the gun weighed 84 pounds (38 kg) and its ground mount tripod 54 pounds (24.5 kg).

Challenged to produce an air-cooled and gas-operated machine gun to compete with Hiram Maxim's guns in the international markets, Colt Industries hired Browning, a young Mormon gunsmith from Salt Lake City, to develop machine gun prototypes in 1895. Browning's designs matured in World War I, although few reached the battlefields of France before the Armistice in 1918. The Army adopted Browning's .30- caliber light machine gun in water-cooled (M1917) and air-cooled (M1919) versions as a mobile infantry support weapon. The M2 heavy machine gun made its debut as the M1921, a .50-caliber air-cooled machine gun with a durable, heavy barrel designed as a defensive weapon against aircraft, vehicles, and massed infantry. An earlier version was water-cooled with a high ground mount for antiaircraft roles against low-flying planes.

The technical characteristics of the M2 were impressive. Its effective range was over 2,000 yards (1,800 m); its muzzle velocity was almost 3,000 feet per second (900 meters per second); and its rate of fire was 500 rounds a minute. The M2's ammunition combined accuracy and hitting power, but it was too heavy to carry easily along with its tripod and ammunition, although infantry commanders seldom left one behind. The weapon, variously mounted alone or in pairs, bristled from all sorts of small naval vessels and light craft, amphibian tractors, trucks, tanks, armored fighting vehicles, jeeps, fighter planes, bombers, and self-propelled artillery. The U.S. armed forces accepted more than three million "Fifty Cals" in World War II. The M2 appeared everywhere in U.S. Army and Marine Corps divisions: the three basic Army divisions had 404 M2s (armored), 165 M2s (airborne), and 236 M2s (infantry); the weapons that armed a Marine division included 392 M2s in 1942, but fell to 161 M2s when the Marine Corps reduced the numbers of vehicles in its divisions.

LEFT: U.S. Army trucks and half-tracks bristled with heavy machine guns.

ABOVE: The air-cooled M2HB with ground mount tripod, long-range sight, and flash suppressor.

56 Depth Charge

The object of an anti-submarine weapon is to rupture or pierce the submarine's pressure hull, thereby letting the sea in to sink the vessel. The weapon used by the British (and indeed most other navies) at the outbreak of World War II was the depth charge, which was little changed from those used in World War I. It consisted of a metal canister containing high explosive weighing between 198 and 300 pounds (90 and 136 kg), with small patrol craft carrying the smaller ones. A hydrostatic device detonated the charge at a pre-set depth in both kinds. The British heavy Mk VII had a maximum depth setting of 850 feet (260 m) and a lethal range of 29.5 feet (9 m).

Usually an attacking ship dropped depth charges in patterns like a five of clubs in a pack of playing cards, with a spacing of 120–180 feet (36–55 m); three would be rolled down stern shutes, and one from each quarter would be projected by throwers. The aim was to bracket the submarine both horizontally and in depth. The latter was achieved by using different depth settings on each charge, or by alternating heavy charges, which sank more quickly, with lighter ones.

Depth charges with fins like a conventional bomb could also be dropped from aircraft. In the first years of the war the depth had to be set before takeoff, and if the hydrostatic pistol was set to detonate the charge at depth, and the submarine was on or near the surface, the depth charge would have little or no effect. The problem was, however, eventually solved by devising depth charges with a shallow set hydrostatic pistol. The aircraft would carry both types and the right one would be selected for the job.

The disadvantage of a stern-launched depth charge attack was that the attacker's ASDIC lost contact with the submarine in the final 590 feet (180 m) of the run over the target. That "deaf time," as it was known, together with the time the depth charges took to sink, gave the submarine an opportunity to take evasive action and get sufficiently far away from the explosions to lessen their effect. Despite this, even if the detonations were not close enough to rupture the pressure hull, they could cause damage, frighten the crew, and keep the submarine below periscope depth and hence unable to retaliate.

The solution to "deaf time" was the ahead-thrown depth charge. The first type in service was the Hedgehog, which consisted of 24 light mortar bombs on six rows of spigots, the whole resembling a hedgehog—hence the name. Each spigot was slightly angled to spread the bombs over a circular area, about 130 feet (40 m) in diameter, well ahead of the firing ship to enable the ship to maintain contact with the target. Each row of spigots tilted as the ship rolled to keep the throw straight. The Hedgehog bomb had one disadvantage, however: it exploded only on contact with the target, so if all the bombs missed, there was no explosion to cause the damage and effect on morale that a depth charge could bring about even if it did not sink the boat.

In late 1943, a better ahead-thrown weapon was introduced: a three-barreled mortar known as Squid, which was fitted in pairs aft of the superstructure. Squid fired bombs filled with 200 pounds (90 kg) of a greatly improved explosive called Minol II. The bombs were projected in a high arc right over the ship's superstructure. They sank nearly three times more quickly than a depth charge and exploded at depths set automatically by the improved ASDIC/Sonar, in two depth layers 59 feet (18 m) apart. A depth charge gave you a six percent chance of a submarine kill, and Hedgehog 20 percent; Squid was a huge improvement on its predecessors, raising the kill probability to 50 percent.

ABOVE: A depth charge on its thrower.

RIGHT: A sailor about to fire a depth charge.

⁵⁷ C and K Rations

S eparated from fresh foods and his company cook, the American frontline soldier depended upon field rations, categorized as C or K rations, for energy and good health. The Army's experience in World War I dramatized the fact that pure water and available food offset fatigue, disabling gastro-intestinal problems and fear. As Napoleon observed, armies live and fight on their stomachs or, more accurately, on a preferred food intake of 3,000–4,000 calories a day.

The challenge for the Army was to create a ration that individual soldiers and combat Marines could carry and eat under such adverse circumstances as rain, snow, heat, darkness, enemy fire, and cold. The ration had to be easy to carry and edible without heating. The "C ration, field, individual" came in a cardboard box that held three small

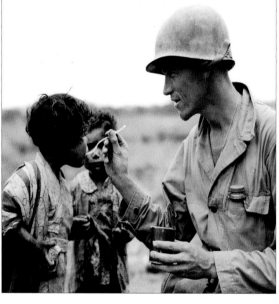

cans and plastic spoons; a well-prepared GI always carried a small can opener, usually on his dogtag chain.

The first can held one of ten different meat-and-vegetable meals (the best meals were pork and beans or hot dogs and beans; ham and lima beans were the least edible, even when heated). The welcome second can contained some sort of fruit like peaches and apple sauce. The third can contained powdered coffee or powdered fruit juice or cocoa, accompanied by candy and chewing gum. A fourth can variant could have cookies, crackers with cheese or peanut butter, or a fruit cake or pound cake. Each meal provided 1,000–1,800 calories. The ration

also included toilet paper in quantities too little or too great for field use. GIs hoarded toilet paper and ration cigarettes in their helmet liners.

The K ration was a lighter, simpler version of the C ration, packaged to be waterproof. Inside a green, very waxed 6.5-inch (16.5-cm) box, one could find a single survival meal, labeled "breakfast," "lunch," or "dinner," a monument to exaggeration. Breakfast was a fruit bar, powdered coffee with sugar, crackers, and a can of ham and eggs. The other two options had cheese and crackers or a can of meat, powdered soup, fruit juice powder, sugar, a chocolate bar, chewing gum, and some other treats.

Heating a ration with an extemporized stove (usually a ventilated ration can) or a pan of hot water helped improve the ration's taste. C-4 plastic explosives made a nice fire but toward the end of the war, rations came with a smokeless heat tab. GIs also carried individual hot sauce or other condiments. If heat was available, adding cheese often improved the meat-and-vegetable meal. No one confused C and K rations with Mom's apple pie; living on K and C rations guaranteed weight loss.

The United States armed forces were the best fed in World War II. Less than 90 days after D-Day, the Army was feeding hot, prepared meals to 70 percent of the troops. The C and K ration supply at the same time reached 60 million meals in France. Army meals also fed liberated Europeans as well as the GIs.

LEFT: American army lieutenant Richard K. Jones shares his food rations with local children found hiding in an abandoned tomb in Okinawa, Japan, May 31, 1945.

ABOVE: Ration boxes given to soldiers in the U.S. Army, including Type K breakfast box, Type K dinner box, and Type K supper box. Also shown are two breakfast cans and a package of cookies.

▣58 The Bridge over the Kwai River

The real bridge over the Kwai River bore no resemblance to the bridge in the movie *The Bridge on the River Kwai* (1957), save that it was built in barbarous conditions, in part by British prisoners of war held by the Japanese. The manner of its building, its appearance, and its location in the movie are all fiction.

There were actually two bridges built in 1943 over the Mae Klong in Thailand (renamed the Khwae Yai in the 1960s): one temporary, made of wood, and a few months later another of steel and concrete. These formed part of the Japanese railroad linking Nong Pladuk in Thailand to Thanbyuzayat in Burma, which enabled the Japanese to move supplies by rail from Singapore to their armies fighting in Burma. The rapid Japanese conquest of South-East Asia had resulted in a serious shortage of shipping to cover a vast area, and the sea route to Rangoon was vulnerable to attack by British submarines and by U.S. and British aircraft.

The construction of this railroad was a daunting feat of engineering. The line had to be cut through 260 miles (420 km) of mountainous jungle situated among some of the most unhealthy regions in the world: malaria, dengue, dysentery, cholera, and jungle sores were just some of the health hazards faced by those living and working there. The first step in construction of the line began in July 1942, when 3,000 Allied prisoners of war were sent from Changi in Singapore to build a base camp. Eventually some 61,000 Australian, British, and Dutch prisoners of war were employed building the line and bridges. In addition, and usually forgotten, the Japanese induced (or more often forced) more than 270,000 laborers from Burma, Malaya, Thailand, and the Dutch East Indies to work on the railroad. The labor force—prisoners of war and laborers alike—were seemingly regarded as expendable. The minimal diet, lack of medical supplies, atrocious working and living conditions, and numerous epidemics resulted in a high death rate. Although figures vary, the most reliable estimates state that some 12,000 Allied prisoners and 90,000 laborers died.

Between February and April 1945, a series of attacks by RAF and USAAF Liberators based in India were made on the railroad and bridges, resulting in sections of the bridges being destroyed. Both bridges were repaired near the end of the war, but the railroad always carried less than the Japanese hoped for. Subsequently the wooden bridge was demolished, but the concrete and steel bridge is still in use today.

The movie *The Bridge on the River Kwai* fails to portray the full extent of the appalling conditions and suffering endured by the prisoners of war, and omits the native laborers entirely. While the senior British officer in the film, played by Alec Guinness, collaborates with the Japanese, the real senior British officer, Colonel Philip Toosey, most certainly did not. In fact, he did as much as possible to delay the building of the bridge, including organizing the collection of termites in huge numbers to eat the structure of the wooden bridge and encouraging acts of sabotage such as mixing concrete as badly as possible. Not content with getting just about everything else wrong, the movie portrays Japanese as being so technologically backward that they are unable to build the bridge without British engineering expertise.

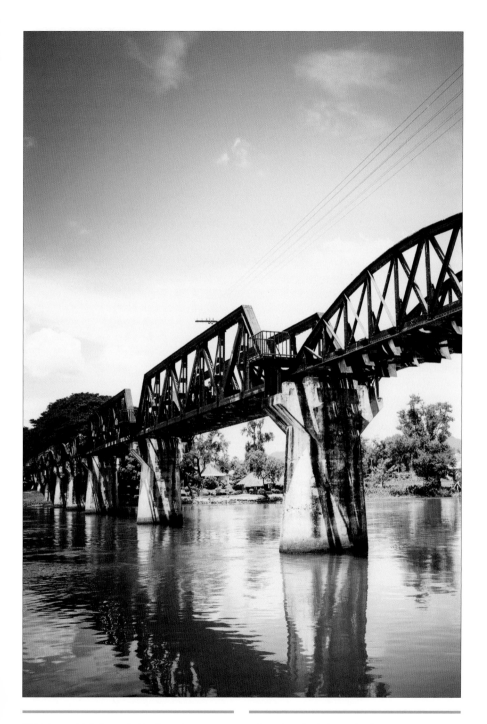

LEFT: A drawing of the bridge over the Mae Klong under construction.

ABOVE: The modern bridge over the Khwae Yai.

59 The Atlantic Wall

Up to the end of 1941, German fortifications along the French coast consisted of seven heavy coastal batteries between Boulogne and Calais, built to bombard England in the prelude to Operation Sealion, the invasion of England. In addition, some fortified U-boat pens had been built with a few naval coastal batteries to protect them.

Following the cancellation of Sealion, Hitler ordered Dr. Fritz Todt, his Minister for Arms and Munitions, to continue construction of U-boat pens and fortify the French Atlantic coast, especially at Brest, Lorient, and Saint Nazaire. Over the succeeding 18 months additional fortifications were erected and in September 1942, Hitler ordered the construction of defenses along the length of the French coast, similar to the Siegfried Line along the Franco–German frontier. This new wall was to consist of 15,000 concrete strongpoints manned by 300,000 men. Hitler designed many of these strongpoints himself, each housing 30 to 70 men equipped with machine-guns and antiaircraft weapons. The intervening ground was covered by interlocking fire from these strongpoints, which were planned to withstand air and sea bombardment. The U-boat pens were to be strengthened first, followed by the fortification of harbors suitable for Allied landings, and finally those beaches most appropriate for amphibious landings. The wall would also be extended to include the Belgian and Dutch coasts.

The task was now undertaken by Albert Speer, the new head of Organization Todt following Todt's death in an air crash on February 8, 1942. Although the Wehrmacht High Command believed the Channel coast to be the most likely place for Allied landings, Hitler decreed that priority be given to portions of the Atlantic Wall defending the V-1 rocket-launch sites. As a result, even the strongest sections of the wall never became the impregnable fortress that existed in Hitler's imagination. He himself never inspected the wall.

Hitler decreed that the German armies in the west must give priority to holding the wall when the attack came. This was also the view of Field Marshal Erwin Rommel, who had been appointed to command the initial phase of resistance to any Allied landing under the overall command of Field Marshal Karl Rudolf Gerd von Rundstedt.

On the eve of D-Day, June 6, 1944, there were 73 large-caliber guns in concrete emplacements, with mines and other obstacles on and behind likely beaches. In late 1943, von Rundstedt, whose views on tactics differed sharply from Rommel's, had ordered a second line to be built a short distance inland to give some depth to the wall—this was in addition to installing stakes in all likely glider-landing zones—but in April 1944, Rommel ordered work to cease on the second line and concentrated on beach defenses. In spite of this, of the 50 million mines needed to provide a continuous belt along the whole coast, only five million had been planted by D-Day. The string of smaller fortifications was still incomplete, especially on the east coast of the Cotentin Peninsula. For example, in the 352nd Division's sector overlooking Utah Beach, only 15 percent of the positions had been bombproofed. Because of Hitler's delay in initiating construction, and shortages of labor and material, the Atlantic Wall was never completed. This was a major factor in contributing to Allied success on D-Day.

One Allied Formation assaulted the Atlantic Wall twice: the 4th Special Service Brigade of Royal Marine Commandos. It landed in Normandy on June 6, 1944, and then, on November 1 the same year, assaulted the island of Walcheren, which guarded the entrance to the Scheldt River, capturing a series of massive coastal batteries in the process.

ABOVE RIGHT: One of the four 15-inch (380-mm) guns at the Batterie Todt near Cap Gris Nez. This part of the wall was never assaulted by the Allies.

RIGHT: The construction of part of the Atlantic Wall.

⬛60 Liberty Ships

The United States made a critical contribution to Allied victory in World War II by building a merchant fleet that could carry men, war materiel, food, and scarce resources like oil to the Allied trans-oceanic battlefronts. As Winston Churchill wrote to Franklin Roosevelt in 1941: "The oceans, which were your shield, threaten to become your cage..." The Liberty ship, a 14,000-ton general cargo carrier, played an important role in breaking out of that oceanic cage.

The merchant fleet sinkings of 1940 showed that German U-boats threatened to make American aid to the British war effort irrelevant. The U.S. Maritime Commission accepted the challenge of building a simple cargo ship that could be assembled rapidly in vast numbers. In December 1940, President Roosevelt authorized $36.5 million of emergency funds to enable the Maritime Commission to develop a general cargo ship on an emergency basis. Congress authorized additional money in February 1941 to build 200 special merchantmen, dubbed "Liberty" ships. By the end of World War II, the Maritime Commission had built and sent 2,710 Liberty ships to sea. This program of "emergency cargo" ships peaked in 1943 when "Liberties" made

up 13 million tons of an annual wartime high of 18.5 million deadweight tons of new merchant ship construction. There was no longer any doubt that American ship construction would outpace U-boat sinkings.

Although the Liberty program began slowly (only seven ships were commissioned in 1941), the Maritime Commission learned that it could not build ships the old-fashioned way and still meet its 19 million-ton goal for 1943. First, it had to finance 107 new shipbuilding sites and encourage production

innovation from its prime contractors, most notably six companies anchored on Henry J. Kaiser Industries of the San Francisco Bay area. Speed of construction demanded radical changes in building Liberty ships; accepting advanced technology was not one of them. Instead Liberty ships were "retro" in design. The key to rapid construction was the production process: to build a Liberty-type cargo ship in 1941 took 355 days, but by 1943 shipbuilders could produce a Liberty in 56 days. The key time savings came from simultaneous modular construction, the introduction of welding over riveting to join sections, the creation of a skilled and well-treated workforce, and the lure of high profits for good management. The basic limitation was the availability of steel.

The Liberty ship program had its share of problems. The ship itself was slow at 11 knots (20.4 km/h) and thus an attractive target in convoys that could travel no faster than their slowest ships, almost always Liberties. The ship could not be loaded and unloaded rapidly because of the outmoded boom-and-winch system. And although Kaiser-built Liberty ships were dependable, others were not.

To encourage rapid production, the Maritime Commission used unbid, cost-plus contracts, which could be exploited by unprincipled managers to enlarge company profits and their salaries. A Congressional investigation found shocking examples of fraud and mismanagement that threatened the entire Liberty program in 1944, but by that time the shipping crisis had passed, and the Maritime Commission could cancel some of its contracts. Liberty ship production fell to 7 million tons in 1944 and 1.5 million tons in 1945.

During the course of the war, the U.S. Maritime Commission accepted delivery of 45 million tons of new shipping. Almost 30 million tons of this fleet were Liberty ships.

LEFT: One of the Liberty ships being fitted out in 1943 prior to being sent to war.

ABOVE: The bow of one of the Liberty ships at Bethlehem-Fairfield Shipyards, Inc., after she had ran aground.

61 Morphine Syrette

For the wounded GI, the medical aidman or "medic" became the person standing between the casualty and insufferable pain. In the Navy and Marine Corps, the hospital corpsman (always known as "doc") played the same role. The principal instrument for killing pain without killing the patient was the morphine syrette.

Based on opium, a narcotic produced by a poppy plant, morphine became a sanctioned painkiller for the wounded in the nineteenth century. In the American Civil War doctors and medical orderlies used laudanum (a mixture of opium and alcohol) as a painkilling sedative during field surgery, usually amputations. Other than its humane function of painkilling, the narcotic immobilized a patient. The risky part of sedation was that it could also kill the patient, although at times a morphine overdose for an incurable wound became an alternative to futile treatment. Morphine narcotherapy could also produce addiction.

In World War II medics, corpsmen, or medical orderlies (the Commonwealth term for emergency medical service personnel) eased the pain of wounds by injecting morphine under the skin of a wounded person from a syrette, a small tube of slightly-jelled liquid morphine with a four-inch (10-cm) attached needle. The needle came covered by a plastic case with a protective cap. After removing the case and cap, a medic would inject the morphine (16 milligrams) by inserting the needle at a shallow angle into the patient's bare arm and then squeezing the tube. Morphine introduced directly into the bloodstream had an effect measured in seconds. A sedated patient became easier to treat and evacuate from the battlefield. The pharmaceutical company Bristol-Myers Squibb developed, patented, and produced morphine syrettes for the American armed forces.

Although morphine could arrest shock, it could also kill a patient by speeding the collapse of blood circulation—a clinical event known as respiratory failure. Morphine was not administered to unconscious patients, who were likely to be in the advanced stages of shock. Careful medics either put an M on a patient's forehead after administering morphine or inserted the empty syrette in the patient's collar (or both) to warn other medical personnel against overdosing. Because of its addictive potential, medical officers restricted the distribution of morphine to combat medics. Sometimes morphine syrettes were issued to GIs when going directly into combat, since casualties to medics and corpsmen were predictably high.

ABOVE: A Navy corpsman administers morphine to a wounded Marine in the Pacific, 1944.

RIGHT: The morphine syrette, the reliable pain killer.

62 The Bouncing Bomb

The Bouncing Bomb was conceived by Dr. Barnes Wallis, the chief designer at Vickers, who had a reputation as an aircraft designer dating back to the 1930s. At the outbreak of World War II, he began designing very big bombs to knock down buildings and other large structures. At that time, the RAF, along with all other air forces, preferred to drop quantities of small bombs rather than one big one. During the course of his work on this project, Wallis set about designing a bomb that would be capable of destroying the dams that supplied water to the population and armaments factories of Germany's Ruhr valley: the Eder, Möhne, Sorpe, Ennepe, Schwelm, and Diemel. The first dam-busting bomb envisaged by Wallis, in 1940, was far too heavy for any aircraft then in service or even on the drawing board. He realized that if a 6,000-pound (2,720-kg) bomb could be placed right by a dam wall, the water would multiply the effect of the charge and blow a hole in the 112-foot (34 m) thick wall of the Möhne Dam and the even larger Eder Dam. The Lancaster could carry such a bomb, but the problem was dropping it exactly in the right place. This led Wallis to design a barrel-shaped bomb, actually a mine or depth-charge, that would bounce across the water like a stone thrown in a stone-skipping game. Before the bomb was released, a mechanism started it revolving, imparting back-spin so that when the bomb hit the dam wall it would roll down it and sink to a predetermined depth where a hydrostatic pistol would set it off. It had to be dropped at an exact height, speed, and distance from the wall. The bomb, it must be emphasized, was designed for use against concrete dam walls, not the earth dam of the Sorpe.

Contrary to popular belief, Wallis was not the only person with designs on the dams. An attack on the Ruhr valley dams had been on the RAF's target list since 1938, but when the proposal was put to the C-in-C Bomber Command, Air Chief Marshal Sir Arthur Harris in early 1943, he said:

> This is tripe of the wildest description. There are so many ifs and buts that there is not the smallest chance of its working. (The Right of the Line: The Royal Air Force in the European War 1939–1945 by John Terraine, Wordsworth Editions Ltd, 1997.)

Nonetheless, Harris was won over. Barnes Wallis's power of persuasion seems to have been the critical factor. It is arguable that the bouncing bomb was used because it existed—on the principle, by no means rare in war, "we've got it, let's use it."

A special squadron, 617, was formed, under Wing Commander Guy Gibson. Rigorous training in low-level flying at night over water took its toll: in one rehearsal, six out of 12 aircraft were damaged. The attack on the night of May 16/17, 1943, resulting in the destruction of the Möhne and Eder Dams, is the stuff of legend, described by the official historian of the RAF's strategic bombing campaign, himself a Bomber Command navigator, as the "most brilliant feat of arms which has been carried out by any air force," a judgement that no one can dispute (Royal United Services Institute Journal, May 1962, page 103). Unfortunately the heavy losses (8 out of 19 of the RAF's best crews) did not justify the result. The Sorpe Dam had to be destroyed to cut the Ruhr's water supplies. It was only damaged. Wallis's bomb was not suitable for this dam, and he knew it. The official historian is clear that neither the special bomb nor the resulting floods were of any importance. What mattered were the low-level and master-bomber techniques devised and executed by Gibson and his crews. These, when adopted by the rest of Bomber Command, were to transform its tactics from about mid-1944 onward.

LEFT: A bouncing bomb in the bomb bay of Wing Commander Guy Gibson's Lancaster before a trial drop.

ABOVE: A bouncing bomb salvaged from Flight Lieutenant Barlow's Lancaster, which crashed, killing the whole crew, after hitting an electricity pylon on its way to attack the Sorpe Dam. A German official standing by the bomb gives a good indication of its size.

RIGHT: A Lancaster of 617 Squadron carrying out a practice drop at Reculver range in Kent.

OVERLEAF: The breach in the Möhne Dam four hours after the raid.

⬛63 Ration Books

All combatant nations in World War II imposed rationing of food and other key materials, but the United Kingdom was the first to do so because the country relied so heavily on imported food and other materials, including oil and gasoline, all of which was transported by sea. In 1939, the United Kingdom imported 22.4 million tons of food a year, amounting to 50 percent of all meat, 70 percent of cheese and sugar, 80 percent of fruit, and 70 percent of cereals. This was a vulnerability of which the Germans took advantage by attacking shipping in an attempt to cripple British industry and starve the population. After the experience of World War I, when German U-boats had brought the United Kingdom close to being starved into surrender, the British government had plans for rationing ready before the outbreak of World War II.

Once war was declared, the first commodity to be rationed was gasoline, but this was followed on January 8, 1940, by food rationing: first bacon, butter, and sugar, and soon after meat, tea, jelly, cookies, breakfast cereal, cheese, eggs, shortening, milk, and canned fruit. A Ministry of Food was established which laid down the system by which rationing was controlled. Every inhabitant of the United Kingdom, including children, was issued with a ration book.

Most ration books held by adults were buff-colored. Pregnant women, nursing mothers, and children under five years old had a green book, which entitled them to first choice of any fruit available, a daily pint of milk, and a double ration of eggs. Blue ration books were issued to children between the ages of 5 and 16, which gave them a higher priority in obtaining fruit than adults, a better scale of meat ration, and half a pint of milk a day.

In order to buy the majority of rationed goods, everybody had to register with a particular store. The details were stamped in the ration book, and you had to buy from this store and no other. This enabled the storekeeper to stock the amount of items required to supply the number of people registered.

The coupons inside the book were either torn out or stamped by the storekeeper each time a rationed item was purchased.

Food wasn't the only thing rationed in Britain. For clothes there was a points system, and the number of points allocated per person was reduced from 66 per year in 1942 to 24 in 1945 (a man's suit took between 26 and 29 points, depending on the amount of lining). No points were required for second-hand clothing or fur coats. The number of buttons, pockets, and pleats on clothes was regulated. Soap was also rationed, to around three bars a month per person—reduced if you also bought soap flakes or powder for washing clothes and dishes. Coal was rationed, and central heating was prohibited in the summer. Paper was also rationed, with newspapers being limited to 25 percent of their pre-war consumption, and wrapping paper forbidden altogether for most store purchases.

Although the Germans imposed some food rationing in September 1939, Hitler did not introduce full rationing until 1943. This was partly because he did not believe the war would last long, and also because he thought it would damage his popularity. Furthermore, any shortages in Germany could be made up by food requisitioned in large quantities from conquered nations; for example 15 percent of French food production was siphoned off. In mid-1943, however, with the war beginning to go badly for Germany, strict rationing was imposed there, with the lowest, almost starvation, scales reserved for the millions of forced laborers and prisoners of war. These people did much of the heavy work in factories and on the land.

The inhabitants of Leningrad during the 900-day siege suffered one of the most stringent rationing regimes of World War II. During the winter of 1941–42 the daily ration was reduced to 8 ounces (225 g) of all types of food for manual workers and 4 ounces (112 g) for all other civilians. Birds, rats, dogs, and cats were eaten, and there were even reports of cannibalism.

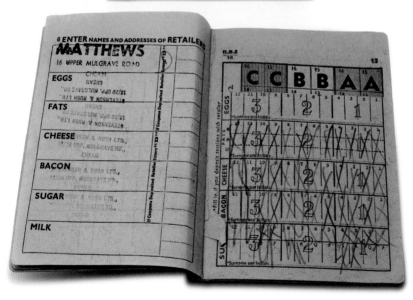

LEFT: A still life of a variety of rationed items. The picture includes a buff (adult) ration book, a red clothing ration book, a package of powdered eggs, and a can of SPAM (processed ham).

ABOVE: The outside cover and inside pages of a ration book.

64 U.S. Marine Corps, Fighting and Utility Knife

ssued to Marine ground combat troops in World War II, the Fighting and Utility Knife, known as the Kabar, became so identified with the Marine Corps that Marines have carried Kabars in every American war since 1945. Even though the Marine Corps now issues a knife-bayonet for the M-16 rifle and M-4 carbine, Marines still buy their own Kabars (the knife is pronounced "Kaý-bar").

The Kabar legend began with courses in close combat taught to Marine lieutenants by Anthony Drexel Biddle Sr., a World War I Marine and martial arts enthusiast. Part of Biddle's course in the 1930s included Asian-style knife fighting. Three of Biddle's disciples took further knife-fighting instruction from William E. Fairbairn and Eric A. Sykes, officers in the Shanghai municipal police. The lieutenants won over more Marines to the Fairbairn-Sykes curriculum, but the knife, a stiletto, had no other use but stabbing people, and was rejected. As adopted by the British commandos, however, the Fairbairn-Sykes knife became a legend in Allied special forces units in Europe in World War II.

In the meantime the U.S. Navy had ordered a utility knife for sailors based on hunting knife styles developed by the Case Cutlery Company. This knife, the USN Model 1, was designed for cutting, not stabbing. The Knife M1, made by Camillus, altered to give it a puncturing tip, remained too short and light for extended field use.

Combat experience in the Guadalcanal campaign in 1942–43 led to wide demand from Marines for a better knife for field work (chopping and cutting) and combat (stabbing). As a Biddle-Fairbairn-Sykes disciple, the project officer, Captain Clifford H. Shuey, knew the requirements well. Working with the Union Cutlery Company of Olean, New York, Shuey and others redesigned a Union Cutlery hunting knife called the "Ka-Bar," (supposedly named for a message from a happy hunter that he had used his Union knife to kill a bear, hence "k a bar"). Designated Navy Fighting Knife Model 2, the knife, built with a razor-sharp 8-inch (20-cm) blade and a sturdy pressed leather handle, went into mass production in December 1942. Union Cutlery shipped the first of one million Kabars to the Marine Corps on January 27, 1943. It was an instant success, and contracts to produce the Kabar went to Camillus and other manufacturers by 1944. In 1952, Union Cutlery became KA-BAR Knives, Incorporated.

Kabars became a common sight on Marine officers, staff NCOs, machine gunners, mortar-men, Navy corpsmen, Browning Automatic Rifle gunners, and almost everyone else not armed with an M-1 rifle and bayonet. Kabar knives also appeared on the hips of sailors and soldiers, since its versatility for non-combat tasks had wide appeal. Even though Marines must now buy their own Kabars, it is still the knife of choice and invokes the heroic service of World War II Marines.

LEFT: Marine artillerymen on Iwo Jima, 1945, open shell casings with Kabars.

ABOVE: A postwar USMC Kabar with a serrated blade for sawing ropes and wires.

65 ASDIC

A SDIC is said by some to stand for Anti-Submarine Detection Investigation Committee, a cover name for highly secret work by the Anti-Submarine Division at the British Admiralty during World War I which aimed to improve techniques for detecting dived submarines. The best that was available at the time consisted of hydrophones to listen for the sound of the U-boat propeller, but these were ineffective unless the vessel operating them halted before lowering them into the water, and remained stationary thereafter. Analysis after the war showed that the total number of U-boat losses credited to detection by hydrophones was just three; meanwhile, German U-boats had sunk so many Allied ships that there was a very real possibility that imports of food and other vital supplies to Britain could have been reduced to a trickle. Fortunately, since Admiralty staff did not manage to find a technical solution to the detection problem before World War I ended, the number of sinkings by U-boats was rapidly reduced by the introduction of the convoy system on April 26, 1917. They did, however, recognize that the answer lay in finding a way to emit a pulse of sound under water which would be picked up when it rebounded off a submarine's hull.

In the interwar years, research continued, and by 1938 the technology of bouncing sound waves off a submerged object had been developed by the British into ASDIC anti-submarine detection equipment. A transmitter encased in a water-filled metal dome on the ship's bottom sent out a series of "pings." The operator sitting in the ASDIC compartment behind the bridge could turn the transmitter head to cover an arc of about 45 degrees each side of the ship's head. When the sound pulse struck an object, it "echoed" with a beeping sound, and the operator alerted the officer of the watch or ship's captain, giving a range and bearing.

Before World War II, the Royal Navy's faith in ASDIC was such that the Naval staff believed the U-boat threat had been largely overcome. There was much discussion in the Admiralty on whether it would be necessary to institute the convoy system in the event of war. Fortunately, merchant shipping was ordered into convoys immediately on the outbreak of World War II, because in operational conditions ASDIC did not perform as well as had been hoped for a number of reasons, including the following: its range was

only 1,500 yards (1,370 m); neither bearings nor ranges could be read accurately—there could be an error of a few degrees in bearings, and a possible error of 25 yards (23 m) in range; it was usually impossible to discriminate between submarine and nonsubmarine targets, such as whales; the operator required much skill and practice, which took time to acquire; the efficiency of the set fell off rapidly at speeds above 20 knots (37 km/h), in rough weather and in waters with layers of large variations in temperature; crafty U-boat commanders learned to hide under a layer that either bent the sound beam or bounced it back; ASDIC could not determine the depth of a submerged U-boat, so it was impossible to set charges to explode at the correct depth; and finally, ASDIC could not detect a submarine on the surface. This last reason was perhaps the most critical failing of all, because the majority of U-boat attacks were at night on the surface, when, as the Naval Staff reported after the war, "the ASDIC was practically useless." The answer was more ships equipped with radar, and radar that was able to pick up a small target, such as the conning tower of a submarine and part of its casing on the surface. As the war progressed, escorts were fitted with such radar sets.

Early in World War II, British ASDIC technology was passed to the US, where work on Sound Navigation and Ranging (sonar) had been in progress for some years. British and American scientists worked together throughout the war to produce more accurate and reliable ASDIC/sonar equipment for both navies. By the end of the war, sonar, as the British now called it, was able to locate submarines more accurately, and this, combined with significant advances in depth-charge technology, played a major part in defeating the U-boat.

RIGHT: The officer of the watch and three ratings on the compass platform of HMS *Anthony*, an "A" Class destroyer. The ASDIC operator is looking out of the ASDIC hut in which he operated.

66 Beach Defenses

The Teller mine was the standard German antitank mine during World War II. Round and plate-shaped (*Teller* is German for plate), it contained about 12 pounds (5.5 kg) of TNT and was exploded by a pressure-operated fuse, usually set to detonate when a vehicle of 200 pounds (90 kg) or more passed over it. This was deliberate, because the mines were laid to damage tanks and destroy lighter vehicles and it would be a waste if one was set off by a person—there were lighter mines for that, which were usually laid alongside antitank mines in a mixed minefield, to make clearing it more difficult. Teller mines could be fitted with "anti-lift" devices that detonated the mine if someone tried to move it. This was well known and added to the time taken to clear a minefield.

In the fall of 1943, Field Marshal Erwin Rommel was commanding Army Group B, responsible for the defense of northern France and the Netherlands, from Nantes to the Zuider Zee. This included the coastal areas most likely to be invaded by the Allies. He had used mines extensively in Africa, and decreed that they should be used in great numbers in his area of responsibility. By October 1943, around two million mines had been laid; by the end of May 1944, the number had risen to more than six million. Not only were mines laid on the ground on all likely beaches, but Rommel also ordered that obstacles be built right out to the low-water spring-tide mark. Wooden or concrete stakes were driven into the sand or clay beach and angled so that they faced seaward. Concrete tetrahedrons 6 feet (1.8 m) high and weighing about a ton were also planted on the beaches. Added to these were "hedgehogs" made of angled girders of 7 feet (2.1 m), riveted together so as to present a sharp point in all directions; when struck they would pierce a craft or turn over, bringing other points up to impale it from beneath. Between these obstacles, or farther out to sea, poles on bipods were placed in such a way that craft trying to avoid the outward-facing poles at high tide would impale themselves on these underwater obstacles.

Many of these defenses of all types had Teller mines attached. If there were insufficient mines, Rommel made use of captured French artillery shells. The purpose of these devices, either with or without mines and explosives attached, was to rip the bottom out of landing craft approaching the beach and to sink them before they could touch down and disgorge their troops or vehicles.

Ever since February 1944, when the Allies discovered that underwater obstacles were being laid, small teams from the Combined Operations Pilotage Parties (COPPs) reconnoitered selected beaches at night to assess the problem. By day, low-flying reconnaissance produced oblique aerial photographs. As a result of the information brought back, the Allies decided they would not land at high tide, which Rommel clearly expected, but at low tide so that assault engineers could clear paths in the obstacle belt before the landing craft came in. This they would do by either demolishing them or pulling them aside with tracked vehicles, which could be achieved only when they stood above the tide level or in less than 2 feet (60 cm) of water. Teams from the Royal Navy and Royal Engineers were formed and trained for the task. At low tide the obstacles would be easier for the landing-craft coxswains to see and avoid.

Fortunately Rommel had neither the time nor the equipment to extend the obstacle belt into the lower half of the tidal range as he had intended. In addition, the Allies had at their disposal the specialist armor of Hobart's "funnies," specifically designed to cope with the problems posed by Rommel's obstacles. Landing at low tide would give the troops a longer run up the beach once they had left their craft, exposing them to enemy small-arms fire, mortars, and artillery, but this was infinitely preferable to being drowned or cut down in the water, which would certainly happen if lanes through the obstacle belts were not cleared.

LEFT: A German prisoner of war clearing a minefield near Stavanger in Norway fixes a charge to a Teller mine to destroy it in situ; it was deemed too dangerous to move.

ABOVE: A metal "hedgehog."

RIGHT: A naval officer, possibly a beach master, and Royal Engineer officer examining a "hedgehog" with Teller mines attached.

OVERLEAF: "Hedgehogs" and obstacle poles along the Atlantic Wall.

⬛ 67 The Nebelwerfer

The Nebelwerfer ("smoke-" or "fog-thrower") was a multi-barreled rocket launcher. The name was a relic of World War I, when it was used to fire smoke or gas shells in large quantities. In its original form it was a mortar, in essence a large drainpipe out of which a bomb was discharged by a small explosive charge. The impact of the charge was low, so big bombs with thin, light cases and packed with large quantities of explosive could be fired, albeit over ranges that were relatively short compared with a conventional gun. A mortar does not need a recoil and recuperating system, so is lighter and cheaper to produce than an artillery piece. Normally, the recoil mechanism absorbs the rearward momentum of a gun, and the recuperator returns the piece to its original firing position.

The size of the bomb makes the mortar a suitable weapon for delivering large quantities of gas or smoke. Normally mortars are high-angle weapons, fired in the "upper register," i.e. from an angle of 45 degrees to almost vertical, allowing for plunging fire onto targets behind hills and woods, and within fortifications.

In 1934 the Germans designed a 10-cm Nebelwerfer, the model 35, to project chemical bombs out to 3,300 yards (3,000 m), but this was not far enough for the army. The result was the 10-cm Nebelwerfer 40, with a range of 6,600 yards (6,000 m). But to achieve this performance the original mortar was converted into a breech-loading piece with a recoil mechanism to absorb the shock of discharge, on a wheeled carriage—an artillery piece in all but name. It weighed eight times as much as the Nebelwerfer 35, and cost about ten times more to manufacture.

Also during the interwar period, the Germans had been working on rocket propulsion, and it was recognized that this was a way to deliver large amounts of smoke or gas. The outcome was the 15-cm Nebelwerfer 41, which came into service just after the Battle of France (May 10–June 25, 1940), and replaced the 35. It consisted of a six-barreled launcher mounted on a trailer, firing a spin-stabilized rocket out to 7,500 yards (6,850 m) and shooting in the lower register like a conventional gun. The rocket warhead, which weighed 75 pounds (34 kg), could be packed with gas, smoke, or high explosive (HE). In the event, the Germans never used gas in World War II, but used plenty of smoke

and HE. A rocket launcher is recoilless, and can therefore dispense with recoil and recuperating systems. The resulting weapon is far lighter than the equivalent caliber artillery piece. Several thousand Nebelwerfer 41s and millions of 150-mm rockets were produced during the war.

Before the invasion of the Soviet Union, two further models were produced: the 28-cm and the 32-cm Nebelwerfer 41. The 28-cm warhead had an HE filling, and the 32-cm an incendiary filling. Both types had a short range: a mere 2,400 yards (2,200 m). They could be fired from their wooden packing cases, or from a towed launcher. These models were quickly followed by the 21-cm Nebelwerfer 42, which had five barrels, a 248-pound (112 kg) HE warhead, and 8,580-yard (7,845 m) range. It was mounted on an artillery-type carriage, and was therefore highly mobile. This saw service in North Africa, as well as in Russia and northwest Europe. The last model to be produced was the 30-cm Nebelwerfer 42, with a massive 277 pound (126 kg) HE warhead. Despite its designation, it was actually introduced in 1943.

Being "stonked" by conventional mortars is an unpleasant experience, all the more so when at the receiving end of a Nebelwerfer barrage. The rocket, fitted with a siren, made a moaning sound as it flew through the air. A multiple launch of a score of rockets produced a long, drawn-out wailing like a pack of banshees; it was extremely unnerving, as the recipients braced themselves for the massive explosions caused by a hail of bombs, each far larger than any Allied mortar bomb with the exception of the later marks of Soviet Katyusha rockets.

RIGHT: A soldier loading a 15-cm Nebelwerfer on the Russian Front.

▣ 68 The WACO Glider

The WACO Glider, made by the Waco Aircraft Company in the United States, was the standard medium glider for use by American airborne forces. It was also used on a number of occasions by British air-landing troops who called it the Hadrian, in keeping with the British glider names: Hengist, Hotspur, Horsa, and Hamilcar. It was a 15-seater troop- and cargo-carrying high-wing monoplane with rectangular wings, manually operated flaps, and landing gear. The cockpit was hinged along the roof where it joined the fuselage, enabling the nose of the glider to be raised and locked in the open position so that a jeep and trailer, motorcycles or light guns could be loaded and unloaded through the front of the glider.

The WACO Glider was employed by both the U.S. and British airborne forces for the invasion of Sicily (July 9–August 17, 1943), and by Wingate's Chindits in Burma. The first use en masse of WACO Gliders in operations in World War II, was the fly-in of the glider infantry, artillery, and headquarters vehicles and heavy radios of the United States 82nd and 101st Airborne Divisions on June 6 and 7, 1944.

Most of the attention on the activities of the U.S. airborne divisions during the invasion of Normandy, and indeed elsewhere, centers on the operations by the more "glamorous" parachute infantry, and the glider infantry tends to be ignored. For the Normandy invasion each division had one glider infantry regiment, each of three battalions, as well as two battalions of glider field artillery with 75-mm guns.

Before the introduction of helicopters, the glider provided the only means of flying soldiers and equipment into battle with a reasonable chance of landing them all together, where they could instantly form up into cohesive fighting units. Soldiers and equipment arriving by parachute were often scattered over miles of countryside, taking hours, and occasionally days, to gather together.

In the case of U.S. airborne forces, each glider was towed to the area of operations by a C-47 Dakota. They were released at a designated point short of the landing zone (LZ), to glide down and land. Most, although not all, glider landings by the U.S. airborne were made in daylight. A trip in a glider was far from being a joy ride, and many soldiers preferred parachuting. The glider wallowed in the wake of its tug aircraft; glider soldiers remember that the floor was often awash with vomit long before arrival at the release point. The lumbering tug-and-tow combination was an easy target for enemy flak and fighters, especially in daylight.

Landing in a glider, described as a "controlled crash," was hazardous, especially in wooded country. With luck, trees would rip off the wings, slowing the glider down. If the nose hit a tree, the result could be disastrous, killing or badly injuring the two pilots and the passengers. A glider loaded with a jeep or artillery was potentially lethal: a bad landing could result in the load shooting forward on impact, crushing the pilots.

Despite these drawbacks, the arrival of the gliders on D-Day and D+1 was critical to the success of the 82nd and 101st Airborne Divisions in achieving their objectives in the Cotentin peninsula and the comparative ease with which the U.S. forces landing from seaward came ashore on Utah Beach.

LEFT: The 1st Battalion 325th Glider Infantry in the second wave of the U.S. 82nd Airborne Division's WACO gliders landing at Landing Zone W 2 miles (3 km) south of Ste. Mère-Eglise in the U.S. sector on the morning of June 6, 1944. C-47 tug aircraft are overhead.

ABOVE: A WACO glider.

69 Landing Craft Vehicle Personnel (LCVP)

The Allied victory in World War II required the projection of military power from the sea to the land in the face of deadly coastal defenses. Amphibious assaults enabled Commonwealth-American armies to campaign against the Axis armies in North Africa, Sicily, Italy, and France. American and Australian-New Zealand amphibious forces played a critical role in defeating Japan.

A successful amphibious landing required the moving of large numbers of assault infantry and engineers ashore along a broad front in order to create a beachhead safe from direct enemy fire. With minimum security assured, the landing force could bring in tanks, artillery, and essential supplies (often preloaded on trucks) to expand the force inland and to meet counterattacks. To land troops, a naval amphibious force needed thousands of small boats capable of taking infantry and small vehicles safely through the surf and defensive obstacles and then retracting for another trip. The workhorse for such operations in World War II became the Landing Craft Vehicle Personnel (LCVP), also known as the Higgins boat after its developer, Andrew Jackson Higgins of New Orleans, Louisiana.

Despite Higgins' claims of it being all his idea, the naval establishments of the United Kingdom and the United States recognized the need for landing craft after World War I. Both navies tested several prototypes, none of which proved satisfactory for a variety of reasons. In a general sense, these early boats were too heavy, underpowered, and not designed for rapid retraction from a beach. The U.S. Navy, prodded by the U.S. Marine Corps, explored the adaptation of a riverine work boat called the Wonderboat or the Eureka, developed by Higgins for commercial use

and for the U.S. Army Corps of Engineers. The Higgins boat had been in use in various forms on the Mississippi River and in the bayous and bays of the Gulf Coast since the 1920s. Its primary appeal was its shallow draft and beaching and retraction capability.

With the enthusiastic support of the Marine Corps, Higgins developed an acceptable landing craft by May 1941, after five years of experimentation. First, the hull and engine design had to be changed to provide adequate power for retractions. To enable rapid disembarkation, the Higgins boat needed a bow ramp, eventually copied from a Japanese craft the Marines had seen in China. Higgins and the Marines also had to persuade the Navy to allow the LCVP to be 36 feet (11 m) in length (not 30 feet/9 m) and to weigh 9–10 tons unloaded, heavier than the original requirement. Higgins met the other demanding specifications. Even with 36 troops or three jeeps, the LCVP drew only 3 feet (90 cm) of water aft. The Navy managed to change the capacity of the davits on its amphibious assault transports to deal with the larger LCVP. The final model had a crew of three and included two machinegun stations aft to be manned by the sailors.

Before the end of the war, the Navy took delivery of 23,398 LCVPs. Half of the boats came from the yards of Higgins Industries, New Orleans. All the LCVPs reflected the basic plans and adaptations made by the Higgins-Marine Corps team. After the conflict ended, General Dwight D. Eisenhower told Higgins that his landing craft had won the war. This assessment was exaggerated, but it recognized the LCVP's essential role in Allied amphibious operations.

Today, there is a full scale LCVP at the National World War II Museum, New Orleans, Louisiana.

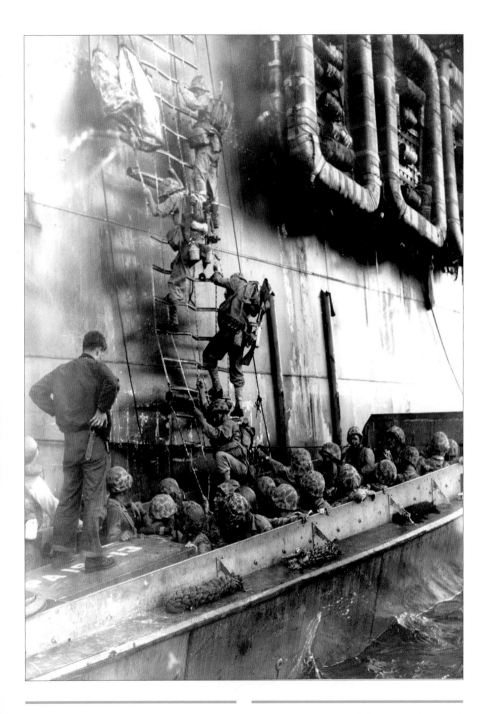

LEFT: An early (1941) version of the LCVP with the essential bow ramp.

ABOVE: A Marine boat team embarks on an LCVP from an attack transport in the Pacific, 1944.

BELOW: U.S. soldiers leave an LCVP late on D-Day, June 6, 1944. A Navy Landing Ship Tank (LST) waits to unload vehicles in the background.

⑦⓪ The LST

The Landing Ship Tank (LST) provided the backbone of all Allied landings in World War II between 1943 and 1945. It could embark tanks, vehicles, artillery, and heavy supplies and land them through its bow doors directly on to a beach. The first Landing Craft Tank (LCT) produced by the British in 1940 was too small for anything other than amphibious operations carried out after a short sea voyage. Churchill demanded a bigger and better ship. In order to produce such vessels as quickly as possible, three shallow draft tankers constructed for use on the Maracaibo River in Venezuela were converted. Their bows were cut away, and a new section with a bow door hinged at the bottom was built on. These three ships served throughout the war, including the Normandy landings in June 1944.

However the main type of LCT used in World War II by both Americans and British was the LST(2) mass-produced in the USA. They began with the "Atlantic tank landing craft," as they were originally designated, which were designed in 1941 to be able to cross the Atlantic under their own power. These LSTs were designed by John C. Niedermair of the U.S. Navy's Bureau of Ships with liquid ballast tanks to enable deep draft for ocean voyages and shallow draft for beaching.

The LST (2) was powered by two General Motors 12-567 V-12 standard locomotive engines connected to twin screws. Maximum speed was 11.5 knots (21.2 km/h) with a cruising speed of 8.75 knots (16.2 km/h). It was designed to take 20 Sherman tanks, or up to around120 small vehicles, plus 170 troops. Tanks could be carried only on the lower tank deck, but lighter equipment such as jeeps, small trucks, and towed artillery pieces could also be carried on the upper deck. The LST was loaded and unloaded through the double bow doors and bow ramp. Vehicles were taken up to and down from the upper deck by vehicle lift. The LST could be beached to allow for unloading, or loads could be disembarked on to Rhino pontoon ferries, which some LSTs would tow to an area off the landing beach. These pontoons were assembled into 175-foot (53 m) barges with detachable outboard engines.

Disembarkation by pontoon ferry overcame the difficulty of getting the LST in close enough if the beach was flat with a very gentle gradient. Its use also avoided the problems caused by letting LSTs dry out at low tide, like beached whales, thus remaining vulnerable to artillery fire and air attack especially in the early stages of a landing. LSTs were, however, designed to dry out and in the later stages of an operation were frequently left to do so, while vehicles drove ashore over the dry sand. Swimming tanks and vehicles, notably the DUKW, were able to disembark straight into the water from the bow ramp and swim ashore. LSTs in British service were fitted with one 12-pounder antiaircraft gun aft and six 20-mm cannon. American LSTs were armed with up to seven 40-mm antiaircraft guns and 12 20-mm cannon.

Some LSTs carried a pair of smaller landing craft on davits; on British ships, usually the Landing Craft Assault (LCA), and the Landing Craft Vehicle and Personnel (LCVP) on American ships. These could be used to land infantry, beach parties and other troops on foot.

Selected LSTs were equipped with medical parties to act as forward mobile hospitals where surgical operations were carried out in the tank deck. Large numbers of wounded carried on stretchers in the tank deck were evacuated by these hospital-fitted LSTs.

For the Normandy landings, LSTs were used to tow pieces of Mulberry harbor across the Channel. On the morning of D+1 onward, LSTs worked a shuttle service from British ports to the beaches, bringing reinforcements, replacement equipment and supplies. One British LST, 416 (LSTs were numbered not named), made 28 Channel crossings between June 6 and September 31. The LSTs were the forerunners of the roll on/roll off ferries of today.

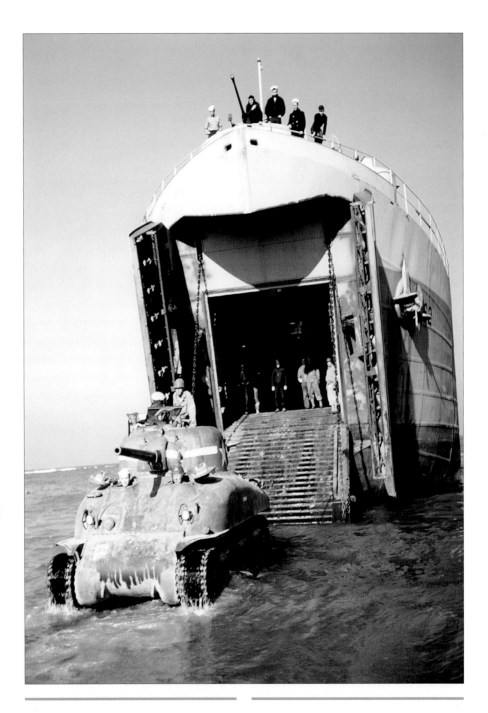

LEFT: LSTs 22 and 206 in the surf at Leyte in the Philippines on October 1, 1944.

ABOVE: A Sherman tank having driven out of the bow doors of an LST and down the ramp, wades ashore.

⁷¹ The Rocket Launcher

Known as a "Bazooka" for its similarity to a musical instrument played by a 1930s vaudeville comedian, the M1/M9 rocket launcher gave the U.S. Army infantry a man-portable anti-armor weapon of modest capability. Its 2.36-inch (6 cm) rocket with a small shaped-charge warhead could not penetrate the frontal armor of a German tank, but if fired at the side and rear, it might cripple one. It was very effective at ranges of up to 200 yards (183 m) against almost all other German fighting vehicles and trucks, and could also be used as a standoff bunker-buster.

The 5-foot- (1.5 m) long launcher accepted the rocket at its open rear where a set of electrical contacts ignited the rocket. When the gunner depressed the trigger, it generated electrical power to the rocket engine. The weapon had no recoil, but the loader had to move clear of the backblast, which also identified the weapon's firing position. Skilled two-man teams did not use the same position more than once if possible.

The 1943 table of organization and equipment for a U.S. Army infantry division allocated 557 launchers throughout the division, but the antitank rocket teams were most numerous in the headquarters of infantry regiments and battalions where they were paired with antitank cannon and mine layers. In actual combat, pairs of rocket launcher teams would be assigned to infantry companies.

Although ordnance experts made modifications to the M-1's sight and trigger mechanism, the M-9 represented the most important change because it divided the launching tube into two parts that could be joined in seconds by twist-locking. This change made the launcher much easier to carry and protected the trigger mechanism.

Impressed by the Bazooka, the German army used it as the model for its own Panzerschreck antitank rocket launcher, which fired an 88-mm warhead that could penetrate seven to eight inches (18–20 cm) of sloped armor. It had twice the destructiveness of the U.S. 2.36-inch warhead and could destroy American tanks with a frontal shot.

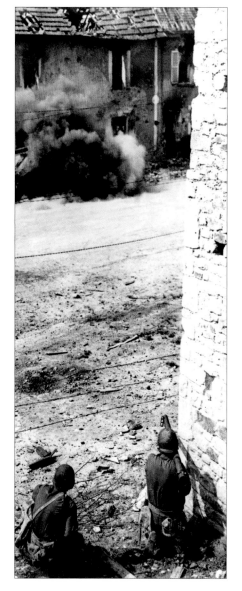

FAR RIGHT: A soldier aims his new Bazooka..

RIGHT: A rocket launcher is used by GIs during street fighting in Normandy in June 1944.

⏹72 Portable Field Radio

The radio communications provided to combat units of the U.S. Army and U.S. Marine Corps proved to be an operational advantage unmatched by either allied or enemy ground combat units. The prewar development of radio technology by the U.S. Army Signal Corps, often in cooperation with the U.S. Navy, paid enormous dividends in the development of radios that could be carried by individuals or teams, or which could be mounted on jeeps. Field radios enabled American infantry units to coordinate their fire and to maneuver and direct supporting tanks and artillery. In World War I, such rapid tactical adjustments had depended on runners and telephone lines, both vulnerable to enemy fire.

Within an infantry battalion, commanders depended upon the SCR (Set, Complete Radio) 300, a line-of-sight FM portable radio that served as the link between the battalion command group, the weapons company, and

the three rifle companies. These six-SCR 300s were the "battalion tac" net. Within the companies, the handheld SCR-536 provided "company tac." A variant of the SCR-300 linked forward observers to the artillery fire direction center. The SCR-300 had a range of 5 miles (8 km), the SCR-536 a range of 1 mile (1.6 km). The SCR-300 and SCR-536 became known as "walkie-talkies."

Higher headquarters units communicated with one another through radios mounted in vehicles or vans, but infantry commanders relied most often on a lone NCO-technician carrying the 34-pound (15 kg) SCR-300 with a long whip antenna and a shorter, collapsible blade antenna. The radio included a handset for voice transmissions. It also had limitations: one was its short range; another its narrow band length; handsets also became wet and damaged if not protected. The most enduring problem was the life of its battery, not always predictable because of usage rates and moisture. Replacement batteries were heavy to carry and could be easily damaged.

Portable field radios did not have the reliability of vehicle-mounted sets, and they could not equal telephones for security and versatility in instant communications. Nevertheless, the SCR-300 and its smaller SCR-536 cousin provided moving combat units with essential voice communications in the heat of battle.

ABOVE: A command group of GIs with an SCR 300 direct a tank-infantry team, France, 1944.

RIGHT: An Army officer somewhere in the Pacific reports his position by SCR 536, the "walkie talkie."

The Tunnelers' Trolley

Perhaps the two best-known escapes by prisoners of war (POWs) in World War II were from Stalag Luft III. The camp was located in Sagan, in Silesia. At the time this was part of Germany. It is now in Poland. It was one of several camps for Allied aircrew, but was the biggest. Eventually it held 10,000 POWs and covered 59 acres (24 ha) with 5 miles (8 km) of perimeter fencing. The POWs at Stalag Luft III included Fleet Arm aircrew and USAAF, plus a few non-aircrew soldiers (the reason for this exception is not easy to establish).

The site was selected for two reasons. First, it was in the middle of occupied Europe so anyone trying to escape would have to travel a very long way to reach a neutral country. Sweden, Spain, and Switzerland were the closest. Second, the sandy soil made tunneling difficult because it caved in easily and the yellow subsoil stood out clearly against the gray surface dust. So it could not be dumped just anywhere without being seen by the camp guards, and was easily spotted on prisoners' clothing, thus giving away the fact that there was a tunnel being dug somewhere. The design of the camp also hindered tunneling. The POW accommodation huts were raised 2 feet (60 cm) above the ground making any tunneling from POW accommodation obvious.

Finally, seismograph microphones were placed around the perimeter of the camp to detect sounds of digging, although only to a very shallow depth.

The first successful escape was in October 1943 using a wooden gym vaulting "horse" as cover for the digging. The vibration caused by men running, jumping, and landing prevented the microphones from detecting the sounds of digging. The "horse" was positioned quite near the perimeter wire, reducing the length the tunnel had to be.

The next partially successful escape was conceived by Squadron Leader Roger Bushell RAF in Spring 1943 and is now called the "Great Escape." He planned to dig three, deep, long tunnels: "Tom," "Dick," and "Harry."

If one tunnel was found, Bushell banked on the Germans assuming that there were no others. He aimed to get more than 200 POWs out. To avoid the problem caused by the raised accommodation huts, Tom's and Harry's entrances were each dug under a camp stove through the its cement and concrete plinth, which extended all the way from the hut floor to the ground. This was a difficult job, taking hours of work with a pick. Dick began in a drain sump in one of the bathrooms. The tunnels were 30 feet (9 m) below the surface in order to avoid the digging sounds being picked up by the seismic microphones.

The tunnel dimensions, 2 feet (0.6 meters) square, were dictated by the material used for shoring: bed boards, just over 2 feet (60 cm) long, 20 under the mattress of each POW's bed. A wooden railway was built along each tunnel. Small wooden trucks or trolleys were pulled along by rope from haulage points positioned at intervals along the tunnel. A ventilation system of empty dried milk cans stuck end to end was laid under the tunnel floor with bellows pumps made from soldiers' bags.

Dick was abandoned when the area planned for the tunnel exit was cleared of trees preparatory to a new compound being built there. It was used thereafter to dump sand from the other two tunnels, to store the huge quantity of escape clothing, false papers, and equipment stolen from the Germans, and as a workshop. Tom was discovered in summer 1943, so all efforts were concentrated on Harry, which was finished in March 1944, 336 feet (102 m) long. But it was not long enough; it did not, as planned, reach the trees some yards beyond the wire: as the escapers would discover.

The breakout occurred on the night of March 24/25, 1944. Seventy-six men got out, before a guard spotted a man lying by the tunnel exit, which was well short of the trees. Three escapers reached safety, 50 were murdered by the Gestapo, and 17 were returned to Sagan, four to Sachsenhausen and two to Colditz.

LEFT: The trolley in "Harry," from which 76 men escaped on the night of March 24/25, 1944. The picture was taken in 2011 by a team of archeologists and veterans who excavated the tunnel and restored part of it.

ABOVE: The restored tunnel.

74 Eisenhower's Unsent Message

D espite his confidence about the cross-Channel attack on June 6, 1944—Operation Overlord—General Dwight D. "Ike" Eisenhower, Supreme Commander of the Allied Forces in Europe, remained concerned about the landings' success. As a student of the history of warfare, and tempered by almost two years of experience as a theater commander in Europe, Eisenhower knew how easily a well-planned operation could become a disaster and how hard it was to turn defeat into victory unless the enemy made even greater mistakes.

Eisenhower had spent much of his career learning how to plan big operations. Although the D-Day landings had been prepared in great detail and simplified where they could be, he faced uncertainties so daunting that only a stupid, pathological optimist would not have been worried. In the first week of June, the Supreme Commander faced uncertain weather, concern about the status of German panzer divisions in Normandy, and some doubts about the air attacks and naval gunfire operations that would precede the landings. He realized that he might be sending three Allied airborne divisions to potential destruction. He weighed all the risks with care, but still commented to an aide: "I hope to God I know what I'm doing." Underneath his serious but outgoing persona, Eisenhower thought about his course of action should Overlord fail.

After a long meeting with his British and American senior commanders and principal staff officers on June 4, General Eisenhower postponed the June 5 landing because of bad weather. When more promising weather reports were received,

he called the same officers to another conference at 4:15 p.m. on June 5, 1944, at his headquarters at Southwick House, just north of Portsmouth. He had his staff meteorologist, RAF Group Captain J. M. Stagg, present the latest forecasts, which offered a window of moderating wind and rain on June 6. Should the landing be postponed again, the expeditionary force would have to wait weeks for more favorable tides, moon phase, and weather. The consensus of advice was "go." After perhaps a minute of pacing, Eisenhower said, "Ok. We'll go."

At this point, Eisenhower could do little but await the results of the June 6 landings and parachute drops. He fretted through his routine paperwork and tried to calm his anxieties by chain-smoking cigarettes and drinking masses of coffee. Some time during the afternoon of June 5, he wrote a brief note to be used if the landings failed, in which he absolved everyone but himself from the failure. He did not, however, offer to resign, a telling sign of his confidence in his own command. Ike tucked the note in his wallet, where it remained for a month until he pulled it out and gave it to an aide. Its message had been overtaken by victorious events.

ABOVE: Although Eisenhower lacked great operational experience, his engaging manner and easy style made him a natural commander.

RIGHT: The day before D-Day, General Eisenhower scribbled a note to be used in the event of failure on the following day, taking all the blame on himself. His state of mind can be gauged by his writing of the wrong date at the end, July 5 instead of June 5.

Our landings in the
Cherbourg – Havre area
have failed to gain a
satisfactory foothold and
~~I have withdrawn~~
the troops. ~~has been~~
~~withdrawn.~~ ~~this particular~~
~~Junction~~ My decision to
attack at this time and place
was based upon the best
information available. ~~and~~
The troops, the air and the
Navy did all that ~~brave troops~~
Bravery and devotion to duty
could do. If any blame
or fault attaches to the attempt
it is mine alone.

——— July 5

75 The Tiger Tank

A popular misconception still exists that the German Tiger Tank was produced to provide an answer to the Soviet armor (the T-34 and heavy KV-1) which the Germans first encountered when they invaded the Soviet Union on June 22, 1941. This is not so. In fact the order for the Panzerkampfwagen VI, Tiger 1, was issued on May 26, 1941. It is true that the shock of encountering the KV-1 and T-34, which were far better than any contemporary German tank, galvanized Hitler into ordering that the production of Tiger be accelerated to provide a counter to the Soviet heavy tank. At the same time he ordered a new medium tank, the Panzerkampfwagen V Panther in order to take on the T-34, then the finest medium tank in the world. Although the Panther must rate as the best tank produced by the Germans, or anyone else for that matter, there is no doubt that the Tiger was the most feared.

The Tiger weighed 64 tons, and was mounted with an 88-mm gun and two 7.92-mm machine guns. The 88-mm gun alone struck dread in the heart of most allied tank crews, mounted as it was in a tank whose mobility turned it into a fearsome weapon. The Tiger's frontal armor was nearly 4 inches (100 mm) thick, and despite a top speed of just over 23 miles per hour (37 km/h) it quickly earned a formidable reputation, helped along by clever propaganda on the part of the Germans. Like all German tanks, the Tiger had a gas engine. It had a crew of five: commander, driver, gunner, loader and radio operator. It had a range of around 120 miles (190 km) depending on terrain and combat conditions, and carried about 80 rounds of 88-mm ammunition.

Any British or American tank could be knocked out by a Tiger (or a Panther) at ranges in excess of 1,000 yards (900 m),

and sometimes more. To knock out a Tiger or Panther, a British or American gunner had to hit the tracks or disable the gun or optics, but a Tiger was usually invulnerable to anything other than a 17-pounder, which only a few British tanks had, or a rocket-firing fighter-bomber. The fear that the Tiger engendered in the British and Americans was known as "Tiger phobia." Word got around that it took five Sherman tanks to destroy a cornered Tiger, and only one Sherman would survive.

The engagement at Villers-Bocage in Normandy on June 13, 1944, provides an example of the deadly nature of a well handled Tiger, especially in the hands of an ace, in this case Lieutenant Michael Wittmann, commanding 2nd SS Panzer Company of 101st SS Heavy Panzer Battalion. By this time, Wittmann was the leading Panzer ace in the Waffen SS, having stacked up 119 armored vehicle kills in Russia. His company at Villers-Bocage was down to five Tigers. The British 7th Armoured Division had been given the task of seizing the town and the high ground beyond.

The leading British battle group drove through Villers-Bocage and halted on the high ground. Wittmann, leaving four of his Tigers with orders to hold their position, drove down the line of British infantry armored personnel carriers, knocking them all out. Motoring on into Villers-Bocage he knocked out nine tanks. Here, in a village without infantry support, and vulnerable to antitank weapons, his Tiger was finally knocked out by a 17-pounder antitank gun. He and his crew baled out and walked back to join his company and at this stage Wittmann's remaining four tanks took a hand. By the end of the engagement, the leading battle group of 7th Armoured Division had been destroyed, losing 60 armored fighting vehicles in the process. Wittmann with five Tigers had brought 7th Armoured Division, the famous "Desert Rats," to a dead stop.

LEFT: A line-up of Tiger II tanks in the first battalion to receive them. Ordered in 1943 and first issued in May 1944, this Tiger had a sloped armor glacis plate and a redesigned turret with a curved frontal plate, and was able to mount the more powerful version of the 88-mm gun, the L/71. The Tiger II eliminated its opponents easily, but too few were produced to have any significant influence on the outcome of the war.

ABOVE: Tiger Mk I; note the flat glacis plate and front turret plate.

▨ 76 Douglas C-47

I f any single aircraft characterized the Commonwealth-American war effort, the ubiquitous C-47 transport aircraft deserved that recognition. It appeared everywhere Allied troops served. By war's end, Douglas Aircraft had built almost 11,000 C-47s, officially known as the "Skytrain" (USAAF) or the "Dakota" (RAF). Many Allied soldiers and airmen knew the aircraft fondly as "the gooney bird." C-47s may still be found flying from primitive airfields in remote areas of the world.

The C-47 began as the DC-3 commercial airliner in 1935, making its first commercial flights in 1936. Its reputation for economical and dependable operation impressed the Army Air Corps enough that Douglas won a competitive military contract in 1940. The C-47 had two Pratt & Whitney R-1830-92 engines, each rated at 1200 hp. Its service ceiling was 23,000 feet (7,010 m), with a maximum speed of 230 miles per hour (370 km/h), but its optimal cruising speed was 185 miles per hour (298 km/h) at half that altitude. The C-47's cabin could hold 6,000 pounds (2,750 kg) of cargo or be reconfigured for 28 passengers in bucket seats along both bulkheads. It could be arranged to carry stretchers for wounded in air evacuation operations or rigged to drop supplies to isolated units. The aircraft had a pilot, co-pilot, radioman-navigator, and crew chief.

The C-47 became the workhorse in two organizations within the wartime U.S. Army Air Forces. The USAAF established its own version of a global commercial airline, the Air Transport Command (ATC). The second grouping of C-47s was in several Troop Carrier Commands, parts of the deployed, numbered tactical air forces. The most visible and busy Troop Carrier Command was the IX TCC, part of the Ninth Air Force supporting the Allied armies in northern Europe in 1944–45. While squadrons of C-47s could be transferred between ATC and the numbered TCCs, the two groupings had different missions.

The Air Transport Command entered World War II as an expanding organization of 11,000 officers and men with fewer than a thousand aircraft. By 1945, ATC had 200,000 members and 3,700 aircraft. Senior ATC officers were recruited from commercial airlines, but junior pilot-officers came from the USAAF multi-engine pilot program. During the war, ATC aircrews showed notable flying skill while dealing with weather and primitive bases, suffering losses of 667 aircraft in crashes and 23,372 personnel from death, wounds, disease, disabilities, and transfer.

The C-47s assigned to the Troop Carrier Commands conducted airborne operations by dropping paratroopers or pulling gliders to landing zones, with either mission calling for a high level of courage and flying ability. The airborne soldiers often criticized the TCC pilots' skill without appreciating the challenges of navigation at night (standard practice until

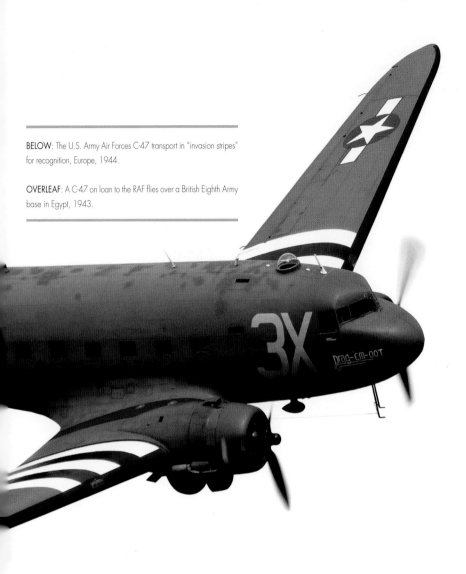

BELOW: The U.S. Army Air Forces C-47 transport in "invasion stripes" for recognition, Europe, 1944.

OVERLEAF: A C-47 on loan to the RAF flies over a British Eighth Army base in Egypt, 1943.

September 1944) and the dangers of enemy flak at the low-level drop altitudes airborne commanders demanded. In the three limited drops in Africa, Sicily, and Italy, the TCC lost eight aircraft to enemy fire and 24 aircraft to Army and Navy "friendly fire" at night, six of these crashing while still full of paratroopers. "Friendly fire" also forced 69 gliders to crash land, killing at least 200 passengers and crew from the 1,100 embarked troops.

The IX Troop Carrier Command made three multi-division drops and one smaller drop in 1944–45, with increasing efficiency. On D-Day (June 6, 1944), 1,000 C-47s of the USAAF and RAF dropped 10,245 paratroopers in the first assault and brought another 14,000 troops to France by day's end. Subsequent drops in Southern France, Holland, and Germany showed that IX Troop Carrier Command and its C-47s had become a useful addition to amphibious and ground offensives. By flying in daylight, protected by fighter-bomber flak suppression operations, IX Troop Carrier Command proved it could deliver airborne troops with speed and in relative safety.

⬛77 Blood Plasma

A mong the many medical innovations exploited by the U.S. Army Medical Department which saved the lives of service personnel, the use of blood plasma rates one of the most important. Used to counterattack the effects of shock and blood loss from traumatic wounds, blood plasma saved thousands of lives. The Army considered plasma, along with sulfa, penicillin, atabrine, and morphine, as drugs of the greatest military utility in World War II.

In the late 1930s Dr. Charles Drew, an expert in blood hematology at the Columbia Medical Center, New York City, experimented in the use of the liquid portion of blood, 55 percent of its composition, in lieu of whole blood in transfusions. Separated from red and white blood cells, plasma is 90 percent water and 10 percent albumin, fibrinogen, and globulin, all of which aid clotting, fighting infection and maintaining blood pressure. Plasma's appeal was that it lasted longer in whole form than blood, could be frozen for preservation and travel, and could be reduced to dried form and later reconstituted. Military bleeding took place

thousands of miles from American blood donors, recruited and processed by the U.S. Red Cross. The development of portable plasma therefore became a high medical priority.

The medical departments of the armed forces adopted plasma for transfusions with a rush and found its use limited only by its supply. The Red Cross eventually turned over 13 million units to the armed forces, which used all but 1.3 million units. Most of the recommendations for improvement focused on the packaging of the liquid plasma and its flow into a patient's veins. One problem was the color of the labels and the suspension systems of the plasma bottles, cans, and flexible pouches. Even the boxes that carried plasma bore too much in the way of white tape and labels; Japanese snipers used these white markings to identify and shoot medics and their patients. All the plasma paraphernalia eventually got a rush coat of olive drab paint.

At the end of the war, General Dwight D. Eisenhower praised the Red Cross and its blood donors for their contribution to saving the lives of thousands of GIs. Plasma, he acknowledged, was a tremendous thing.

ABOVE: An American soldier receives blood plasma behind enemy lines in Italy in 1944.

RIGHT: Private Samuel Atherton is given containers of blood plasma at the British blood bank that was part of a U.S. evacuation hospital on Anzio beachhead in May 1944.

▪️78 The Bailey Bridge

During World War II both sides frequently needed to bridge rivers or ravines, either because the existing bridges had been destroyed, or because part of an army wanted to surprise the enemy by crossing in a place where there was no bridge. The quicker a bridge is built in the combat zone, the better, and engineers are always striving to achieve a design that combines speed of construction with the ability to drive the heaviest vehicles across it. Considerable progress was made toward achieving both requirements in World War II.

The outstanding example of this, and a major engineering breakthrough, came with the invention of the Bailey Bridge by Donald Bailey of the British Military Engineering Experimental Establishment at Christchurch in Dorset in early 1942. The Bailey Bridge girders were constructed from identical steel lattice panels held together by metal pins. Each girder could be doubled or tripled for extra length and strength, and could be increased up to two additional stories for very large spans. The bridge could carry a roadway on the lower transoms. The complete structure could be launched on rollers over the gap to be bridged, using a counterweight.

The Bailey Bridge was first used operationally to bridge the Medjerda River near Medjez el Bab in Tunisia on the night of November 26, 1942, during the North African campaign. It became the main bridging equipment of the U.S. and British Armies, and later the Soviet Army. To bridge wide rivers, all armies used a system of floating pontoons or boats anchored side by side across the river. The Bailey Bridge would be laid across the "bridge of boats." The British and Soviets used wooden pontoons, while the Americans used more vulnerable, but more easily transported, inflatable rubber boats. For bridges carrying loads up to 10 tons, the British also used easily transported light folding wooden boats on which to lay the Bailey Bridge. For loads up to and including 78 tons, pontoons were used.

The Bailey Bridge was carried in trucks in pieces. When an obstacle was encountered, the parts would be brought forward and the bridge assembled. It was preferable to have some warning that bridging was required in order that the bridging trucks were positioned well forward in the advancing column of vehicles. This was particularly important in the case of Operation Market Garden, the attempt to seize crossings over a series of rivers and canals including the bridge over the River Rhine at Arnhem in September 1944. On the morning of September 18, the Germans blew up the bridge over the canal at Zon, north of Eindhoven, holding up the Allied advance. The trucks carrying the Bailey bridging were well back in the column advancing on one narrow road, and they had furthermore to be driven through the large town of Eindhoven, whose streets were crammed with Dutch people celebrating their liberation. Eventually, the bridging arrived, the bridge was constructed, and the tanks of the Guards Armoured Division crossed the canal. But the delay in bridging the canal at Zon was a major contributor to the failure of the British 1st Airborne Division to hold the vital Arnhem Bridge long enough for the relieving force to arrive.

The biggest bridging operation carried out by the British and Americans was during the Rhine crossings in March 1945, but Bailey Bridges were used in all theaters of war, sometimes as ferries, with bridge sections on pontoons. This was especially useful to get armor across in the initial phase of a crossing, while the main bridge was being built. In Italy and Sicily the British and Americans built over 3,000 Bailey Bridges, the longest being over the Sangro River at 1,126 feet (343 m); while one built over the Chindwin during the 14th Army's advance to the Irrawaddy and Mandalay in Burma, was 1,154 feet (352 m) long.

ABOVE RIGHT: Trucks of British Eighth Army crossing the Sangro River in Italy over a Bailey pontoon bridge.

RIGHT: Bailey Bridge spanning sections of bridge destroyed by the Germans during their retreat in Italy, and using the original piers.

79 High Altitude Flying Uniform

In 1942–1945, the high altitude bomber crews of the 8th and 15th Air Forces, U.S. Army Air Forces, faced two enemies—German air defenses and the cold and limited oxygen. On missions into Germany, B-17s and B-24s on daylight raids normally flew at altitudes above 20,000 feet (6,000 m), where the air temperatures reached -40° F (-40° C). Only the four officers in a heated cockpit (pilot, co-pilot, navigator, and bombardier) could fly in relative comfort; the seven enlisted aircrew dressed for aerial combat and the enervating cold.

All members of a bomber crew wore some common clothes and flight equipment: long underwear, woolen trousers and shirts, and B-3 inflatable life vests for water ditching. All crew-members had oxygen masks, necessary for flights above 8–10,000 feet (2,400–3,000 m). After 1942, the Type 14 mask with a built-in intercom microphone became standard, along with a regulator that eased breathing. All crew members also wore parachutes, either attached to their backs or designed as seat cushions. Both types used harness systems that encased the torso for a tight fit. Air crewmen also had access to a chest parachute that snapped on to a torso harness.

The officer members of a bomber crew were able to dress for limited comfort and ease of movement, essential for their flying duties. They could choose hats or flying helmets (usually service caps), flight coveralls, and the iconic leather, lined "bomber" jackets. Officers normally wore field shoes inside rubber overshoes ("galoshes") unless

they could beg, borrow, buy, or steal lined RAF flight boots. The seven enlisted air crewmen, in contrast, dressed for the cold. They wore an electrically heated, two-piece flight suit worn in layers and made of lightweight insulating fabric. Before the dependable F-3 electrical suit became standard in 1944, bomber crews depended on a flight suit of gloves, hat, jacket, trousers, and boots made of heavy leather-like synthetic fabric and lined with different types of fleece. The outfit assumed that the air crewmen would not move much, true for the five pure aerial gunners. The flight engineer and radioman, however, had jobs that required movement to and from their guns and had to be careful about exposing their hands, protected by liners. The gunners also could wear a torso-protecting vest of body armor, built around steel plates, and a wide steel helmet (designed to accommodate earphones) and flight helmets and oxygen masks.

Other than accidents that exposed crewmen to frostbite and hypothermia, the main disadvantage of the bomber flying suit was its weight (up to 60 pounds/27 kg) and bulk, which inhibited movement. Bailing out of a crippled bomber could be a challenge under the best of circumstances, but even reaching the ground safely, the heavy flight suit made escape almost impossible unless the American airman could disrobe and find suitable footwear. Cold-resistant, bulky flight suits did not work well for cross-country travel. Warm clothing, however, helped POWs survive.

ABOVE: The crew of a USAAF B-17 goes through a mission briefing in Europe, 1944.

RIGHT: A B-17 bombardier, dressed for a high, cold mission, checks out his oxygen mask in the nose of a B-17.

■80 The DUKW

The DUKW, or "Duck," is a dual-drive amphibious truck that provided Allied ground forces with a vehicle for administrative over-the-beach landings and for river crossings. The DUKW did not have enough armor or overhead cover to be a combat vehicle like the amphibian tractor or LVT. It was essentially a 2½-ton truck with a propeller and a boat body (including bilge pumps), which could re-engage its wheels on land and drive its cargo to an inland destination.

GMC and other truck manufacturers produced more than 25,000 DUKWs during World War II. Most of them went to U.S. Army engineering and transportation battalions, but the Navy and Marine Corps also used DUKWs as logistical vehicles on Pacific beachheads. DUKWs also appeared in Commonwealth units in every theater of war.

The basic DUKW weighed eight tons, had six pneumatic tires, and could carry a 5,512-pound (2,500 kg) payload. Powered by a standard 90 hp, six-cylinder truck engine, it could reach a top speed of 6 miles per hour (9.7 km/h) in water and 50 miles per hour (80 km/h) on land with a range of 175 miles (282 km). The hull was designed and built by a commercial builder of barges and utility boats, Sparkman & Stephens Inc., and it had no permanent weapons station.

Whenever someone pressed the DUKW into tactical service, the results were not good. The worst case of misuse occurred during the D-Day landing on Omaha Beach when the Army V Corps attempted to land six batteries of 105-mm howitzers using DUKWs. The rough seas and imbalance caused by the heavy guns swamped the DUKWs, sending 17 guns and their crews into the water. The optimal use of DUKWs came from their assignment to U.S. Army Amphibious Special Brigades, where they could be used for over-beach resupply missions, demolition and beach clearance missions, and as emergency ambulances.

As long as DUKWs were not used as combat troop carriers, they provided excellent service. U.S. Navy and Royal Navy Beachmaster units used their DUKWs to rescue broached small craft and to pull stalled vehicles from the surf. The vehicle made an excellent mobile radio station during beach operations. Its ability to move over soft sand made the DUKW a vehicle of choice for emergency missions on beachheads. Today, DUKWs still serve to take tourists on amphibious trips throughout the world.

"Ducks"—amphibious fighting vehicles—used for the first time in the Mediterranean landings.

BACK THEM UP!

ABOVE: A British poster promoting the American "Ducks."

RIGHT: A DUKW in Fort Sheridan, Illinois. Designed in 1942, these vehicles were used to take troops ashore in amphibious operations in the Mediterranean, Pacific, and D-Day landings.

⬛81 The Bangalore Torpedo

The Bangalore Torpedo had been in use since before World War I. It was invented in 1912 by Captain R. L. McClintock Royal Engineers, who was stationed in Bangalore, India, attached to the British Indian Army's Bengal Sappers and Miners, and he published details in the *Royal Engineers' Journal* of March 1913. A narrow metal pipe filled with explosive, the Bangalore Torpedo was designed to be pushed under barbed wire obstacles and subsequently detonated; the resulting explosion would then clear a path through the wire. The first record of its use was in clearing obstacles and booby traps left behind after the Second Boer War (1899–1902) and the Russo–Japanese War (1904–05).

It was used extensively during World War I to clear gaps in barbed wire obstacles, especially on the Western Front. In World War II it was also employed to blast a path through minefields.

The World War II version consisted of light steel tubing 1.5 or 2 inches (3.8 or 5 cm) in diameter, issued in sections 8 feet (2.4 m) long and packed with 10–12 pounds (4.5–5 kg) of explosive. These could be fitted together to penetrate the entire depth of the obstacle. As each section was pushed in, the next section was attached, and the whole was pushed forward again. A bullet-shaped nose plug was fitted to the head of the pipe to make it easier to push through barbed wire, and a detonator was inserted in the base of the pipe, initiated by a time-delay fuze. Depending on the type of terrain, undergrowth, and so forth, a pipe longer than 24 feet (7.3 m) was difficult to handle, so deeper obstacles would have to be blown in stages. A Bangalore Torpedo would blow a path about 10–20 feet (3–7 m) wide through wire or an antipersonnel minefield; the width depended on the density of the obstacle or the types of mines employed.

Bangalore Torpedoes were normally considered to be specialist engineer equipment, though infantry assault pioneers, U.S. rangers, and commandos were all trained to use them. They were deployed in all theaters of war, but perhaps the best-known example of their deployment was at Omaha Beach on June 6, 1944. Here, the soldiers of the U.S. V Corps were pinned down by fire from Germans dug in on top of a 150-foot- (45 m) high bluff that dominated the beach. Barbed wire and antipersonnel mines also blocked the small gullies which offered the best beach exits for infantry. In small unit actions made memorable by the movie *Saving Private Ryan* (1998), U.S. rangers eventually blasted their way through the obstacles to fight their way on to the top of the bluff and engage the enemy.

Bangalore Torpedoes were packed in boxes and could sometimes be a hazard to those in the vicinity. Lieutenant "Scotty" White, a platoon commander of the 9th Battalion the Durham Light Infantry, part of Montgomery's 8th Army at the Battle of Mareth in Tunisia in March 1943, remembered: "At H-hour the attack started and we were shelled from the beginning. The sappers [engineers] in the truck with the Bangalore Torpedoes were hit by a shell and blown up." (Imperial War Museum Sound Archive.)

If Bangalore Torpedoes were not available, they could be improvised: two 6-foot (2 m) angle-iron pickets, normally used in erecting a barbed wire fence, could be lashed together with wire to form a tube around lengths of plastic explosive. This would be exploded using a detonator and a length of fuse. It was not as effective as a tailor-made Bangalore Torpedo, and could be used only on small obstacles, but in some situations it was better than nothing.

RIGHT: Assault Engineers push a Bangalore Torpedo forward under enemy barbed wire in order to create a space for the advancing infantry to move through.

82 The Tallboy Bomb

Following the success of Barnes Wallis's cylindrical bouncing bomb in the dambuster raid of May 1943, the RAF, who hitherto had rejected his designs for big bombs, showed renewed interest in the idea. Accordingly, Barnes Wallis began work on the Grand Slam, a monster 22,000-pound (10,000 kg) bomb, the heaviest used in the war. The bomb, which was 26.5 feet (7.7 m) long and 3.8 feet (1.2 m) in diameter, contained 9,135 pounds (4,145 kg) of Torpex explosive (used for torpedoes, hence its name).

Before the Grand Slam came into service, Barnes Wallis developed a smaller version — the 12,000-pound (5,445 kg) Tallboy, intrinsically the same design. The Tallboy, like the Grand Slam, was designed to be a deep-penetration bomb. It was 21 feet (6.4 m) long and 38 inches (97 cm) in diameter, containing 5,200 pounds (2,540 kg) of Torpex explosive. The streamlined Tallboy could reach the speed of sound during its descent, and its angled fins made it spin rapidly. Like a corkscrew, this spin exacerbated the effect of its weight and speed of descent to enable it to penetrate 16 feet (5 m) of concrete. Furthermore, the ignition could be delayed by up to 11 seconds, and by penetrating before exploding, the bomb sent out shock waves that wrought massive internal destruction, as well as collapsing adjacent buildings and installations.

Only one of these bombs could be carried at a time, and then only by the Lancaster, which had to be modified for the purpose. The Tallboy was first used operationally on the night of June 8/9, 1944, when Lancaster bombers of 617 Squadron (The Dambusters) attacked the Saumur railway tunnel. The object of the hastily planned raid was to close the railway line to delay the arrival of German armored reinforcements for counterattacks

on the newly formed Allied bridgehead in Normandy. One Tallboy pierced the roof of the tunnel; the resulting mass of debris blocked the line for several days.

RAF Bomber Command dropped 854 Tallboys on German targets during World War II, of which 77 were dropped in three attacks on the battleship *Tirpitz* between September and November 1944. The most successful of these was on November 12. Between February 1941, when the ship was completed, and the successful raid, there had been no less than ten attacks on her by RAF and Fleet Air Arm aircraft, and by submarines. These had damaged *Tirpitz* but not sunk her. An RAF attack with Tallboys on September 15, 1944, left the *Tirpitz* unfit to go to sea, and she was towed to an anchorage off Tromsø. Another Tallboy attack on October 29 damaged the *Tirpitz* again. Finally, on November 12, 1944, Lancasters of numbers 9 and 617 Squadrons achieved three direct hits on the *Tirpitz*. Smoke and steam rose in a great pillar, the *Tirpitz* began to list, and some minutes later she capsized, with only her hull above water.

The first Grand Slam raid was carried out by 617 Squadron on the Bielefeld viaduct on March 14, 1945, collapsing more than 100 yards (90 m) of the structure thanks to the "earthquake" effect of the bomb. On a raid against submarine pens near Bremen, two Grand Slams penetrated over 14 feet (4.2 m) of reinforced concrete. A total of 41 Grand Slams were dropped during the war, mainly against bridges and viaducts. The accuracy of bombing at the time would not guarantee a direct hit on such slim structures, but with the Grand Slam it didn't matter. Provided the bomb landed quite close, and depending on the nature of the soil, the earthquake effect would bring down part of a bridge or viaduct.

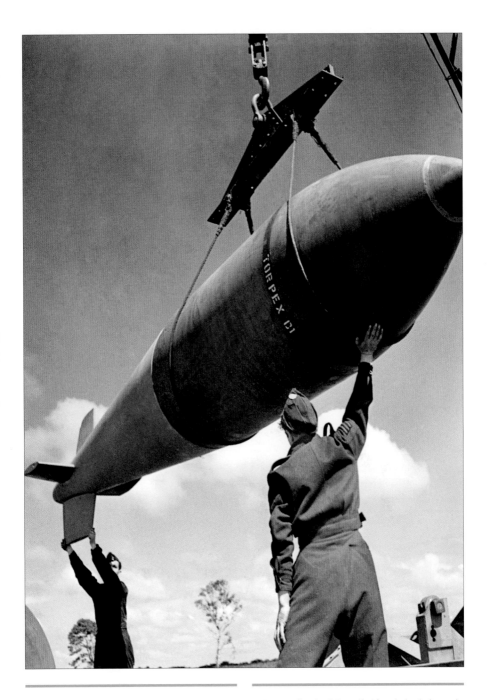

LEFT: The Tallboy bomb in the air.

ABOVE: A Tallboy bomb being lifted from the bomb dump to be loaded into a Lancaster of 617 Squadron RAF for a raid on a V Weapon site at Wizernes France.

83 The Grumman F6F Hellcat

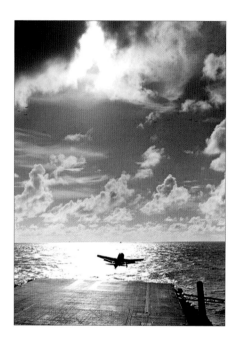

The Grumman F6F Hellcat joined the U.S. Pacific Fleet in early 1943, replacing the Grumman F4F Wildcat as the Navy's standard carrier-based fighter. The first fighter squadron to fly the Hellcat in combat (VF-9) had been assigned to the first of a new class of aircraft carrier, the U.S.S. *Essex* (CV-9), the 33,000-ton warship that became the dominant vessel in the Pacific naval war from 1944 to 1945. Designed for extended operations at sea and to destroy the Japanese A6M (Zero) fighter, the Hellcat was powerful, with a 2,000 hp Pratt & Whitney engine, and heavy—the maximum takeoff weight was 15,000 pounds (6,800 kg). Its normal armament consisted of six wing-mounted .50-caliber machine guns, and it could be altered to carry bombs and rockets for attacks on ships and ground targets.

For taking off and landing on carriers, naval aviators preferred the Hellcat to the Vought F4U Corsair because of its cockpit visibility. During the war, Grumman built 6,500 F6F-5s, the final production model, and 1,200 F6F-5Ns, a night fighter variant with special avionics. The total of all Hellcats produced numbered 12,275 aircraft. The U.S. Navy and Marine Corps claimed that their pilots flying the Hellcat shot

ABOVE LEFT: A Grumman F6F Hellcat shown taking off from the U.S.S. *Lexington* during operations in the Marshall and Gilbert Islands in November 1943.

ABOVE: The Grumman F6F Hellcat in flight.

down 5,156 Japanese aircraft or 75 percent of all the naval services air-to-air kills.

The Hellcat played the central role in the Pacific War's greatest aerial engagement, the Battle of the Philippine Sea (June 18–20, 1944). Task Force 58, which included 15 carriers, engaged a Japanese carrier and a land-based aviation force of 500 aircraft. On June 19 alone, about 500 Hellcats shot down an estimated 400 Imperial Japanese Navy carrier aircraft with a loss of only 29 aircraft. The next day the Hellcats escorted the dive-bombers and torpedo planes that sank a Japanese heavy carrier. After this,

Japanese naval aviation ceased to be a major problem since the United States could replace pilots, aircraft, and carriers in numbers Japan could not match.

Durable, and armored to protect the pilot and gas tanks, the Hellcat could survive air-to-air combat with greater ease than the faster, more agile Zero. Almost 1,000 Hellcats served in the Royal Navy's Fleet Air Arm, and toward the end of World War II other Hellcats joined the aviation forces of the French navy.

◼84 105-mm Howitzer M2

German and Japanese soldiers called American artillery the most formidable weapon they faced on the battlefield. The backbone of the U.S. Army artillery establishment was the 105-mm howitzer in the field artillery battalions of every American division. The U.S. Marine Corps began the war employing a 75-mm howitzer, but switched to the 105-mm M2A1 by war's end.

In U.S. Army divisions the 105-mm howitzer appeared in three basic models. The M-2A1, the most numerous fieldpiece, was a towed gun with a barrel and two supporting tubes for recoil control and gas evacuation. The cannon had two pneumatic tires, a splinter shield, and twin trails. It weighed 4,260 pounds (1,930 kg) and had a crew of six cannoneers. The next most common model was the same gun without a shield, wheels, or trails mounted on an M-4 tank chassis and designated the M-7 "Priest" self-propelled howitzer or Howitzer Motor Carriage. This became the standard cannon within the Armored Field Artillery battalions of American armored divisions. The third model, the M-3, combined a

105-mm howitzer of reduced weight (2,495 pounds/ 1,130 kg) with the strengthened wheeled chassis of the 75-mm howitzer. The M-3 served as the direct support cannon for airborne divisions. It arrived at the landing zones by glider, pulled by a jeep, and it could even be dropped in a protective cage with two parachutes. It could be easily be manhandled.

One strength of the 105-mm howitzer, in addition to its durability and ease of operation, was the variety of shells developed for it by the Ordnance Department. The standard shell had a high explosive, fragmentation warhead with a bursting radius of up to 50 yards (45 m). It could be fuzed for airbursts or point detonation. Among the

other shell varieties were white phosphorus (WP or "Willy Peter"), smoke of many colors, and an antitank round for use in desperate situations. The howitzer could also fire illumination rounds, flares attached to small parachutes. In 1944, American artillery battalions introduced the variable time (VT) or proximity fuze, which carried a small radio transmitter that detonated the shell at a predetermined distance from a target by returning radio signal or radar.

The normal organization of a U.S. Army 105-mm howitzer battalion was three firing batteries of four guns each. The battalion headquarters and headquarters battery provided communications, manned the fire direction center, and managed the battalion training and administration. The same battery was responsible for vehicle maintenance, ordnance handling, equipment and gun repairs, field engineering, and logistical support for the battalion. A 105-mm howitzer battalion (towed) had 33 officers and 462 men.

Although it lacked the antiaircraft or tank-killing lethality of the German 88-mm gun, the 105-mm howitzer had no equal as a durable, accurate high angle-of-fire artillery piece. Through the use of forward observer teams, direct support artillery could provide fire missions within minutes, with the forward observers making adjustments before the final "fire for effect" by an entire battery or even a whole battalion. Sometimes the observers became an airborne spotter, prowling above the battlefield in a light overwing plane (with the cockpit below the wing) nicknamed a "birddog" or a "grasshopper." It was also standard for infantry officers and NCOs to learn how to call for artillery fire. One postwar criticism of American tactics was that the GIs became too artillery-dependent. At the time, tactical theory gave way to good sense.

LEFT: The 105-mm Howitzer M2 in action defending the Kasserine Pass, North Africa, February 20, 1942.

ABOVE: The 105-mm Howitzer M2.

⬛85 The DD Tank

The Duplex Drive (DD) tank was developed in time for the invasion of Normandy. It was designed to meet the requirement for armored support with high-velocity firepower on the beach as early as possible, to deal with the enormous defense works built by the Germans. Based on the Sherman chassis, it could be propelled by its tracks on land or by twin propellers mounted in the rear in water. A canvas screen mounted around the body of the tank could be raised to enable it to float. Once it arrived on the beach, the screen was lowered to enable the tank to use its gun.

The British were the first to develop the floating tank using a Tetrarch, which was trialed in June 1941 at Brent Reservoir. After sea trials, the go-ahead was given to produce the first operational models, this time based on the Valentine tank. The Valentine was used for training crews and a number were lost, some with their crews. The man most at risk was the driver, because getting out through his small hatch in a hurry was so difficult. Crews were equipped with emergency breathing sets offering a five-minute "window" to get out and surface. Furthermore, the Valentine tank had to train its gun to the rear to enable the screen to be raised. This led to the Sherman tank being the final selection for this role, because it could swim with the screen up and its gun trained forward, ready to fire as soon as it arrived on the beach.

The base of the screen was fixed to a metal frame welded to the tank's hull. The screen was fitted with horizontal metal hoops and a number of vertical rubber tubes. It was inflated by compressed air, and could be erected in 15 minutes and collapsed quickly on arrival on the beach. Some units discarded the skirt as soon as possible after landing, while others kept it on their tank. DD tanks often supported infantry well inland, both on D-Day—June 6, 1944—and afterward, with screens still attached. DD tanks could swim at about 4 knots (7 km/h). The driver steered under the directions of the commander by swiveling the propellers using a specially fitted hydraulic system. The commander stood on a platform in the turret to enable him to see over the screen and, if necessary, steered using a tiller overriding the driver's control.

It was intended that all DD tanks in the Normandy landings would launch down the bow ramp of LCTs about 2 miles (3 km) offshore, with screens already up, and swim to the beach. The DD tanks should have arrived on the beach first, followed by the AVREs (Armoured Vehicle Royal Engineers), with the infantry arriving next. On all beaches except Omaha, most DD tanks got ashore, although, thanks to rough seas, with varying degrees of success; only some were ahead of the infantry as planned. The DD was designed to swim in waves up to 1 foot (0.3 m) high, but off Normandy the waves were 6 feet (1.8 m) high. Some swam in, while others were landed directly onto the beach or in shallow water a few yards off.

At Omaha the lowering position (where landing craft start the run-in to the beach) selected by the U.S. naval commander was so far offshore that craft had to start the run-in in darkness. The confusion was considerable. LCTs carrying DD tanks straggled badly, and in many cases headed well off to the flank of the correct beach, or turned away having launched DDs too early. Of 32 DD tanks launched some 6,000 yards (5,500 m) from the shore (far too far out), 27 foundered. Without AVREs, which the Americans were offered but rejected, and with most artillery swamped in craft launched too far offshore, the infantry at Omaha suffered badly. Only by their own courageous exertions did the U.S. infantry finally get off the beach to overcome the defenders.

DD tanks were used successfully in subsequent operations in northwest Europe and Italy, notably at the 7-mile (11 km) wide Scheldt river crossing in October 1944; at the Rhine (March 23, 1945) and Elbe (April 29, 1945); and at the Po and Adige rivers in Italy in April 1945.

LEFT: A Valentine DD tank with screen raised, alongside a landing craft at the 79th Armoured Division Training School at Gosport in January 1944.

ABOVE: A Sherman Duplex Drive (DD) tank with screen lowered.

■86 A German Prison- Camp Watchtower

The popular image of a prison-camp watchtower or guard tower, as portrayed in numerous movies and on TV, is of a small open-sided hut on legs, built of wood, metal, or both. There were actually a number of designs for Nazi camps—not surprisingly, bearing in mind the number of camps in Germany, Poland, and parts of occupied Europe. There were three classes of German camp: POW camps constituted by far the greatest number—counting those in Italy, there were 260 of these, including transit camps and sub-camps (often used as temporary camps for housing working parties from main camps); there were also 23 concentration camps, and six extermination camps.

Concentration camps were instruments of Nazi terror, conceived by Hitler as early as 1921. The original prisoners were political opponents of National Socialism, but in 1939, people from all German-occupied territories began to join them. To start with, the camps were run by the *Sturmabteilung* (SA), but in 1934 the SS took control. They were not built as death camps, although large numbers of people died in them from malnutrition and disease, as well as by execution, and from being used as guinea pigs in "medical experiments." Belsen, for example, was a concentration camp, not an extermination camp. The numbers imprisoned, and subsequent deaths, in concentration camps are not known with any degree of accuracy. The number of registered prisoners is thought to be around 1,600,000, and 450,000 deaths are documented, although a figure exceeding 600,000 is thought to be more likely. The round numbers are an indication of the imprecise nature of the statistics, but in no way exaggerate the scale of the horror.

Death or extermination camps were set up in 1941 for implementing the "final solution," *Endlösung*, the term used for the murder of six million Jews during World War II. Six sites for extermination camps were chosen in remote locations: five in German-occupied Poland (Belzec, Chelmno, Sobibor, Treblinka, and Auschwitz) and one in occupied Russia (Maly Trostenets, near Minsk). About 300,000 European Jews survived the camps and death marches, but those murdered comprised one-third of the world's Jewish population in 1939.

Some camps, especially the older ones, had brick or concrete watchtowers with rooms underneath. These were to be found in camps such as Dachau, the first concentration camp in Germany, opened 51 days after Hitler came to power. As more camps were created, less permanent structures were erected as watchtowers, of the huts-on-legs type. A common feature of most watchtowers was a sentry or sentries, whose job was to keep a watch on the inmates. Depending on the nature of the camp, he would be armed with a rifle or a machine gun, more often the latter. Most watchtowers were equipped with searchlights and connected to a central guardhouse by telephone. A handful of camps had only a few watchtowers. The most famous POW camp, Colditz Castle, had just one custom-built guard- or watchtower in a corner of the outer perimeter wire, although sentries with machine guns were posted around the perimeter and on prominent parts of the walls, and the whole of the exterior of the castle was covered by searchlights at night.

Many camps of all sorts had warning fences set up at about knee height several yards inside the perimeter fence. Stepping over this fence usually ended in the person being shot, unless—as occasionally happened, although probably only in POW camps—the sentry shouted a warning, in which case the prisoner made a fast retreat.

LEFT: A watchtower at Mauthausen concentration camp. This is an example of one of the more permanent types of watchtower.

ABOVE: A watchtower at Auschwitz extermination camp.

■87 The M-1 Rifle

The standard rifle of American infantrymen in World War II, the M-1 designed by John Garand became the iconic weapon of both the GI "dogface" and the "jarhead" Marine of the U.S. armed forces. It was the perfect individual weapon for a mass army of relatively untrained citizen-soldiers. Before the last M-1 was issued in 1957, the military's armory in Springfield, Massachusetts, and private manufacturers like Winchester had made 5.5 million of these rifles.

It was a pioneer weapon because Garand designed it for semiautomatic fire, which meant that the rifle reloaded itself without the manual operation of its bolt. Until then, bolt-action rifles remained the global standard for infantry rifles, as they had been in World War I. The M-1 however could fire a clip of eight .30-06 caliber cartridges. This feature depended upon channeling gases, created by firing from the barrel, to a piston that drove the bolt to the rear (extraction) and then enabled it, with

the help of a recoil spring, to ride forward and load a fresh cartridge. When all eight cartridges had been fired, the empty clip sailed clear of the breach with a reassuring "cling."

The M-1 had many attractive features as a combat rifle. It doubled the rate of fire for a trained rifleman from ten rounds a minute with the bolt-action M1903 Springfield rifle, to 20 aimed rounds a minute. It sacrificed nothing in accuracy compared to the older weapon, over open sights to 300

yards (275 m) and with a peep sight to 500 yards (460 m). The ammunition was the same for the Springfield 03, the Browning Automatic Rifle, and the Browning M1917 and M1919 machine guns. Some GIs found the rifle heavy at 9.5 pounds (4.3 kg), but the weight also reflected durable manufacture and reduced recoil when used with a proper sling. The rifle was also easy to disassemble and clean: it had two compartments in the butt of the stock that held a cleaning rod in sections, and a container for bore cleaner and lubricating oil as well as patches and a bore brush. The moving parts at the breach could be brushed clean without taking the rifle apart. In summary, the rifle had been designed to be "soldier proof."

The rifle could also be adapted to more specialized use. With a mounted scope and blast suppressor, it could be used by snipers. Using a special clip-on launcher and blank cartridges, it could even launch a grenade with stabilizing fins, turning it into a small mortar.

The M-1 became the most common weapon in a U.S. Army infantry squad in which ten of 12 members carried them. In a Marine squad, this was ten of 13. Cut-down M-1s often appeared in motorized and mechanized units as personal defense weapons, rather than the .30-caliber carbine. The standard U.S. Army infantry division carried over 6,000 M-1 rifles in its table of equipment (1942–45) for a force of around 14,000 officers and men.

LEFT: At Camp McClellan in Alabama in July 1945, a new recruit receives instruction from a sergeant on how to fire the M-1 Garand rifle.

RIGHT: An M-1 as manufactured by Springfield Armory, complete with leather sling.

■88 A Mulberry Harbor

One of the problems facing those planning the invasion of Europe was was the unlikelihood that a port could be captured intact early enough to supply the Allied armies during the first days or even weeks of the operation. The landing of supplies over open beaches was likely to be slowed down or even halted completely by bad weather. As early as 1942, Churchill had sent a note to Vice Admiral Lord Louis Mountbatten, then Chief of Combined Operations, telling him to devise piers that would float up and down with the tide, concluding, "Don't argue about it, the difficulties will argue themselves." It was over a year before the problem was solved. Captain John Hughes-Hallett, then on Mountbatten's staff, wrote in 1947 to a civil engineer:

You overestimate the part played by Lord Mountbatten… The project was decided upon at a stage when an operational staff headed by General Morgan [Chief of Staff to the Allied Commander (COSSAC)] had been established to plan the invasion. It was this staff, of which I was the naval head, which had responsibility for deciding and advising on such matters… It was either 13.6.43 or 20.6.43 (probably the former) that I decided to rely on a port of some magnitude (The idea came to me oddly enough during the singing of the Anthem at the Abbey)… Between that date and 27 June 1943 the Port was a cardinal point of the COSSAC Plan.

Hughes-Hallett proposed that an artificial harbor be constructed by sinking blockships off the Normandy coast. A harbor plan was drawn up by Lieutenant Commander I. G. Steele, who selected a site at Arromanches.

From D-Day on, the intention was to land as much as possible of the stores over the five assault beaches, using an array of craft ferrying from merchant ships anchored offshore. To give some protection to these craft it was decided to establish five craft shelters, code-named Gooseberries. At each beach 12 old merchant ships were to be sunk in a line in about 15 feet (4.5 meters) of water (at low tide), giving about 1 mile (1.5 km) of breakwater. Without these Gooseberries, if a gale blew in from the north, the craft would be driven ashore and damaged beyond repair, cutting the lifeline to the armies ashore.

Eventually some of the Gooseberries would grow into Mulberries; "no mean agricultural feat," commented a senior naval officer (*The Imperial War Museum Book of Victory in Europe: The North-West European Campaign 1944–1945,* Julian Thompson, Sidgwick & Jackson Ltd 1994, page 4.) The Gooseberries were to be positioned thus:

US

Gooseberry 1	Varreville	Utah Beach
Goosebery 2	St. Laurent	Omaha Beach

Gooseberry 2 became Mulberry A

British

Gooseberry 3	Arromanches	Gold Beach

Gooseberry 3 became Mulberry B

Gooseberry 4	Courcelles	Juno Beach
Gooseberry 5	Oustreham	Sword Beach

The Mulberries were to consist of a breakwater made up of large concrete boxes, code-named Phoenix, sunk in deep water—up to 33 feet (10 m) at low tide. Outside each harbor it was intended to place 1 mile (1.5 km) of floating breakwater, code-named Bombardon, to give additional protection to the harbor. There was also an arrangement of piers capable of taking a 28-ton load, and one capable of berthing an LST and bearing a load of 45 tons, the weight of a Cromwell tank.

By D+12 (June 18, 1944) both Mulberry harbors were in use. A gale on June 19 destroyed most of the American Mulberry, and its remnants were used to repair the British Mulberry, which had not been so badly damaged. However, thanks to the Gooseberries on the U.S. Beach, ships were still able to discharge direct to the open beach if the weather allowed. By mid-July, the British Mulberry had reached its planned capacity of 7,800 tons a day.

During the 10 months that the Arromanches Mulberry was needed, a total of some 2.5 million men, 500,000 vehicles, and 4.5 million tons of supplies passed through the artificial harbor.

ABOVE RIGHT: The artificial harbor in operation at Colville sur Mer near Omaha beach in the U.S. sector on D-Day.

RIGHT: Phoenix concrete boxes being towed into position.

89 Patton's Pistols

Commander of the U.S. Seventh Army in Sicily in 1943 and the U.S. Third Army in northern Europe (1944–45), General George S. Patton Jr. (1885–1945) set the standard for eccentricity among American generals in World War II. His only rival in attracting publicity was General Douglas MacArthur. Patton's operational brilliance impressed his German opponents and dissuaded his superiors, Dwight D. Eisenhower and Omar N. Bradley, from relieving him for his embarrassing public behavior, such as striking two sick GIs in Sicily for "cowardice."

Patton expressed his flamboyance in many ways, none more memorable than his choice of personal sidearms. Most senior American generals did not carry pistols at all, but had well-armed bodyguards when traveling in hostile territory. If they felt the need to be armed, they carried the U.S.-issue .45-caliber Colt automatic pistol, the M1911. The alternative would most likely have been a .38-caliber Colt or Smith & Wesson revolver, common to American police and an issue weapon in the U.S. Army before the adoption of the .45 automatic.

Plagued with low self-esteem, depression, and wild mood swings, complicated by dyslexia and a troubled childhood, Patton had to be different. Since he and his wife Beatrice had family wealth, he could afford to be so. Throughout his military career, Patton bought expensive cars, sailboats, polo ponies, household help, tailored uniforms, and personal weapons. He gloried in his prowess with the U.S. Army cavalry saber and won matches up to Olympic standards. He even designed a saber, the M1913, which was adopted by the army.

George Patton relished his ability to shoot rifles and pistols with accuracy, because he thought a true combat leader should have exceptional skill with individual weapons. Although he could be brilliant with the real tools of his trade—a brain, maps, compass, and telephone—Patton retained a compulsion to be well-armed with handguns of his own choosing. The Colt automatic was not one of them. At a dinner party in Texas in 1916, Patton, dressed in civilian clothes, put a loaded and cocked .45 in his right trouser pocket. The pistol fired and nearly shot off his genitals. Shaken by the experience, Patton thereafter carried holstered revolvers with the hammer resting on an empty chamber, a standard safety precaution.

Over the course of his military career, Patton collected many handguns, but as a colonel of cavalry and general, he most often carried a chrome-plated, ivory-handled, single-action .45 caliber Colt revolver, Model 1873, with a five-inch barrel, a pistol most associated with the American western frontier. Patton's pistol had his initials, G.S.P., etched into the handgrips. The pistol itself had been extensively engraved. Patton carried the weapon in an open black leather holster that matched his black leather U.S. Army general's belt. Upon occasion, usually for showmanship, Patton also carried another expensive revolver, a Smith & Wesson .357 Magnum with a 3-inch (7.5 cm) barrel, also engraved and fitted with ivory handles. Patton's photographs from North Africa and Sicily also show him carrying a .22-caliber automatic pistol, popular for plinking at non-human roadside targets. Contemporary photographs also often show Patton without any sidearms.

Patton's pistols are on display at the George S. Patton Museum, Fort Knox, Kentucky.

LEFT: George S. Patton Jr. photographed ca.1942.

TOP: Patton with pistols, Europe, 1945.

ABOVE: Patton's M1873 .45-caliber Colt revolver—the "Peacemaker," which he carried throughout World War II. It has two notches on the handle, placed by Patton himself, after an encounter with Mexican bandits where he shot two men.

OVERLEAF: American troops seen through a wall advancing during the Battle of the Bulge, one of Patton's finest hours.

◼90 The Sherman Tank

Assessing tank development in Europe from 1939 to 1941, the U.S. Army's Armored Force Board approved the adoption of a new medium tank, the M4 "Sherman," which married an existing chassis with a new cast hull and a fully rotating turret that mounted a 75-mm gun. The basic consideration was to speed up production of the thousands of medium tanks that the British and the U.S. armies might need to fight German Panzers.

The tank had serious limitations compared with the German tanks they eventually faced—shortcomings which were well understood by U.S. armor officers—but the need for an adequate medium tank was urgent. The men who selected the M4 assumed the basic tank would be modified and improved and indeed, the tank went through six major changes before the war ended. In the meantime, the Sherman in many variants fought in every theater of the war in the hands of American, Commonwealth, and Soviet tank drivers. None of them were very happy with the M4 except that they were numerous and easy to maintain. By 1945, the United States had built more than 40,000 Shermans. The Soviets fielded an estimated 40,000 of their basic tank, the T-34. In comparison, Germany produced 10,500 PkW (*Panzerkampfwagen*) IVs and 5,500 PkW Vs, the Sherman's most numerous foes. In the end German manufacturing excellence could not compensate for Allied numbers.

The Sherman weighed 30 tons and had a crew of five. With experience and availability, the power plants gradually improved. The tank engines came from the aircraft industry and from automotive companies: Continental, Wright, General Motors, Ford, and Caterpillar. From the crew's perspective, a diesel engine did a better job than a gas engine since the

latter tended to explode and burn too rapidly for the crew to escape; survivability was a serious concern, since the M4's armor was vulnerable to most German tank and antitank guns. This reality put a high priority on tank team tactics and the use of terrain for hull-down cover.

The Sherman's main gun could not match German shells of higher velocity and greater penetrating power in frontal engagements, and the tank had to maneuver to get killing shots. In 1944, a new M4 variant was introduced with a higher velocity 76-mm gun. The Commonwealth tank corps replaced the 75-mm gun with the British 17-pounder antitank gun, an even better solution. This "Firefly" M4A4 Commonwealth tank gave Allied tank units greater punch against Panzers.

To improve hull durability, tank manufacturers abandoned cast hulls and joined heavier plates by welding. Another change widened and strengthened the tracks, which gave the M4 improved traction on soft ground and better incline-climbing ability. The vehicle's two .30-caliber machine guns could be fired from inside the turret and driver's compartment, though the external .50-caliber machine gun exposed the gunner.

For all its design flaws, the M4 had a battlefield durability that made it an attractive platform for tactical variations. M4s became flamethrowers, mine-clearers, rocket-launchers, and command vehicles. Some M4s acted as troop carriers with the turret removed; others carried forward air controllers. One variant exchanged a tank gun for a 105-mm howitzer and became a self-propelled artillery piece. An M4 with a bulldozer blade, or "hedgecutter," became a standard part of Allied armor units in Europe in 1944. In the end, the M4 proved as versatile as its sponsors hoped.

LEFT: Sherman tanks move through the bombed town of Flers, following the D-Day invasion.

ABOVE: The late war M4A4 "Firefly" with the British 17-pounder antitank gun mounted on the new turret.

◼91 The Victoria Cross

By the start of World War II the Victoria Cross had been established for 83 years as the highest award for bravery by a member of the armed forces of the United Kingdom, British Empire, and Commonwealth. A holder of the Victoria Cross takes precedence, irrespective of rank, over holders of all other orders, including the Garter.

The Victoria Cross was authorized by Royal Warrant in 1856 by Queen Victoria, who wanted the bravery of her sailors and soldiers, regardless of rank, to be recognized by the award of a medal. The warrant made the award retrospective to include the war against Russia in the Crimea and Baltic (1854–56), the conflict that had kindled the Queen's concern. Until then, only officers were awarded decorations for gallantry. Between 1858 and 1881, the Victoria Cross could be awarded for acts in circumstances of extreme danger. The regulation was changed in 1881 to award it only for gallantry in the face of the enemy. There have been occasions over the years when it has been open to debate whether the enemy was present or not. If there is doubt, the Victoria Cross is not awarded. This led to the institution of the George Cross during World War II.

The Victoria Cross has been awarded 1,356 times to 1,353 people, three of these having been awarded a bar to the medal, denoting an award for two separate actions. Only one of these VC-and-bars was awarded during World War II, to Charles Upham, a New Zealander; thus during World War II the Victoria Cross was awarded 182 times to 181 people.

The first Victoria Cross of World War II was awarded to Lieutenant Commander Gerard Roope, captain of the destroyer HMS *Glowworm*, for an action on April 8, 1940. The *Glowworm* was on patrol off Norway, and having attacked and put to flight two German destroyers, encountered the German heavy cruiser *Admiral Hipper*. Roope attacked with torpedoes, and scored one hit,

but the *Glowworm* was sunk, with heavy loss, including Roope. Although awarded later, the Victoria Cross received by Commander John Linton was for his command of the submarine *Turbulent* from September 1939 to March 1943, when he sank one cruiser, one destroyer, one U-boat, and 28 supply ships, and destroyed three trains by shell fire.

The last Victoria Cross of World War II was posthumously awarded to Lieutenant Robert Gray, Royal Canadian Naval Volunteer Reserve, serving with 1841 Squadron Fleet Air Arm, for his actions in an air strike on Japan. The last Victoria Cross awarded to a soldier in that war was to Private Leslie Starcevich of the 2nd/43rd Australian Battalion in Borneo.

Twenty-six Indians and Gurkhas received the Victoria Cross in World War II, the last two on the same day: Sepoy (Private) Ali Haidar, 13th Frontier Force Rifles, and Sepoy Namdeo Jadhao of the 5th Mahratta Light Infantry for their actions on April 9, 1945, during the crossing of the River Senio in Italy.

The only member of the Special Air Service to receive the Victoria Cross was Major Anders Lassen of the 1st Special Air Service Regiment attached to the Special Boat Service, for his actions during the Battle of Lake Comacchio on the night of April 8/9, 1945. He is one of only three Danes to be awarded the medal. Thirteen of the 23 Victoria Crosses awarded to air crew of Bomber Command were posthumous, including the last, to Captain Edwin Swales, South African Air Force, serving with 582 Squadron RAF.

Nine submariners were awarded the Victoria Cross in World War II, the last two being Lieutenant Ian Fraser and Leading Seaman James Magennis for their successful attack in midget submarine *XE3* on the Japanese heavy cruiser *Takao* in the Johore Strait off Singapore on July 31, 1945. Magennis was the only Northern Irishman to win the Victoria Cross in World War II.

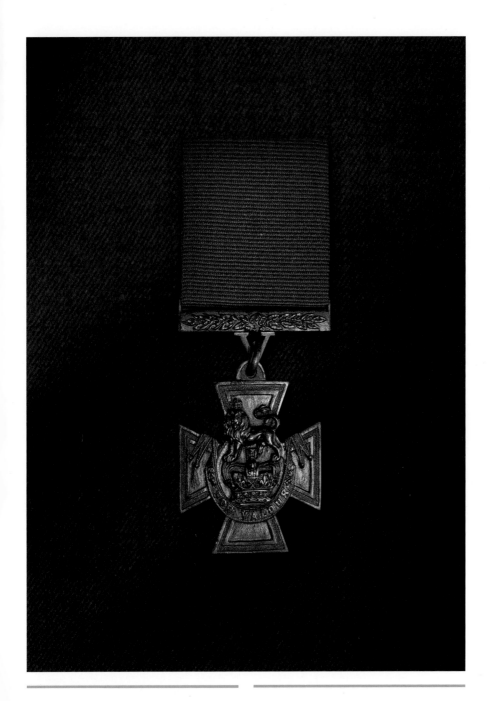

LEFT: The New Zealander Charles Upham, the only recipient of a VC twice in World War II, standing in front of King George VI at the investiture at Buckingham Palace on April 7, 1945.

ABOVE: The bronze Victoria Cross.

■92 The Goliath German Mini-Tank

The first German small, remotely controlled "tank," though not a mini, was the Minenräumwagen (Sd Kfz 300) BI, an expendable mine-clearing vehicle designed in 1939. It weighed 1.7 tons, was radio-controlled, and towed mine-detection rollers. Up to May 1940, some 50 of the BI model were produced. This was superseded by the heavier BII, but only prototypes were completed, both types being replaced by the smaller, wire-guided Goliath.

During the Battle of France in 1940, the German army captured some French mini-tanks, and based on these, the Goliath was designed to meet a specification issued at the end of 1940 for a smaller vehicle which could be used for applications beyond minefield clearance. Between April 1942 and January 1944, 2,650 Goliaths were produced, their official designation being Leichte Ladungsträger Sd Kfz 302 (E-Motor), Gerät 67 "Goliath," or expendable remote-controlled tracked demolition charge. It was tracked with four small wheels, a driving sprocket at the front and an idler at the back, weighed .4 tons, and was 4 feet (1.2 m) long, 2.7 feet (0.82 m) wide, and 1.8 feet (0.55 m) high.

Power came from two Bosch 2.5 kW electric engines, with one forward and one reverse gear, a speed of 6 miles per hour (9 km/h), and a range of just under 1 mile (1.5 km). Guidance was via a three-strand wire, two for steering and one to detonate the charge. The hull had three compartments: explosive charge at the front, control unit in the center, and drum of wire at the back. The two 12-volt batteries and electric motors, one for each track, were stowed in sponsons on the side of the tank.

The first units to be issued with the Goliath were the armored pioneer companies, part of the motorized army engineer battalions, and the armored storm brigades. The

Goliath saw a great deal of service on the Russian Front, being used extensively at Kursk for minefield clearance. It was also used during the Warsaw Uprising of 1944 against the Polish Home Army. Because the Home Army had very few antitank weapons, volunteers showing great bravery were sent out to cut the control wires before it reached its target. A few Goliaths were used against the Normandy beaches in June 1944, but Allied troops found most already immobilized before the actual landing. They had been in the zone under heavy preliminary bombardment, which cut their cables; the bombardment had not been planned with them in mind at all.

In 1942 an improved version of the Goliath was ordered, the Sd Kfz 303 (V-motor), to enable a heavier charge to be carried over a greater distance. Two models were built, the 303a and 303b. The 303a was smaller and lighter than the 303b. The latter weighed 0.48 tons. Its 703 cc gas engine gave it a top speed of 7.5 miles per hour (12 km/h) and a range of 7.5 miles (12 km), although its battle range was limited by the length of control wire on the drum—just over 700 yards (640 m). For transport to the battle area, the Goliath was carried on a two-wheeled trailer.

Goliaths were in production until January 1945, but it was not the only remotely controlled demolition vehicle produced by the Germans. The 4-ton Schwere Ladungsträger Sd Kfz 301 Ausf. A and B were produced from April 1942 to November 1943 and could drop a heavy demolition charge on to or close to a target to demolish fortifications, as well as being used for minefield clearance. After the charge was dropped via radio control, the vehicle was backed off, again via radio control. With a speed of 23 miles per hour (37 km/h) and a range of 131 miles (211 km), it was used to great effect for mine clearing on the Russian Front.

LEFT: A Goliath on the Eastern Front in March 1944.   ABOVE: A Goliath.

93 Prophylaxis Kit

Through history, field armies have been weakened by sexually transmitted venereal diseases. Although not immediately fatal, syphilis and gonorrhea induced distracting pain and discomfort among soldiers and resisted even temporary treatment until the nineteenth century. In World War II, the medical departments of the U.S. armed forces made dramatic progress in treating venereal disease (VD), but preventing it in the first place was a much more appealing option than the expensive, prolonged, painful, and resource-consuming treatment of patients.

The extent of venereal disease in the U.S. armed forces during World War I alerted the Army to its World War II challenges. Even with preventive medicine programs, the Army alone treated almost 400,000 VD cases and lost 6.8 million man-days of service through VD treatment admissions in 1917–1918. Only respiratory infections topped VD for disease-related hospital admissions in the Army.

The armed forces declared war on venereal disease in 1940 and by 1945 had won a limited victory. By 1945, the global incidence of venereal disease in the armed forces was 18 per 1,000 servicemen, or one-third the rate in World War I. The introduction of sulfa drugs (1941) and penicillin (1943) reduced days lost to hospitalization. The armed forces also tried with considerable success to stamp out prostitution in American territory and with less success abroad by policing.

The most direct way to control VD was to change GI behavior towards sex. Commanders and medical officers stressed the virtues of continence, accompanied by lurid training movies. Troop education programs, dramatized with visual examples of ruined genitalia, had some effect. Keeping troops well-fed and tired and isolated in camps helped too. Some GIs believed mandatory medications for tropical diseases and certain foods had been introduced to subvert

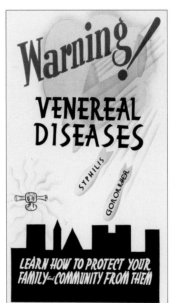

their libidos. At the preventive disease frontlines of VD control stood public health tools that assumed a serviceman would have sex: the latex condom and the postcoitus, chemical urethral flushing syringe. Together they made up the GI Prophylaxis ("Pro") Kit.

Although limited in use by notions of virility and religious convictions, condoms had entered American life as much for birth control as for VD prevention. However, many of the young males that flooded the ranks did not always want to use them. The armed services deluged them with information about condom use, required PXs to stock condoms, and eventually issued them on the basis of six per man per month. The major contractors were Young's Rubber Corporation ("Thins") and Trojan, Incorporated. Since combat troops were least likely to have sex, infantrymen found condoms most useful to keep water out of the barrels of their rifles.

With the appearance of GIs in Australia and the British Isles in 1942, individual "pro kits" and prophylactic stations became part of the American military presence abroad. The "pro kit" provided postcoitus sanitary measures, centered on a syringe to be inserted in the urethra that would flush it with an ointment of calomel and sulfathiazole. The individual kit also contained soap and cleansing tissue. A pro-station provided individual pro-kits, but also bulk supplies and attendants for those GIs who sought help and repetitive treatment. Medical departments checked on the use of prophylactic measures by holding "short arm" inspections. Servicemen could not leave a foreign shore or be discharged without clinical proof of being VD-free. Many GIs found VD control a memorable part of their wartime experience.

FAR LEFT: Venereal disease prevention throughout the United States was a public health issue.

ABOVE LEFT: VD prophylaxis reduced GIs hospitalized for treatment.

ABOVE: An Army "pro" station.

■94 Canadian Army Insignia

Unlike during World War I, when Canadian battalions in France simply wore numbers as unit identifiers and a division patch, the Canadian ground forces of World War II wore battalion, regimental, and special corps badges, as well as division and corps patches on their field uniforms. This system of unit identification mirrored that of the British army and included special headgear, cap badges, and other regimental affectations that reflected local, provincial, and national pride. The common national symbol was the maple leaf, but the practice of unit identification reflected the influence of the British army regimental system. Since Canadian soldiers wore British-style uniforms and field kit and carried British army weapons, a simple Canadian unit designator was often the only thing that reflected Canadian national identity. The single uniform patch said "Canada."

The Canadian army provided three infantry divisions, two armored divisions, two independent armored brigades, a parachute battalion, and many combat support (engineers) and combat service support (medical units) to the Allied expeditionary forces in Europe. The Canadian Army of World War II numbered 700,000 of the one million Canadians who served in uniform. Until 1945 this force was all-volunteer and rich in local pride, accommodated by distinctive unit identifiers. Whatever

their formal unit titles, Canadians loved particularistic regimental symbols and names.

The standard (meaning most likely) way to show one's "regiment" was the cap badge and the sleeve strip worn just below the shoulder seam, which announced that the wearer belonged to a battalion of the Princess Patricia's Canadian Light Infantry or the Highland Light Infantry of Canada or the Fusiliers Mont-Royal. Below the regimental "slash" and above enlisted rank insignia, the Canadian soldier wore color-coded division patches of rectangular cloth, but without a special division coat-of-arms as became common in the U.S. Army.

Early in World War II, Canadian soldiers wore a color-coded circular patch above the division rectangle to designate which brigade in the division they belonged to. Another modification was for members of specialized units to wear a service corps badge instead of a division patch—for example, the Royal Canadian Signals, a communications service.

ABOVE: A German sergeant lights the cigarette for a captured Canadian officer in Dieppe, France, on August 19, 1942. Visble on the Canadian soldier's left arm is the Canadian Army insignia.

ABOVE: The insignia for the Royal Canadian Air Force.

OVERLEAF: Canadian infantry moving slowly through a street in Campochiaro, Italy, in 1943.

229

95 The *Volkssturm* Armband

Hitler established the *Deutscher Volkssturm* on September 25, 1944. It was first announced in a secret decree on October 18, the anniversary of the great victory of the Prussians, Saxons, Poles, Swedes, and Russians over Napoleon at Leipzig in 1813, dubbed the "battle of the nations." Hitler was fond of identifying himself with selected events in Prussian history that suited his purpose, either for propaganda, or as self-delusion, or both. The Battle of Leipzig marked an important stage in the revival of Prussia after its disastrous defeat by Napoleon at Jena in 1806.

Hitler wished to draw a comparison with the Prussia of then and Germany now, the message being that although the country was being attacked on two fronts, all would come right in the end. A nation under arms would mirror the work of the Prussians who reformed the country and revitalized its army during the Napoleonic war. But the call to arms of the *Volk*, the people, did not strike quite the same chord in 1944 as it had in 1813 when the Prussian *Landsturm* had fought, often as guerrillas, against Napoleon.

Hitler ordered Martin Bormann, Head of the Party Chancellery and his private secretary, to raise six million men. This number was based on the fact that in May 1944, there were over six million men exempted from military service among the German workforce. However, the *Volkssturm* never achieved this strength. The basic unit was a battalion

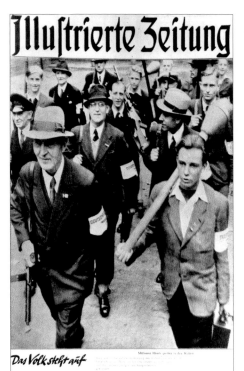

Illuſtrierte Zeitung

Das Volk ſteht auf

of men ranging in age from 16 to 60. The 16-year-olds were predominantly Hitler Youth, while the older men were mostly veterans invalided out of service or graded as unfit for military duty. They were supposed to be employed only in their own districts, but in fact many found themselves sent to the Eastern or Western Fronts once advancing Allied formations arrived on German soil. The *Volkssturm* was commanded by Heinrich Himmler in his capacity as commander-in-chief of the Replacement Army. While still in their districts, the *Volkssturm* came under command of the local Nazi party hierarchy. Once deployed, they came under army command.

War work still had priority, so training was carried out for four hours on Sundays. The men had to bring their own uniforms if they had them, otherwise they wore civilian clothes, and trilbys or flat caps. Arms and ammunition were in short supply. The most numerous weapons were panzerfausts, the German handheld antitank weapon. During the final months of the war the Germans produced a *Volkssturmgewehr* (People's Assault Rifle). There were several marks of this weapon; most were crudely manufactured bolt-action rifles, some without a magazine, so each round had to be loaded manually after the previous one was fired. Some had fixed, i.e. non-adjustable sights. From January 1945 to the end of the war, a more sophisticated semiautomatic rifle was beginning to be produced with a magazine. It is not known exactly how many were made, though the figure of around 10,000 seems

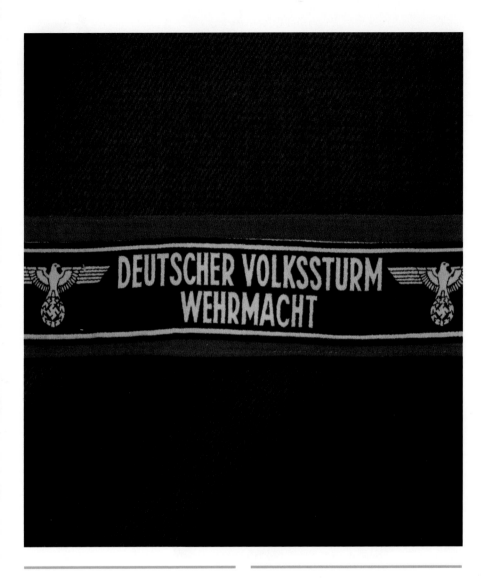

LEFT: The cover of the *Berliner Illustrierte Zeitung*, November 2, 1944, announcing "*Das Volk steht auf*" ("the people arise").

ABOVE: The *Volkssturm* Armband.

OVERLEAF: These *Volksturm* soldiers are not wearing armbands, because all are in uniform, perhaps because they are being inspected by Goebbels, pictured here shaking the hand of a boy.

credible. Few exist today.

The *Volkssturm* units in East Prussia were the most effective. It was here that the Landsturm had been raised in the previous century, so there was already a tradition for a people's army. Furthermore, it was in the east that the territory of the German homeland was first threatened in World War II, by the Red Army, and they were guarding their homes against the invaders. Right to the end, many Germans clung to the belief that the Red Army might be held at bay while an accommodation was arrived at with the Americans and the British in order that the war should end with the smallest possible portion of Germany occupied by the Soviets. All these factors combined to make the Landsturm fight harder in East Prussia than elsewhere, though there were also cases of them putting up a stout resistance in the west.

96 The P-51 Mustang

onceived by the Royal Air Force as a ground attack fighter-bomber in 1940, the P-51 Mustang became one of the best air superiority fighters—designed specifically to engage enemy aircraft—of World War II. It turned into the mainstay of the U.S. Army Air Forces' 8th and 15th Fighter Commands, which escorted American bombers deep into Germany to strike urban-industrial targets in 1944–45 and thus weaken the Third Reich. In one or another of its three basic models, the Mustang saw action over six years of global warfare in every theater.

In April 1940, with its own facilities overtaxed producing Hurricanes and Spitfires for Great Britain's air defense, the Royal Air Force and British Purchasing Commission negotiated with North American Aviation in the United States to produce a single-engine, single-pilot aircraft that ensured air superiority over the battlefield and attacked ground targets.

Based on earlier design experience, North American Aviation produced an advanced aerodynamic airframe in 117 days, but construction of an 1100 hp Allison engine slowed testing. The engine problem also ensured that the Mustang I (or Model A) had limited use except as a ground attack aircraft. It had many marvelous combat flight characteristics—speed, range, and maneuverability—and eight .30-caliber machine guns. The aircraft looked so promising that the RAF ordered 320 before it had evaluated the aircraft. After the Mustang's initial use in a ground reconnaissance role for the Army Cooperation Command, the RAF ordered 300 more aircraft.

Testing and operational experience during 1940–41 however, dramatized the Mustang's basic limitation, which was that it lost power and speed as it tried to reach 20,000 feet (6,100 m). The Mustang could fly into Germany but only

at low altitudes on reconnaissance missions. When the USAAF evaluated its own version of the Mustang in 1942, it improved the aircraft within its low altitude missions, with self-sealing wing tanks, four wing-mounted 20-mm cannon, and better cameras. The USAAF also developed bomb racks for the aircraft and changed the cannon to six .50-caliber machine guns. A slightly improved Merlin engine went under the cowling.

Both the RAF and USAAF saw the need for an air superiority fighter with ranges greater than the Spitfire's, and aerodynamic qualities superior to the USAAF's P-38 and P-47. Engines developed by Rolls-Royce and Packard showed great promise as a substitute for the Allison power plant. A hybrid Rolls-Royce/Packard engine, the Merlin V-1650-3, actually generated greater power (and speed) as the aircraft climbed and reached its maximum airspeed of 441 miles per hour (910 km/h) at 28,000 feet (530 m). It also climbed more rapidly than its competitors.

The USAAF desperately needed a long-range air superiority fighter to protect the B-17s and B-24s of Eighth Air Force, a role being pioneered by the P-47 with gasoline drop tanks. In December 1943, the new P-51B and P-51C, identical aircraft built at different plants, entered combat over Europe. More air combat experience brought a D-Model on line in 1944, with a special canopy and other aerodynamic modifications suitable for air-to-air combat. The P-51's final range was over 2,000 miles (3,200 km), and the service ceiling was 41,000 feet (12,500 km). Paired with growing numbers of experienced USAAF pilots, the P-51 ruled the skies in the war's last year in Europe and Asia. Before the war was over, North American built 15,586 P-51s, including 7,956 D-Models.

LEFT: Captain D. S. Gentile poses for a photograph on the wing of his P-51B Mustang in England on April 10, 1944.

ABOVE: North American Aviation P-51 Mustang fighter planes over France on July 20, 1944.

🔳97 V-Weapons

The Germans called them *Vergeltungswaffen* (retaliation weapons), conceived as revenge for Allied bombing of German cities. The British called them V-weapons. There were three types.

The V-1 flying bomb, a small pilotless aircraft powered by a pulse-jet engine, was an early cruise missile. It could be catapulted from a ramp, or air-launched by a Heinkel III. It first flew at Peenemünde on the Baltic under the direction of Wernher von Braun. The first flying bombs were launched against London on June 13, 1944. By the end of June, 2,452 V-1s had been targeted on London. About a third, 800, crashed in Greater London. Another third crashed or were shot down by fighters or antiaircraft fire before reaching the coast, and the remaining third crashed or were shot down before reaching the intended target.

A minority of V-1s were launched from Heinkel IIIs. Nearly half failed to fly and crashed soon after launch. Those that did stay airborne were very inaccurate compared with ground-launched V-1s. From October 1944 until March 1945, the V-1 effort was switched to Antwerp, the main supply port for the Allied armies in northwest Europe. The attacks on London resumed from launchers in Holland on March 3, 1945, finishing at the end of March when the launching sites were overrun. Just over 10,000 V-1s were directed at England. Of these, 7,888 crossed the coast, 3,957 being shot down before reaching their targets. London was hit by 2,419 V-1s, 30 reached Southampton and Portsmouth, and one hit Manchester. They caused 6,184 deaths and injured 17,981 people.

The V-1 rocket, also known as the "Doodlebug" or "Buzz Bomb" because of the sound of its engine, would cut out over its intended target, lose flying speed, and dive into the ground. All in the vicinity would hear the sudden silence and wonder where it would hit.

The V-2 rocket was even more terrifying. Not only did it deliver more explosive (2,150 pounds/975 kg compared with the V-1's 1,875 pounds/875 kg), but, it arrived without warning, and could not be shot down. It was the forerunner to the intercontinental ballistic missile. It had a maximum velocity of 3,600 miles per hour (5,800 km/h), could climb 60 miles (96 km) above the earth, and had a maximum range of 200 miles (320 km). It was first fired successfully in October 1942, but fortunately for the Allies, and Britain in particular, it was hugely complicated to develop and produce. A succession of bombing raids on Peenemünde by the RAF and USAAF seriously delayed work on the V-2 by forcing production to be moved to an underground factory at Nordhausen in the Harz Mountains in May 1944. The first V-2 to reach England landed in Chiswick on September 8, 1944, killing three and injuring 17, the last on March 27, 1945. A total of 1,054 V-2s landed on England, around five a day, of which three a day hit London, killing 2,700 Londoners. Antwerp was hit by 900 V-2s during the last three months of 1944.

The V-2 was launched from a small concrete pad that was easy to hide. All the launch equipment was easily moved from place to place. Even if the sites were found, there was little for attacking aircraft to hit.

The V-3 was a long-range gun, which from two firing sites at Mimoyecques, near Calais, was capable of firing a 4.3-inch (10.92 mm) shell at the rate of ten per minute on London. One of the sites was abandoned after an air attack by the RAF in November 1943, and the surviving site likewise in July 1944. Allied troops overran the area soon afterward. The Germans persisted with work on a simplified version of the gun, which shelled Antwerp and U.S. troops in Luxembourg, but to little effect. Shortly afterward, the Germans demolished the guns to prevent them from falling into Allied hands.

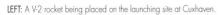

LEFT: A V-2 rocket being placed on the launching site at Cuxhaven.

ABOVE: A V-1 "Doodlebug" in flight.

RIGHT: V-2 rockets being prepared for launch.

OVERLEAF: London July 1, 1944, rescuers working among the ruins of a building demolished by a V-2 rocket.

98 Hitler's Eagle's Nest and the Berghof

The Eagle's Nest and the Berghof were part of Hitler's mountain-top estate in the Obersalzberg, overlooking the town of Berchtesgaden in southeastern Bavaria. This mountain property was purchased by Hitler using money from sales of his book *Mein Kampf* (*My Struggle*), which set out his political message.

The biggest and original building was the Berghof (Mountain House). Its huge, richly carpeted rooms were designed by the Führer himself, and reflected not only his taste but also his youthful hankering to be an architect, as well as his image of himself as a Wagnerian warrior chief. The buildings, which were constructed by slave labor, consisted of a central chalet situated in the middle of a compound that included barracks for 20,000 troops, and there were five rings of protective fortifications around it. Only the top floor was above ground; like an iceberg, the majority of the space in use, another 12 floors, was dug deep into the mountain rock. On this top floor, which afforded wonderful views of the mountains and the valley floor below, the most impressive of all the rooms was the great reception room, with its vast picture window. Adjacent to this was the banqueting hall. The underground floors contained the guardroom, kitchens, bedrooms, larders, and wine cellars.

Hitler's cronies—Hermann Goering, Joseph Goebbels, and Martin Bormann—lived in smaller houses nearby. Camps for additional troops were situated within a short distance of the Berghof, and a special road was cut through to the complex from Berchtesgaden.

The Eagle's Nest, also known as the Kehlsteinhaus, was a separate chalet atop the Kehlstein, a peak about 4 miles (6.5 km) from the Berghof. Built as a 50th birthday present for Hitler, it was presented to him on April 20, 1939. The road to the Eagle's Nest went through five tunnels, climbing 2,600 feet (79 m). Access to the building itself was through a tunnel some 400 feet (120 m) long bored into the mountain, and from there by lift up the final 400 feet (120 m). Its official designation was the Diplomatic Reception Haus, or D-Haus for short, sometimes corrupted to "teahouse" by English speakers. As a result it is often mistaken for the teahouse at the Berghof, which Hitler walked to after lunch on most days when he was in residence, whereas he rarely visited the D-Haus.

Hitler's regular visits to the teahouse were so well known that the plan to assassinate him while he was at the Berghof was put together by the British SOE. A sniper would be concealed in the forests adjacent to the road, ready to shoot Hitler on his walk. The plan was never put into effect because after the attempt on his life in July 1944, Hitler never visited the Berghof again.

As the war in Europe drew to an end, Allied leaders feared that Hitler, or one of his fanatical Nazi deputies, might command a last stand in the Bavarian Alps from the Berghof complex. On April 25, 1945, Lancasters of 617 Squadron RAF bombed the area, and at least two bombs hit the Berghof itself, smashing the top floor into ruins. In a race between the French 2nd Armored and the U.S. 101st Airborne Divisions to be first to capture the place, the French won. Four days later, the 506th Parachute Infantry were the first Americans to arrive. On their heels came soldiers of the 321st Airborne Artillery and the 327th Glider Infantry of the 101st Airborne Division, followed by other units of the 101st. The lower 12 floors of the Berghof were almost untouched by the bombing, and although the French had looted the place, there was plenty of the Führer's champagne and cognac left for the American airborne soldiers to enjoy. In one of the lower rooms, soldiers of B Company of the 506th Parachute Infantry discovered a Gruppenführer (SS major general) still in uniform. He refused to surrender and was shot. The paratroopers stripped him of his insignia and decorations, laid his body on a bed, and left, telling nobody until years later. He was found by other troops later, leading to a popular myth that he had shot himself.

The Eagle's Nest was undamaged by bombing and was also occupied by the 101st, who followed the example of their comrades in the Berghof and had their photographs taken among the ruins of Hitler's lair.

ABOVE: The Eagle's Nest on the Kehlstein.

RIGHT: Hitler with Dr. and Mrs. Goebbels and their three children at the Berghof.

BELOW: The entrance to the access tunnel for the Eagle's Nest.

OVERLEAF: The Great Hall at the Berghof.

■99 The Boeing B-29 Superfortress

The largest strategic bomber of World War II, the B-29 Superfortress devastated Japan's cities in 1945 and provided an important incentive for its surrender on August 15, 1945. Given the distances from U.S. Army Air Forces (USAAF) bases in China and the Pacific to Japan, no other bomber could have mounted this campaign.

Even before America's entry into the war, General Henry H. "Hap" Arnold, commanding general of the-then Army Air Corps, saw a requirement for VHB-VLR (Very Heavy Bomber-Very Long Range) aircraft. He thought that the United States might have to wage war alone against a victorious Axis coalition and defend the Western Hemisphere against invasion fleets or armies based in Latin America. Both the Boeing and Douglas aircraft companies were already working on an aircraft for commercial air travel capable of transoceanic flight and therefore had the capability to design such a plane for military use.

The Air Corps called for proposals for the VHB-VLR plane in January 1940 and awarded design contracts to four companies. Only Boeing remained in the competition at the end of 1940 with the promise that it would have a prototype ready for flight testing in two or three years. On September 21, 1942, Boeing pilots flew the XB-29 Model 341 for the first time. Desperation and haste characterized the $3.7-billion program that produced 3,970 bombers by 1947 at an individual cost of $930,000.

The B-29 was capable of bombing either Japan or Germany, provided it had overseas bases. It could fly 3,250 miles (5,230 km) at altitudes up to 31,000 feet (9,500 m), with a cruising speed of 220 miles per hour (355 km/h), and carried a maximum bomb load of 10 tons. It had 40,000 separate parts and was outfitted with state-of-the-art avionics for bombing accuracy, navigation, communications, defense, and damage control. The aircraft had two new features: a heated, pressurized cabin and crew stations to ease the discomforts of long flights and four powered, remote-controlled turrets for air defense guns. Only the tailgunner actually aimed his guns by sight.

Boeing's commitment to exploiting new technologies and the speed of its development process made the B-29

a troubled aircraft. The plane's accident rate per 100,000 miles (160,000 km) flown was twice that of other USAAF heavy bombers. In testing and training flights, B-29s had 272 accidents that destroyed 119 aircraft and killed 461 crewmen. The worst culprit was the Wright R-3350 2,000-hp engine, four for each aircraft. To save weight, the engine designers used aluminum and magnesium-based alloys for the engine parts. Prone to overheating on the ground, the engines caught fire during long, high-altitude flights. The engine had 18 pistons and twice the number of surfaces to be cooled as a B-17, while only having a cooling airflow equal to it. Moreover, the engine fire suppression systems could not cope with a magnesium fire.

When B-29s became operational in late 1943, General Arnold felt compelled by his own publicity about the bomber to deploy the B-29 somewhere, even in limited numbers. Operation Matterhorn—their first deployment—in India and China was a logistical nightmare. When American forces captured the Mariana Islands in the summer of 1944, the India-based B-29s redeployed to Saipan, Guam, and Tinian, where they joined new groups from the United States to become the 21st Bomber Command. The China-based B-29s had already bombed Japan in June 1944, setting-off a Japanese ground offensive that drove them inland. The round-trip from the Marianas to Japan was a shorter 3,200-mile (5,150 km) journey and much safer.

From the winter of 1944–45 until the Japanese surrender, 21st Bomber Command devastated Japan's cities. High-altitude bombing of industrial targets with high explosives produced poor results, and in March 1945, Major General Curtis E. LeMay, recognizing that winds and weather could not be overcome, adopted the RAF concept of night-time, low-altitude bombing with incendiaries. The March 9–10 raid on Tokyo set off a fire storm that killed almost 100,000 people and left more than a million homeless. In August 1945, B-29s dropped two nuclear weapons on Hiroshima and Nagasaki. This air campaign was not cheap for the USAAF, which lost 439 bombers and 3,000 aircrew in bombing of Japan.

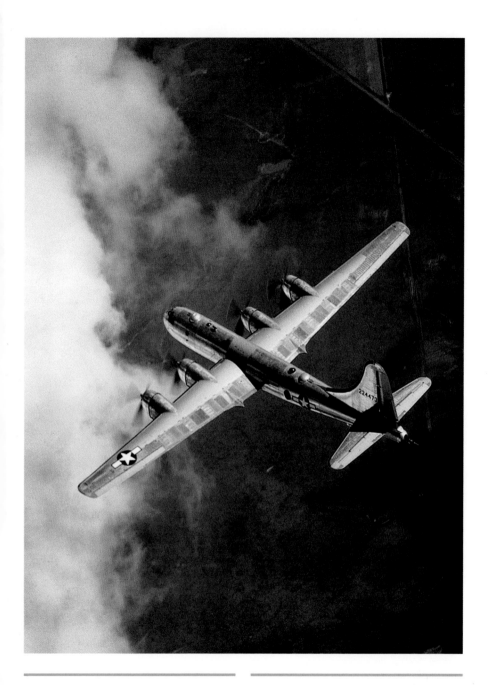

ABOVE: The U.S. Army Air Forces B-29 heavy bomber program gave the USAAF a plane that could bomb Japan from mid-Pacific bases.

OVERLEAF: Built by the Boeing Aircraft Corporation, the B-29 exploited advanced technology in its engines, avionics, defense systems, and metallurgy. Its rapid development created design flaws that resulted in engine failures.

100 The Atomic Bomb

The first atomic bomb was tested in New Mexico on July 16, 1945. Three weeks later, on August 6, the first-ever nuclear attack in history took place when the atom bomb code-named "Little Boy" was dropped on the Japanese city of Hiroshima. This was followed three days later by the dropping of "Fat Man" on Nagasaki. Japan surrendered on August 15, 1945. The Japanese Instrument of Surrender was signed on September 2, 1945, bringing World War II to an end.

The idea that atomic fission might form the basis of a large bomb was first proposed by two British scientists, Ernest Rutherford and Frederick Soddy in 1903, but very little progress was made in this field until the outbreak of World War II saw a renewed interest in the possibility of such a weapon. Work in Britain began in 1940, assisted greatly by German and Austrian Jewish physicists who had escaped from Nazi Germany. Little research on nuclear fission weapons took place in the United States until 1941, when American scientists visited Tube Alloys, the cover name for the project in Britain. Impressed by the progress made, the Americans set up their own research and development program, code-named the Manhattan Project, to which British scientists were transferred when America entered World War II.

In the meantime, German scientists began working on the production of "heavy water" in Norway, believing that the key to nuclear fission lay in developing this substance.

The Soviet Union also wished to develop a nuclear weapon, devoting much effort to espionage activities in the United States in order to steal the necessary knowledge from the Americans and British. The Soviet Union did not acquire an atomic bomb until 1949, the technology being aquired through spying.

Two major efforts were made to frustrate the German research, although the ending of the war with Germany revealed that they were well behind the British and Americans. The first attack was a successful commando-style raid on the heavy water plant at Rjukan in Norway on the night of February 27/28, 1943, which damaged most of the plant and machinery. Follow-up raids by RAF bombers starting in November 1943 persuaded the Germans to transfer the remaining plant and heavy water to Germany. On February 20, 1944, the SOE planted a bomb on the railway ferry across Lake Tinnsjø in Norway, sinking the ferry.

Meanwhile, joint work by the British and Americans (though mainly the latter) resulted in the production of two bombs, "Little Boy" and "Fat Man." Each used different nuclear technology, that of "Fat Man" being an improvement on "Little Boy."

Some 70,000 people, mostly civilians, died in Hiroshima, and around 40,000 in Nagasaki. Also on August 9, the Soviet Red Army invaded Manchuria, having declared war on Japan the previous day. It is perhaps an indication of the state of mind of the Japanese leadership that, despite these events, it would take until August 15, six days later, before Japan agreed to accept unconditional surrender terms.

To this day the debate continues on the morality of using atomic bombs on Japan. They caused fewer casualties than the firebombing with "conventional" weapons that preceded the attacks on Hiroshima and Nagasaki. Starting on March 9, 1945, with an attack on Tokyo that killed 100,000 people and made over a million homeless, the ensuing firebomb attacks

LEFT: The mushroom cloud from "Fat Man" rises over Nagasaki. This was the second bomb dropped on Japan.

ABOVE: "Fat Man" the 22 KT atomic bomb dropped on Nagasaki on August 9, 1945.

resulted in the destruction of large areas of 67 Japanese cities, costing around 500,000 civilian deaths, and about five million homeless in five months. Add to this the thousands of Japanese civilians killed on Okinawa alone, as well as on other islands inhabited by the Japanese during the final months of the war in the Pacific, and the carnage wrought by the atom bombs

pales by comparison with what had gone before, let alone the expected losses to civilians had the Allies invaded Japan. Still, the results of using the bombs were severe. The number of deaths and of people affected by illnesses continued to grow even after the event due to the effects of the bombings.

Glossary

ampoule A small glass container used to hold a solution for an injection.

belligerent A country or group engaged in war.

Bonhams A British auction house that is one of the oldest and largest fine art and antique auctioneers in the world.

casemate A fortified room or an armored enclosure from which guns can be fired through small openings.

clandestine Done privately or secretly.

fuselage The main part of an aircraft, designed to hold the crew, passengers, or cargo.

howitzer A large gun or cannon used to fire shells high up in the air for short distances.

in situ In the original place or position.

materiel Equipment and supplies, such as weapons, used by soldiers.

metallurgy The branch of science and technology that deals with the nature and uses of metals.

ordnance Often refers to artillery, but can also include other military supplies such as weapons, ammunition, vehicles, tools, and equipment.

propaganda Ideas or statements that are often exaggerated or untrue and that are spread with the intention of helping a certain cause, group, or leader.

quay A structure built on land next to a body of water used for the landing, unloading, and loading of boats.

reconnaissance Military activity that involves finding out information about an enemy.

sextant An instrument used for measuring the angular distances between objects and for taking altitudes in navigation, used especially to determine the position of a ship or airplane.

siren suit A one-piece item of clothing meant to be easy to put on, originally intended for use during air raids.

theodolite An instrument used to measure horizontal and vertical angles. Modern versions involve a telescope that can rotate horizontally and vertically.

transom A beam that helps to carry the load on a structure such as a bridge.

trawler Usually refers to a boat used for fishing with a large net; at wartime, such boats have been armed and fitted for naval use.

Tube A system of trains that run underground in London, also called the London Underground.

Further Information

Books

Bains, Alisha. *World War II*. New York, NY: Britannica Educational Publishing, 2017.

Ellis, Catherine. *Key Figures of World War II*. New York, NY: Britannica Educational Publishing, 2016.

Hamen, Susan E. *World War II*. North Mankato, MN: ABDO Publishing Company, 2014.

Langley, Andrew. *Stories of Women in World War II: We Can Do It!* Chicago, IL: Heinemann Raintree, 2015.

Langston-George, Rebecca. *Fearless Spies and Daring Deeds of World War II*. North Mankato, MN: Compass Point Books, 2017.

Marsico, Katie. *World War II: Why They Fought*. North Mankato, MN: Compass Point Books, 2016.

Ringstad, Arnold. *World War II Weapons*. Minneapolis, MN: ABDO Publishing Company, 2016.

Roberts, Russell. *World War II Leaders*. Minneapolis, MN: ABDO Publishing Company, 2016.

Servin, Morgan. *World War II Close Up*. New York, NY: Rosen Publishing Group, 2016.

Websites

The MacArthur Memorial
www.macarthurmemorial.org

National Museum of the US Airforce
www.nationalmuseum.af.mil

National World War II Museum
www.nationalww2museum.org

Smithsonian National Postal Museum: Victory Mail Online Exhibit
postalmuseum.si.edu/victorymail/index.html

Index

Picture Credits

The publishers would like to thank the following sources for their kind permission to reproduce the pictures in this book.

6. Getty Images/Central Press, 7. Getty Images/Topical Press Agency, 8–9 Getty Images/Popperfoto, 10. Getty Images/Universal History Archive, 11. Carlton Books/IWM, 12. Getty Images/AFP, 13. Getty Images/Galerie Bilderwilt, 14. Scala/BPK, Berlin, 15. Science Museum/Science & Society Picture Library, 16. Corbis, 17. Alamy/Interfoto, 18. AKG-Images/Ullstein Bild, 19. (top) AKG-Images, 19. (bottom) Corbis/Bettmann, 20. AKG-Images/IAM, 21. Getty Images/Popperfoto, 22. Getty Images/Time & Life Pictures, 23. Getty Images, 24. IWM (HU 40239), 25. Photo12.com/Collection Bernard Crochet, 26. Getty Images/IMAGNO/Austrian Archives, 27. (top) Getty Images/LAPI/Roger-Viollet, 27. (bottom) Getty Images/Keystone, 28. Getty Images/Eric Harlow/Keystone, 29. (top) IWM (PST 13861_2), 29. (bottom) Alamy/John Joannides, 30. Getty Images/Time & Life Pictures, 31. U.S. Air Force, 32. Getty Images/Hulton Archive, 33. Topfoto.co.uk/The Board of Trustees of the Armouries/HIP, 34. Corbis/Hulton-Deutsch Collection, 35. Alamy/Itdarbs, 36–37. Photo12.com/Ann Ronan Picture Library, 38–39. Getty Images/Dorling Kindersley, 39. Alamy/Lordprice Collection, 40–41. Alamy/Chris Pancewicz, 41. Corbis/Bettmann, 42–43. Getty Images/Fox Photos, 44. Getty Images/Keystone, 45. Getty Images/Fox Photos, 46. Getty Images/H.F. Davis/

Topical Press Agency, 47. (top) Getty Images/Keystone-France/Gamma-Keystone, 47. (bottom) Getty Images/Central Press, 48. Getty Images/Tunbridge, 48–49. Getty Images/Popperfoto, 50. & 51. Paradata.org.uk, 52. Alamy/The Art Archive, 53. Alamy/Interfoto, 54. AKG-Images/RIA Novosti, 55. (top) AKG-Images/RIA Novosti, 55. (bottom) AKG-Images/Voller Ernst, 56–57. Getty Images/Slava Katamidze Collection, 58. Getty Images/Hulton Archive/Fox Photos, 59. The Churchill Archives Centre, 60–61. Getty Images/Hulton Archive, 62–63. 7.62x54r.net, 63. AKG-Images, 64–65. Getty Images/Michael Ochs Archive, 66–67. Getty Images/Popperfoto, 68. IWM (MH 4647), 69. IWM (E_MOS 1439), 70. & 71. Myrabella/Wikimedia Commons/CC-BY-SA-3.0 & GFDL, 72–73. Heritage-Images/National Archives, 74. Getty Images/Hulton Archive, 75. Wilson History & Research Centre, 76. Getty Images/Roger Viollet, 77. Author collection, 78. Getty Images/PhotoQuest, 79. Topfoto.co.uk 80. Getty Images/SSPL/Bletchley Park Trust, 81. Getty Images/SSPL, 82. Topfoto.co.uk/The Granger Collection, 83. Alamy/The Art Archive, 84. Getty Images/David E. Scherman/Time Life Pictures, 85. Alamy/Antiques & Collectables, 86–87. Private Collection, 88. Getty Images/Kurt Hutton/Picture Post, 89. Private Collection, 90. Topfoto.co.uk/Ullstein Bild, 90–91. Alamy/Interfoto, 92. Getty Images/Popperfoto, 93. IWM (T 54), 94. National Archives & Records Administration, Washington, 95. IWM (UNI 13161), 96. Getty Images/Frank Scherschel/Time & Life Pictures, 97. Getty Images/Dmitri Kessel/Time & Life Pictures, 98. National Archives & Records Administration, Washington, 99. Corbis/Bettmann, 100. AKG-Images/Interfoto, 101. AKG-Images/Interfoto, 102–103. AKG-Images, 104. Getty Images/Bernard Hoffman/Time & Life Pictures, 105. (top) Getty Images/E.F. Joseph/Anthony Potter Collection, (bottom) Getty Images/Margaret Bourke-White/Time Life Pictures, 106. IWM (A 30568), 107. (top) Corbis/Bettmann, 108–109. AKG-Images, 110. Getty Images/Popperfoto, 110–111. Getty Images/Hulton Archive, 112. Getty Images/Time & Life Pictures, 113. (top) IWM (INS 7209), 113. (bottom) IWM (INS 7210), 114–115. Getty Images/Keystone-France, 116. IWM (E 14948), 117. (top) IWM (INS 5110), (bottom left) IWM (5499), (bottom right) IWM (5114), 118. Getty Images/Roger Viollet, 119. National Archives & Records Administration, Washington, 120. AWM (042011_1), 121. (top) & (bottom) Carlton Books/IWM, 122–123. Topfoto/Ullstein Bild, 124. Corbis, 125. National Archives, Washington, 126. Alamy/Interfoto, 127. IWM (FEQ 415), 128. Getty Images/PhotoQuest, 129. Alamy/Daniel Templeton, 130. Corbis/Bettmann, 131. Getty Images, 132. Alamy/Interfoto, 133. Getty Images/Keystone, 134. Topfoto, 135. Getty Images/Time Life Pictures/US Navy, 136-137. National Archives & Records Administration, Washington, 138. Corbis/Bettmann, 139. Getty Images/SSPL, 140. National Archives & Records Administration, Washington, 141. Photo provided courtesy of James D. Julia Inc., 142. Getty Images/Popperfoto, 143. Corbis, 144. Getty Images/Time Life Pictures/US Signal Corps, 145. Alamy/Interfoto, 146. IWM (ART 16884), 147. Corbis/Ocean, 149. (top) Getty Images/Hermann Harz/Photoquest, (bottom) Getty Images/LAPI/Roger Viollet, 150. Getty Images/Buyenlarge, 151. Getty Images/Frederic Lewis/Hulton Archive,152-153. National Archives & Records Administration, Washington, 154. IWM (HU 69915), 155. (top) IWM (HU 62922), (bottom) IWM (FLM 2340), 156–157. IWM (HU 4594), 158. IWM (ART 16345), 159. (top) Getty Images/Popperfoto, (bottom) Alamy/Art Directors & TRIP, 160. National Archives & Records Administration, Washington, 161. lameducouteau.fr, 163. IWM (A 22617), 164. IWM (BU 9757), 165. (top) Alamy/Interfoto, (bottom) Topfoto.co.uk/The Granger Collection, 166–167. Topfoto.co.uk/Ullstein Bild, 169.

Topfoto.co.uk/Ullstein Bild, 170. Getty Images/Keystone, 171. Corbis, 172. Getty Images/Ed Clark/Time Life Pictures, 173. National Archives & Records Administration, Washington, 174–175. National Archives & Records Administration, Washington, 176. Getty Images/US Coast Guard/FPG/Hulton Archive, 177. Getty Images/Galerie Bilderwelt, 178. Getty Images/Keystone-France/Gamma-Keystone, 179. Getty Images/Hulton Archive, 180. Getty Images/Corporal Angus Robertson/US Marine Corps/FPG/Hulton Archive, 181. Getty Images/W. Eugene Smith/Time Life Pictures, 182. & 183. Rex Features/Geoffrey Robinson, 184. & 185. National Archives & Records Administration, Washington, 186. AKG-Images/Ullstein Bild, 187. Alamy/Jack Sullivan, 188-189. Alamy/Paul Heinrich, 190–191. Getty Images/Time Life Pictures/US Signal Corps, 192. Corbis/Hulton-Deutsch Collection, 193. Corbis/Bettmann, 195. (top) Getty Images/George Rodger/Time & Life Pictures, (bottom) Getty Images/Margaret Bourke-White/Time & Life Pictures, 196-197. National Archives & Records Administration, Washington, 198. Corbis/Heritage Images, 199. Topfoto.co.uk/Curt Teich Postcard Archives, Lake County HistoryArchives/HIP, 201. National Archives & Records Administration, Washington, 202. Topfoto.co.uk/The National Archives/HIP, 203. IWM (CH 15363), 204. Corbis, 204–205. Getty Images/PhotoQuest, 206. Alamy/The Art Archive, 207. HMVF, 208. IWM (H 35181), 209. IWM (MH 2210), 210. Getty Images/Imagno, 211. Corbis/Michael St. Maur Sheil, 212. Getty Images/PhotoQuest, 213. Alamy/Interfoto, 215. (top) Getty Images/Three Lions, (bottom) Getty Images/Popperfoto, 216. Getty Images/Time Life Pictures/US Signal Corps, 217. (top) Getty Images/PhotoQuest, (bottom) Gen. Patton Museum. Fort Knox, 218–219. Corbis/DPA, 220. Getty Images/Popperfoto, 221. Istockphoto.com, 222. Getty Images/Kurk Hutton/Picture Post/Hulton Archive, 223. Private Collection, 224. Getty Images/Keystone-France/Gamma- Keystone, 225. Deutsches Panzermuseum Munster, Germany, 226. National Archives & Records Administration, Washington, 227. (left) Private Collection, (right) National Archives & Records Administration, Washington, 228. Alamy/Interfoto, 229. (top) IWM (INS 7993), (bottom) IWM (7994), 230–231. Corbis/Hulton-Deutsch Collection, 232. AKG-Images/Ullstein Bild, 233. Private Collection, 234–235. AKG-Images, 236. Getty Images/Popperfoto, 237. 238. Getty Images/Fox Photos, 239. (top) Getty Images/Keystone/Hulton Archive, (bottom) Getty Images/Roger Viollet, 240–241. Getty Images/Mansell/Time & Life Pictures, 243. (top) Photo12/Cabinet Revel, (bottom left) Getty Images/Three Lions, (bottom right) Getty Images/AFP, 244–245. Photo12/Cabinet Revel, 247. Corbis/Bettmann, 248–249. Corbis, 250. Corbis/Nagasaki Atomic Bomb Museum/epa, 251. IWM (MH 6810)

Every effort has been made to acknowledge correctly and contact the source and/or copyright holder of each picture and Carlton Books Limited apologizes for any unintentional errors or omissions, which will be corrected in future editions of this book.